GROWTH THROUGH REASON

VERBATIM CASES IN RATIONAL-EMOTIVE THERAPY

ALBERT ELLIS

Published by

WILSHIRE BOOK COMPANY
12015 Sherman Road
No. Hollywood, California 91605
Telephone: (213) 875-1711

Printed by

HAL LEIGHTON PRINTING CO.
P. O. Box 1231
Beverly Hills, California 90213
Telephone: (213) 346-8500

Library of Congress Card Number 77-153850 **ISBN 0-87980-264-2**

Contents

Contents

Contributors

BEN N. ARD, JR., PH.D., is a psychologist in private practice in San Francisco and also Professor of Counseling at San Francisco State College. Dr. Ard has edited two books, *Counseling and Psychotherapy* (Science and Behavior Books, 1966) and *Handbook of Marriage Counseling* (with Constance C. Ard; Science and Behavior Books, 1969). He has published articles in *Rational Living, Sexology, Family Coordinator, Marriage Counseling Quarterly,* and *Personnel and Guidance Journal.*

ALBERT ELLIS, PH.D., is Executive Director of the Institute for Rational Living and Director of Clinical Services of the Institute for Advanced Study in Rational Psychotherapy in New York City. He is an associate editor of several scientific journals, has published more than 350 articles, and has authored 30 books and monographs, including *Reason and Emotion in Psychotherapy* (Lyle Stuart, 1962), *The Art and Science of Love* (Lyle Stuart, 1969), *Sex Without Guilt* (Lyle Stuart, 1970), *The Encyclopedia of Sexual Behavior* (with Albert Abarbanel; Hawthorn Books, 1961, 1967), and *A Guide to Rational Living* (with Robert A. Harper; Prentice-Hall, 1963).

H. JON GEIS, PH.D., is a clinical psychologist in private practice in New York and Director of Training at the Institute for Advanced Study in Rational Psychotherapy where he supervises the professional staff and gives public lectures. Dr. Geis formerly taught on the graduate faculties of New York University, Yeshiva University, and Teachers College, Columbia University. He has written articles for *Dissertation Abstracts* and *Rational Living.*

JOHN M. GULLO, M.A., is a consulting clinical psychologist for the Illinois Department of Mental Health. He is also engaged in the private practice of individual and group psychotherapy and marriage, family, and pre-marital counseling. Mr. Gullo has participated with Dr. Ellis in holding professional workshops and in conducting marathon weekends of Rational Encounter. He is the author of *Murder and Assassination* (with Albert Ellis; Lyle Stuart, 1971), several articles in professional journals, and two tests in the training-teaching field.

PAUL A. HAUCK, PH.D., is a clinical psychologist in private practice in Rock Island, Illinois. He was formerly chief psychologist, Peoria Mental Health Center, and Director of the Western Mental Health Center, Marshall, Minnesota. Dr. Hauck has published twenty-four professional papers and was the first editor of *Rational Living*, the journal for the Institute for Rational Living. He has written *The Rational Management of Children* (Libra, 1967).

MAXIE C. MAULTSBY, JR., M.D., is Director of the Psychiatric Out-Patient Department of the University of Kentucky. He was formerly Assistant Professor of Medicine at University Hospitals in Madison, Wisconsin. Besides doing clinical research, Dr. Maultsby has conducted many workshops and seminars in rational-emotive therapy. He has written articles for the *American Journal of Psychiatry*, *Psychological Reports*, *Rational Living*, and *Psychotherapy: Theory, Research and Practice*.

CHAPTER 1

Introduction

ALBERT ELLIS, Ph.D.

Rational-emotive psychotherapy has many unique features that differentiate it from most other forms of psychotherapy. One of these in particular will be emphasized by the cases that are included in this book: namely, that it is not only a relatively short-term procedure (taking from one to thirty sessions in most instances, where the conventional forms of therapy take considerably longer), but it usually fosters gains within gains. That is to say, when a rational-emotive therapist is working with a client on a major problem—such as the typical symptom of feelings of severe inadequacy or worthlessness—there tends to occur (a) a significant diminution of this problem before the symptom is completely eliminated and (b) an amelioration of certain other of the client's emotional complaints, even though some of them may have hardly been mentioned during the therapy sessions.

This kind of treatment bonus, moreover, often occurs with startling rapidity. When I practiced psychoanalysis and psychoanalytic psychotherapy some years ago, I warned my clients that before they improved as a result of seeing me, they might well get worse. And I was frequently right! Many of them ultimately got better—but only after they had undergone considerable suffering concomitantly with, and quite probably as a direct result of, treatment. For revealing to an individual some of his hidden traits and motivations may finally do *him* some good, but in the short run it aggravates his suffering.

This can happen in rational-emotive therapy (RET, for short), too; but it usually doesn't. RET not only quickly reveals to the individual many important things of which he is, at best, only dimly aware; but it almost immediately begins to undercut and disembowel the conscious and unconscious irrational assumptions that make him and

1

keep him emotionally disturbed. This is particularly true of his unsubstantiable negative assumptions about himself, which create his "feelings" of inadequacy, worthlessness, anxiety, guilt, and depression. From the very first therapeutic session, the therapist is showing the client exactly what his self-defeating values and philosophies are, how these make him anxious and self-hating, and precisely what he can do to question and challenge them in order to minimize or exterminate their effects.

In the distinct majority of instances, then, RET begins to work promptly and to produce some beneficial results. This does not mean that all rational-emotive clients, or even the majority of them, become significantly improved or "cured" in a brief period of time. Not so! Some of them make little or no advance for many weeks. Others make progress but take a long time before they finally make important inroads against their basic self-sabotaging philosophies and thereby become better.

Nor is the rational-emotive therapist usually interested in what is called a "symptom cure"—although the so-called "depth" therapists like to think so ad nauseam. On the contrary, he normally tries for what he considers to be the most elegant cure imaginable: that is, a radical restructuring of the client's value system and the semi-automatic internalization by him of a scientific, logico-empirical attitude toward himself and the world that will effectively prevent him from ever becoming seriously disturbed again. Unless the client is in some special, restricted category—is, for example, very young or old, or of quite limited intelligence—the therapist vigorously endeavors to induce him to surrender some of his basic philosophic nonsense, and not merely his annoying symptoms. If this can't be accomplished, too bad; but almost always this is the rational-emotive therapeutic goal.

That is why the incidental, and often amazingly quick, gains achieved in RET are so startling: they are almost a by-product rather than a direct aim of the therapy process. In my own case, for example, I generally assume that my new client probably is capable of fundamental personality change rather than only relatively slight behavior modification. I also assume that although most individuals have great difficulty in changing their fundamental views and behaviors, this particular client may be one of the relatively few who is able to do so with some degree of ease and speed. If I am wrong, then he and I have lost little or nothing. If I am right, then we both are saved considerable time, and he gains a shortcut to release from pain. So why not experiment and see?

Experiment? Why, of course! One of the brightest aspects of psychotherapy, and the prime element in keeping it (at least for myself) from becoming a blasted bore, is the fact that each client is in many respects quite singular, different from the many others who have gone before him; and therefore there is no damned way of knowing, save clairvoyantly, how he is going to react to the same kinds of methods that the therapist has used many times before or to different techniques that he improvises for this current encounter. Even, therefore, when the therapy of choice is far from being eclectic and is based on a clear-cut theory and practice (as is RET), each session is still highly experimental. Although I have realized this to some degree for many years, I am grateful to Gerald C. Davison and his associates (1970) at the State University of New York at Stony Brook for recently emphasizing this point in a more formal manner.

Anyway, as I experiment with the new client who is before me, I try many maneuvers to try to achieve a consistent goal: to see how quickly I can get him to see what is *really* bothering him, to understand exactly what he is doing to make this thing bothersome, and to discover what he can do to stop bothering himself. If I can get him to see these things, and then to act on them quickly, fine. If not, too bad. But almost always, if he works at all at helping himself along the lines I outline for him, he will improve to some extent, usually, within a short period of time.

That is what most of the cases in this book demonstrate: that rational-emotive psychotherapy tends not only to work, but to have fairly immediate as well as long-range effects. *Why* it works this well is, of course, open to various interpretations. Relationship-oriented therapists, such as Arbuckle (1967) and Patterson (1966, 1969), and psychoanalytically-oriented therapists, such as Greenwald (1967), tend to "explain" RET results by hypothesizing that it is not the rational-emotive therapist's didactic content and philosophic analysis that really affect the client, but rather it is his warmth, his relating, or his transference connections with the client. This is a little far-fetched, since, as will be seen in the cases in this book, he frequently has a minimum relationship and a maximum teaching alliance with his client. Moreover, if the RET "relationship" works so quickly, even when little or no effort is made to achieve it, how is it that the client-centered, experiential, existential, and psychoanalytically-oriented relationships work so slowly, even when therapists who subscribe to these schools take such great pains to establish them?

Other critics of RET, such as Pottash and Taylor (1967) claim that it really gets its good results because it is a kind of behavior therapy that conditions the client to react better and to surrender his symptoms. This is partly true since the rational-emotive therapist does reinforce the client's more efficient behavior, and he does make liberal use of *in vivo* homework assignments that help force the client to act differently. However, systematic desensitization, operant conditioning, and other forms of behavior therapy generally take a number of sessions to produce good therapeutic results (Wolpe and Lazarus, 1966), whereas RET may help create significant behavioral change in as little as one or two sessions. Moreover, as some of the less doctrinaire leaders in the field of behavior therapy have been increasingly pointing out, cognitive processes are really explicitly or implicitly included in most effective behavior therapy cases, and rational-emotive psychotherapy, in particular, is one of the best means for supplementing traditional desensitizing or operant conditioning methods (Davison & Valins, 1969; Eysenck, 1964; Lazarus, 1971).

Are cognitive processes and didactic teaching the core of the rational-emotive technique? Yes and no. Actually, as its name implies, RET is a truly comprehensive method of treatment, which includes cognitive-explicatory, evocative-emotive, and behavioristic-active-directive methods. As noted in the previous paragraph, it is strongly oriented toward homework assignments, as well as to other active-directive techniques, such as role-playing, assertion training, and conditioning and counterconditioning procedures. It also makes use of many dramatic-emotive exercises, particularly in the course of group and marathon encounter therapy, including honest expression of feeling, direct confrontation, risk-taking experiences, uninhibited language, love experiences, and the use of unconditional positive regard. Its unique essence, however, especially when it is employed in individual psychotherapy and in marriage and family therapy, is a Socratic-type dialogue through which the client is calmly, logically, forcefully taught that he'd better stop telling himself nonsense, accept reality, desist from condemning himself and others, and actively persist at making himself as happy as he can be in a world that is far from ideal.

RET also differs from the vast majority of other schools of psychotherapy in that it consciously strives to help the client achieve the most elegant solution to the problem of human worth or self-acceptance. Theoretically, virtually all systems of therapy aim for the client's self-acceptance; but actually they tend to fall down sadly.

Thus, Carl Rogers (1961, 1971) has done a great service to psychology by emphasizing the value of unconditional positive regard; and in this respect, as Bone (1968) incisively points out, client-centered and rational-emotive psychotherapy are oriented toward the same goals. In actual practice, however, almost all Rogerian and existentialist therapists seem to assume that their clients can only improve through highly conditional positive regard: through the therapist's relating warmly to the client and, by his existential encounter with the client, showing him that he is a worthy person *because* the therapist accepts him and *because*, presumably, others will therefore accept him as well. Consequently, the "successfully" treated Rogerian client normally gains "self-esteem" or "ego strength" by entering therapy with the irrational idea, "I am no good unless other people accept or love me," and leaving therapy with the slightly better but still basically insane idea, "I am now worthwhile because my therapist cares for me, and presumably others can care for me as well." It is exceptionally difficult to see how this client has gained any appreciable kind of *un*conditional positive self-regard.

Conditional self-acceptance is similarly achieved by the client in most other types of therapy—including experiential, basic encounter, sensitivity training, reality, Gestalt, Synanon, and operant conditioning therapy. For all these schools go along with the individual's basic irrational belief that it is not only preferable that others approve of him but that he absolutely needs this approval if he is to accept himself. Essentially, therefore, these forms of therapy "help" him by showing him better techniques of relating rather than disabusing him of the idea that he has to relate well in order to consider himself a worthwhile human being.

These schools, as well as several other systems of psychotherapy also do not forthrightly and unequivocally attack and uproot the individual's other important disturbance-creating notion: that is, the idea that he must achieve notably or perform well in life in order to have confidence in himself. Thus, Adlerian therapy (Adler, 1927, 1929, 1931; Ansbacher and Ansbacher, 1956) shows the client that he has to have considerable social interest if he is to be a worthy member of the human race. Branden's biocentric-objectivist approach (1969) bases the individual's self-esteem on the conviction that he is competent to deal with reality effectively and that he is morally worthy. Behavior therapy often teaches the client that he really can master certain situations at which he has a prior history of failure and that therefore he can have confidence in himself. (Bandura, 1969; Wolpe and Lazarus, 1966).

On the other side of the fence, RET now seems to be almost the only kind of psychotherapy that is based on the assumption that the individual can fully, unconditionally accept himself whether or not he is approved by others and whether or not he performs well in life; that clearly distinguishes between the client's *preference* and *need* to be popular and achieving; and that specifically teaches him that he doesn't have to rate or evaluate his *self* or his *being*, even though he'd better objectively perceive and measure his *traits* or his *abilities*. It sharply differentiates between the person's achievement-confidence and his approval-confidence, on the one hand, and his self-acceptance, on the other; and it presents a radical solution to his "ego" or "identity" problem by essentially eliminating his "ego" (Ellis, 1971a, 1971b, in press c).

RET is also rigorously scientific—meaning that it is based on and consistently uses the principles of empirical validation and logical analysis rather than the principles of magic, mysticism, arbitrary definition, religiosity, and circular thinking. It shows the individual that whenever he upsets himself at point C (the emotional consequence), it is not (as he almost always thinks is the case) because of what is happening to him at point A (the activating event). Rather, it is because of his own irrational and unvalidatable suppositions at point B (his belief system). More precisely, when a person feels terribly depressed at point C, it is not because he has been rejected by someone or has lost a job at point A, but because he is convincing himself, at point B, of both a rational and an irrational hypothesis.

His rational belief (rB) is usually of the order: "I don't like being rejected, because it has real disadvantages. I wish, instead, that I were being accepted. But because I am being rejected, that is unfortunate, unbeneficial, and frustrating." If asked to sustain or verify this rational hypothesis or belief, the individual can easily present empirical, observation-backed data to prove that it *is* unfortunate that he is being rejected. Thus, he can show that rejection leads to (1) lack of love and approval, (2) loss of companionship, sex fulfillment, or job advancement; (3) knowledge by others that he has been rejected and their consequently being influenced to reject him, too; and (4) various other kinds of real inconveniences. He can also show that if these inconvenient consequences of rejection occur (and it is highly likely, though not necessary, that they will), it is inappropriate for him to feel delighted and joyous, while it is most appropriate for him to feel sorrowful, regretful, frustrated, and annoyed. His feelings of sorrow and frustration are appropriate because (1) it is hardly appropriate for him to feel unfrustrated and joyous when he is truly rejected and inconvenienced, and (2) feelings of sorrow and annoyance usually encourage him to work at *changing* the conditions that occur at point A (that is, rejection), so that in the future he is more likely to be accepted.

The individual's irrational belief (iB) is usually of the order: "I can't *stand* being rejected! It is awful, horrible, and catastrophic for me not to be accepted! I *should* have been approved rather than rejected, and the fact that I was not proves (*a*) that I am a worthless individual and/or (*b*) that my rejector is a rotter and a bastard!"

This irrational belief (iB) is really a magical, empirically unverifiable hypothesis because there is no possible way of proving or disproving it. Thus (1) he cannot prove that he can't *stand* being rejected, since this is a tautological assumption and consists of circular thinking. He cannot stand being rejected because he *thinks* he cannot stand it; he thinks he cannot stand it because he *decides* not to stand it; and when he thinks and decides that he cannot stand being rejected, he *feels* that he cannot stand it. (2) It is awful, horrible, and catastrophic for him not to be accepted only because, once again, he *thinks* it is awful, horrible, and catastrophic. The words "awful," "horrible," and "catastrophic" have surplus bombastic meaning and cannot truly be defined. They mean, first, that it is inconvenient for him to be unaccepted (which he already proved and accounted for in the course of his rational belief [rB] about nonacceptance); and they mean, second, that he *should* not, *ought* not, *must* not be inconvenienced. But why should, ought, or must anything not exist? Only because, by arbitrary fiat, he *thinks* and *declares* that it must not exist! Only because he absolutistically, definitionally believes "What I *want* to exist, *ought* exist!" Only because his wish is father to his thought. Only because he grandiosely, Jehovahistically ordains: "When I prefer to be accepted, I should be!" (3) He is a *worthless person* when he is rejected because he insanely decides or dictates that he is worthless under those circumstances. (*a*) As indicated a few paragraphs back, he doesn't have to rate or measure his *personhood*, his entire being, his total self at all; and he could merely decide to fully accept rather than to crassly rate himself. (*b*) When he dogmatically asserts that he is a worthless person because some of his main traits or characteristics are rejected by another individual, he is obviously illogically overgeneralizing. Just because someone else finds some of his aspects rejectable is hardly evidence that he, totally, is of no value. (*c*) Even if his rejection by another indicates that this other person finds him completely valueless, he would still be wrong if he concluded, "Because I am totally worthless to this *other*, I have to consider myself totally worthless to *me*." (4) If he concludes that the person who rejects him is a rotter and a bastard, he is making the same illogical overgeneralization about this individual as he makes when he puts himself, as a person, down when he experiences rejection; for his rejector has numerous—probably hundreds—of traits, many of which are desirable or efficient and many of which are undesirable or inefficient. At most, therefore, he can justifiably conclude that his rejector has some important traits or characteristics that are rotten, but not that he, as a total human being, is rotten.

For many reasons, such as those listed in the previous paragraph, the individual who feels (at point C) anxious, depressed, ashamed, or hostile when he is rejected by another (at point A) is creating these upsetting feelings by his own highly irrational beliefs at point B. In addition to sane beliefs, he has a number of interlocking insane beliefs, all of which are really tautological and definitional, and are not truly related to reality. But as long as he devoutly holds on to these irrational beliefs, he will strongly tend (1) to feel depressed and/or angry; (2) to be obsessed with his own circular thinking; (3) to mull his thoughts around, sometimes for hours or days on end, in his own inappropriate emotional juices; (4) usually to behave in such a manner that he enhances his chances for continued rejection; (5) to conclude after a while that he is hopelessly upsettable; and (6) to bring on various other unfortunate symptoms, disturbances, and psychosomatic reactions.

In the course of rational-emotive psychotherapy, many emotive, experiential, and behavioristic methods of psychotherapy are employed—but they are not used in a hit-and-miss eclectic manner. They are consciously utilized in order, in many vigorous and clear-cut ways, to interrupt the individual's irrational belief system and to teach him how to keep attacking it himself, not merely for the duration of therapy but for the rest of his life. Most uniquely, as will be shown in the verbatim therapy transcripts included in this book, cognitive and didactic methods of therapeutic intervention are employed. Although these are only a part of the RET armamentarium, they are in some ways its most distinctive and effective part.

After the therapist has shown the client the A-B-C's of how he has been and still is disturbing himself, he then goes on to point D—disputing the irrational beliefs that the client devoutly holds at point B. Thus, in the case we are examining, where the individual is horrified because he may be or actually is rejected, he is shown how to dispute as follows: "Why can't I stand being rejected? Where is the evidence that it is awful, horrible, and catastrophic for me not to be accepted? Why should I have been approved rather than rejected? How does my rejection prove that I am a worthless individual or that my rejector is a rotter and a bastard?" At the same time that he is shown how to dispute his irrational beliefs, the client is shown why his rational beliefs are legitimate, how he can learn from them, and what he can do about using them to effectively change some of the noxious conditions—like rejection—that keep occurring at point A.

If the client actively starts to dispute his irrational beliefs and to substantiate his rational ones, he normally arrives at point E—the effect of his disputing. First, he achieves a cognitive effect (cE), or a revised philosophy about A. Thus, he will tend to conclude: "There is no reason why I can't stand being rejected, though I may well never like it. It is clearly *not* awful, horrible and catastrophic, although it may be highly inconvenient, for me not to be accepted. The only reason I absolutely *should* have been approved is because I foolishly *think* I should; it is *better*, but hardly *necessary*, for me to be approved. My rejection does not in the least prove that I am a worthless individual, but merely indicates that I may well have some ineffective traits and that some people may wrongly consider me worthless for having them. My rejector may be acting unfairly or stupidly in rejecting me, but he is entitled to his disagreeable behavior and is not a total rotter for displaying it."

Finally, if the client persists in this new cognitive effect or philosophy, he will tend to develop, according to RET theory and practice, a new behavioral effect (bE), which consists of a radically changed emotion or symptom. Thus, instead of feeling depressed, anxious, or hostile, as he originally did at point C, he will now tend to feel only disappointed, sad, and frustrated. He may still be highly emotional—since it is appropriate that he feel emotional when an important rejection occurs in his life—but he will not be truly disturbed, upset, or destroyed.

Through the cognitive aspect of RET, then (as well as through its experiential, emotive, and behavioristic aspects), the client is specifically taught how to be *discriminatingly* emotional—or to control his own emotional destiny and truly to run his own life. This kind of cognitive-emotional discrimination (which has often been inaccurately labeled "emotional insight") is, of course, produced in other types of therapy, too. But it is my hypothesis that it is learned much more readily and thoroughly by active teaching, as is usually done in RET, than by less cognitively-oriented kinds of therapeutic encounters. In fact, I would hypothesize that so far no one has invented any method of helping troubled individuals to make some of the finer distinctions and utilize some of the more elegant solutions to their problems than the RET method of very specifically and concretely teaching them rational sensitivity and emotional discrimination.

RET can even be more briefly (though not entirely adequately) explained by noting that, according to its formulations, virtually all human disturbance is self-created by the human individual because he pig-headedly and devoutly believes in two nonsensical words and their equivalents: "It's terrible!" The person who is easily and consistently upsettable more specifically believes that (1) *"It's terrible* when I fail to do some important task well or when significant others do not approve of me; and I am a pretty *worthless person* when these kinds of failures or rejections occur!" (2) *"It's awful* when you fail to treat me fairly or to give me the kind of favors I strongly desire you to give me; and you are a *rotten individual*, a *louse*, when you deal with me in that fashion!" (3) *"It's horrible* when the world is rough and things around me are quite difficult; and *I can't stand it* when life is that hard!"

As long as he maintains these magical, unscientific, definitional beliefs, it is virtually impossible for the individual not to be frequently emotionally disturbed. If he wants to be minimally disturbable and maximally sane, he'd better substitute for all his absolutistic *It's terrible*'s two other words which he does not parrot or give lip-service to but which he incisively thinks through and accepts— namely, "Too bad!" or "Tough shit!" Or, more precisely, in terms of the three basic "terrors," "awfulnesses," and "horrors" listed in the previous paragraph: (1) *"Too bad* that I fail to do some important tasks well or that significant others do not always approve of me! But that's the way I am and will in all probability always be: fallible and partially unlovable." (2) *"Tough shit* when you fail to treat me fairly or to give me the kind of favors I strongly desire from you! But that's the way you are: often unfair and ungiving." (3) *"Tough luck* when the world is rough and things around me are quite difficult! But even though I may never like it, that's the way it is, and I can definitely stand it if I can't change it for the better."

Will this rather simplistic, utterly realistic, and fully grown-up philosophy of life really eliminate all serious emotional disturbances to which humans always seem to have been and still very much are heir? Possibly not; but I would somewhat conservatively guess that it would minimize at least 90 percent of them. I could, of course, be wrong about this. But so far, in the clinic and in the research laboratory, I seem to have been surprisingly right.

As for the clinic, conclusive results are by no means in yet and probably will not be until a large-scale study comparing the effectiveness of rational-emotive therapy with various other major forms of psychotherapy is completed. Unfortunately, although I would be delighted to conduct such a study, it is not at the moment feasible, because it would require at least a million dollars to execute, and no research fund or agency has been ready to grant me and my associates at the Institute for Advanced Study in Rational Psychotherapy even a small part of such funds to carry on this kind of an experiment.

Meanwhile, however, a number of smaller studies have been done that indicate that RET is quite effective when used with disturbed individuals, and particularly when it is used with clients who have had a considerable amount of psychoanalytic or client-centered therapy and made little or no improvement until their therapist switched to RET techniques. Thus, clinical papers showing the effectiveness of rational-emotive methods with various types of clients have been published by many therapists, including Ard (1966, 1967a, 1967b, 1968, 1969); Bedford (1969), Breen (1970), Callahan (1967), Diamond (1967a, 1967b), Geis (1970), Glicken (1967), Grossack (1965), Gullo (1966a, 1966b, 1968), Harper (1960a, 1960b, 1967), Hartman (1967), Hauck (1966, 1967a, 1967b, 1968, 1969), Hudson (1967), Konietzko (1968), Maultsby (1968, 1969d), and Wagner (1963, 1966).

Experimental studies of RET, showing that it is clinically effective when used with control groups or procedures, have also been done by a good many researchers, including Bard (1965), Burkhead (1970), Conner (1970), DiLoreto (1968), Ellis (1957), Gustav (1968), Hartman (1968), Karst and Trexler (1970), Krippner (1964), Lafferty (1962), Maes and Heimann (1970), Maultsby (1969a, 1969b, 1969c), O'Connell (1970), Raskin (1965, 1966), Shapiro, Neufield, and Post (1962), Shapiro and Ravenette (1959), Sharma (1970), Taft (1965), and Zingle (1965).

Many independent researchers, most of whom were not even particularly aware of RET hypotheses and procedures, have published findings that confirm some of the major assumptions and principles of rational-emotive therapy. This is particularly true of the basic RET theory that emotions are largely caused, not by the stimuli or activating events that occur to people at point A, but by the cognitive evaluations, mediating processes, or belief systems that they engage in at point B. There is now a huge mass of experimental evidence to support this hypothesis, including studies by Beck (1967), Beck and Hurvich (1959), Beck and Stein (1967), Becker (1960), Becker, Spielberger, and Parker (1963), Brainerd (1970), Breznitz (1967), Carlson, Travers, and Schwab (1969), Cassidy, Flanagan, and Spellman (1957), Davison (1967), Davison and Valins (1969), Davitz (1969), Deane (1966), Folkins (1970), Frank (1968), Friedman, Cowitz, Cohen, and Granick (1963), Fritz and Marks (1954), Garfield et al. (1967), Geer, Davison, and Gatchel (1970), Geis (1966), Glass, Singer, and Friedman (1969), Gliedman et al. (1958), Gordon (1967), Grossack, Armstrong, and Lussiev (1966), Jordan and Kempler (1970), Kamiya (1968), Kilty (1968, 1969, 1970), Lange, Sproufe, and Hastings (1967), Lazarus (1966), Loeb, Beck, Diggory, and Tuthill (1967), Marcia, Rubin, and Efran (1969), McConaghy (1967), Miller (1969), Mowrer (1938), Nisbett and Shachter (1966), Nomikos et al. (1968), Pastore (1950, 1952), Paul (1966), Salzinger and Pisoni (1960), Schacter and Singer (1962), Steffy, Meichenbaum and Best (1970), Sullivan (1969), Valins (1966, 1967, 1970), Valins and Ray (1967), Wenger, Averill, and Smith (1968), and White, Fichtenbaum, and Dollard (1969).

A great many other studies have also been done that more specifically show that when individuals are given concrete suggestions regarding emotional and behavioral changes, either with or without hypnosis, they significantly modify their behavior. Included among scores of studies of this kind are those by Barber (1966), Barber and Calverley (1965, 1966), Hampson, Rosenthal, and Frank (1954), Jellinek (1946), Levitt, Den Breeijen, and Persky (1960), Levitt, Persky, and Brady (1964), Meath (1954), Roper (1967), Rosenthal and Frank (1956), Sparks (1962), Wolf (1950), and Wolf and Pinsky (1954).

Still another group of experiments have been performed that present impressive evidence that when human beings have emotional disturbances, they have specific irrational ideas, especially those which I have been hypothesizing since I gave my first talk on rational-emotive therapy in 1956. These include studies by Appleton (1969), Argabrite and Nidorf (1968), Beck (1967), Conklin (1965), Dua (1970), Jones (1968), Kemp (1961), Lidz et al. (1958), Meehl (1966), Overall and Gorham (1961), Payne and Hirst (1957), Rimm and Litvak (1969), Rokeach (1964), Spielberger, Parker, and Becker (1963), Tosi and Carlson (1970), and Velten (1968).

Further evidence favoring some of the basic principles and practices of RET has been presented in several studies that show that the kind of live, active-directive homework assignments that are an integral part of rational-emotive procedures are not only quite effective in aiding personality change but are usually more effective than more passive kinds of desensitization, such as those frequently employed by Wolpe (1958) and his followers. The efficacy of in vivo homework procedures has been experimentally validated by a good many researchers, including Cooke (1966), Davison (1965), Garfield et al. (1967), Jones (1924), Litvak (1969a, 1969b), Rimm and Medeiros (1970), Ritter (1968), and Zajonc (1968).

I could present a great deal more evidence that cognitive-behavior therapy, in general, and rational-emotive therapy, in particular, not only works but is probably more effective than any other major system of therapy thus far devised. Let me, however, conclude this introduction by making the important point that although RET procedures were originally invented to help individuals who had already become afflicted with serious emotional problems, they are so allied to the field of education that they have enormous implications for emotional prophylaxis as well as treatment. A number of clinicians and other professionals have now shown how rational-emotive psychology can be applied to "normal" or little disturbed individuals, especially to young children, in order to help prevent them from ever becoming as seriously upsettable as they presumably would otherwise become in the course of modern living. Articles and books vouching for the effectiveness of what I call emotional education using RET principles have been published by a number of writers, including Austin (1964), Ellis (1969d, in press c, in press d), Ellis, Wolfe, and Moseley (1966), Glicken (1966, 1968), Hauck (1967a), Lafferty, Dennerll, and Rettich (1964), McGrory (1967), Pollaczek (1967), Rand (1970), Wagner (1966), and Wolfe et al. (1970).

As a result of the good results so far obtained with using rational-emotive psychology in educational settings, the Institute for Advanced Study in Rational Psychotherapy in New York City has established the Living School, a private school for nondisturbed children, where a concerted effort is being made to teach all the pupils, in the course of their regular academic program, some of the main principles of rational living. By giving this kind of emotional education to the youngsters and their parents, it is hoped that methods will be worked out by which any public or private school in the world can eventually employ rational-emotive psychology to enhance the personal growth and enjoyment, as well as the academic performance, of its pupils.

To return to this casebook, the cases herewith presented are all fairly typical of RET procedures and are included to show what

the rational-emotive therapist does to help his clients think more
clearly and sanely about themselves, about others, and about the
universe, and to indicate how they can thereby help themselves
"emotionally." These cases by no means display all the many techniques that are frequently employed in RET; but they do highlight
some of its main or most unique aspects. They also show what can
be done by an effective rational-emotive practitioner to help some
people in a relatively brief period of time, in spite of the fact that
they have a number of serious emotional difficulties.

CHAPTER 2

The Case of the Black
and Silver Masochist

BEN N. ARD, JR., Ph.D.

The excerpts from the following case involve a twenty-four-year-old, single, handicapped woman who was referred to Dr. Ard by her counselor at the rehabilitation center where she was staying at the time of her referral. (She had been at the center only a short while since her recent release from a state mental hospital, where she had been for about seven years. There she had been diagnosed as having a schizophrenic reaction. Her counselor rightly believed that she needed more psychotherapy and so referred her to the therapist.)

Because she was not in a position to afford extended treatment and because the therapist was familiar with rational-emotive psychotherapy, an attempt was made to see what could be accomplished within a few sessions.

The case had many unusual aspects to it and perhaps goes against what many professionals have been taught in their professional training. The therapeutic approach is direct, active, hard-hitting, even relentless. The client's religious assumptions, which have been unquestioned for many years and which seem to be at the base of her problems, are attacked in a straightforward manner. Attacking a person's religious beliefs is a form of heresy in many circles of the helping professions. Yet, as this case illustrates, just such steps are sometimes desirable, if the client is to be helped on the road to better mental health.

The client was seen for a fifty-minute hour at intervals of once a week, sometimes every two weeks, from spring through fall of 1969.

Here, then, is the case of a very unusual human being who has had a hard life and adopted rather unusual methods of adaptation to her harsh treatment by several people. This case is not an ideal one; many probable mistakes were made in these therapy sessions.

But the young woman does make some progress. Perhaps this record at least shows that some help can be given to a client who many would feel was practically hopeless.

This young woman had previously been labeled the "Black and Silver Masochist," since she had adopted the practice of paying men to beat her with black and silver belts to assuage her guilt feelings, which derived from her unquestioned religious assumptions. Prior to the present treatment, she had seen a number of therapists and had many shock treatments, none of which she felt had been very helpful.

FIRST SESSION

T¹: You said over the phone that you had had some other help?

C²: I spent seven years in——State Hospital.

T³: Did you feel you got some help there?

C⁴: A little bit. I got help in that I realized I needed it. I had thought it was kinda normal going around cutting up with razor blades.

T⁵: You cut yourself with razor blades?

C⁶: Yeah, I've cut myself (reveals many, many scars on both arms, from the wrists up past the elbow). It's just lately that I've turned to razor blades because I couldn't get what I really want.

T⁷: What do you really want?

C⁸: I term it as "black and silver."

T⁹: When you say "black and silver," will you tell me what that means?

C¹⁰: A belt.

T¹¹: A belt?

C¹²: I had a list of guys who would use it, but the thing is they don't do it for free. I gave them the money that they want. But it's kind of a rotten deal.

T¹³: Let me see if I understand this: you want men to use a black and silver belt on you?

C¹⁴: Yeah. A black leather belt with a silver buckle. Just before I did this last job with the razor blade, I went out and bought me a black belt. It cost me five dollars. It's a real neat one. I have several of them.

T[15]: Umm.

C[16]: I lived with this guy who did it for me for two weeks. I did anything he wanted me to. He had a lot of grass floating around. I had a couple of bummers on it. I let him take pictures of me, nude.

T[17]: Why do you want these men to beat you with these black belts?

C[18]: I don't know; it's fun.

T[19]: How do you mean, "It's fun"?

C[20]: It makes me feel better for the things I've done.

T[21]: It sounds like pretty rough punishment for yourself. Is that fair?

C[22]: Yeah, it's fair. I told my counselor what a tramp I was.

T[23]: You think you are a tramp?

C[24]: Yeah.

T[25]: Why do you think you are a tramp?

C[26]: Various things. I think it started with my mother. Because she used to beat us up, you see. She was sick herself, you know. The more my father said against her, the more I had to justify her. He didn't do anything about her for five years. If anyone is to blame, he is the one. Because he didn't do anything about it for five years. After all the damage has been done, big deal! So he got a divorce, wow!

T[27]: May I interject something right here? You just touched upon something that might be pretty basic to what you have been doing to yourself in your life. You talked about blaming. You mentioned your father and your mother, and you have previously been talking about yourself. One of the things that I hear in what you have been saying so far is that you have been blaming yourself, pretty badly.

Although this first session has only gone on for a few minutes, Dr. Ard zeroes in on what he considers the client's main problem to be: blaming herself. He does this largely on theoretical grounds, since RET theory hypothesizes that whenever people are seriously disturbed, they are almost invariably blaming themselves, blaming others, or blaming the world. And by "blaming" the rational-emotive therapist means not only (a) insisting that certain people or things are responsible for or cause unfortunate results but also (b) demanding that they should undoubtedly be damned as individuals (that is, rated as being *bad people*) and severely punished for their misdeeds. Although in this particular instance, since the client has such as unusual history, the therapist gets sidetracked for awhile before he returns to the essence of her disturbance, her blaming tendencies, he quite properly raises this important issue very early in the therapy sessions.

C^{28}: I don't blame myself without good reason. I don't do anything without good reason.

T^{29}: But is the reason you have been giving yourself such a bad time entirely justified?

C^{30}: Yeah, why not?

T^{31}: You said you were beaten as a child by your mother?

C^{32}: Yeah, that's how I became handicapped. And my brother had seven fractures of the skull. He's mentally retarded.

T^{33}: Your mother injured you?

C^{34}: Yeah.

T^{35}: How?

C^{36}: I had a brain hemorrhage.

T^{37}: From the beating?

C^{38}: Yeah. From being thrown against the wall.

T^{39}: But you are continuing to want to hurt yourself today. Is that right?

C^{40}: Well, yeah.

T^{41}: I am interested in what you are saying about your past; it may make the present more understandable. But I am also interested in us getting to work on the present and the future, as fast as we can.

C^{42}: Yeah; ooh, I agree. It isn't all my mother. I have done things that I know were wrong.

T^{43}: Who have you killed?

C^{44}: Oh—this guy. I didn't kill him; he committed suicide.

T^{45}: You drove him to it, you mean?

C^{46}: Yeah. I had an affair with him when I was fourteen. He was sixty-three. All I wanted him to do was to get him to stop because I was having these dreams. And at that time I thought they were a sign from God that he had told. Because I was hung up on religion. Because I was raised a Seventh-Day Adventist. I just wanted him to stop. When he found out I told, he committed suicide and left a note saying "May God forgive you." So when you say, "Who have you killed?" you're not far off.

T⁴⁷: But you didn't kill him.

C⁴⁸: But I feel I made him commit suicide.

T⁴⁹: You feel you should be punished forever?

C⁵⁰: It's been ten years—

T⁵¹: You are still trying to punish yourself, aren't you?

C⁵²: Yeah, but the problem that goes along with it is that it has been turned into—somewhat—pleasurable. So that makes it harder to give up.

T⁵³: Do you really want to give up these things that give you pleasure?

C⁵⁴: More than I did even last year. Last year I was seeing a psychiatrist, and one of the reasons I quit—there were two main reasons. One was that I felt I wasn't getting anywhere, and secondly I wasn't all that ready to give it up. I don't dig hypocrites. And I don't like to be one, and I felt I was being hypocritical.

T⁵⁵: By continuing to see the psychiatrist when you didn't really want to work on getting better?

C⁵⁶: Yeah. Yeah. Yeah.

T⁵⁷: Are you ready to work on getting better now?

C⁵⁸: Yeah.

T⁵⁹: It's going to be hard work. Damned hard work.

C⁶⁰: Ooh—Yeah, I know because I have tried to do it myself.

T⁶¹: It isn't easy, is it?

C⁶²: No. I used to carry a razor blade around with me all the time in my key case, just for security reasons. I could take it or leave it, but when the time came, oh man, I failed.

T⁶³: You were going to use it to hurt yourself with, right?

C⁶⁴: Yeah, sure. Why not?

T⁶⁵: Well, one of the things you and I might find out, if we are going to work together, is what are going to be the understandings, the rules of the game, the commitment we have to each other here. I may operate a little differently from some of the other people you have seen.

C⁶⁶: Yeah. I don't want to go around and around like with a psychiatrist. I'm fed up.

T⁶⁷: Well, let's see if you think you would want to work with me.
       Let me tell you a little bit about the sorts of things we might
       do. One of the things we might do is talk about what you
       are doing to yourself. And in so far as it's helpful, I am all
       for encouraging you. But in so far as it is self-defeating for
       you, I am going to work against that.

C⁶⁸: What's "self-defeating"?

T⁶⁹: Anything harmful you do to yourself such as cutting yourself
       with razors—

C⁷⁰: Or drinking nail polish remover?

T⁷¹: I don't want to go into specifics such as razor blades right
       now because that is not the problem, but rather what you
       are thinking inside your head which causes you to turn to
       razor blades or whatever you might turn to. I am going to
       offer you a little proposition and see if you think it's worth
       looking at. If you want to work with me, and I am willing
       to work with you, I would look upon you somewhat as a
       partner. That is, you and me as partners. Specifically, the
       healthy part of you working together with me, working on
       the problems you have been having. That means that the
       healthy part of you has to agree to work with me. Does that
       make sense to you? That is, there are some things within
       you that are working to your detriment, if I hear you right.

C⁷²: Um-hm.

Quite properly, Dr. Ard sees that he can easily get lost in the
fascinating details of the client's story. But the purpose of RET
is not to track down the gory details of her history and thereby
show her how to "understand" herself. Rather, the main purpose
is to demonstrate to her what thoughts she is thinking inside her
head that cause her to have a long and checkered history of cutting
herself, drinking nail polish, driving an older man to suicide, being
beaten with belts, and so on. So in T⁷¹ and several subsequent responses, the therapist tries to get away from history-taking and
to structure the therapeutic relationship with the client as a collabo-
rative problem-solving kind of relation.

T⁷³: But there is also a healthy part of you. The fact that you
       are in here right now, talking about possibly doing something

differently in the future, says to me that you may be ready—
or fixin' to start, as some people might say—to do something
about it.

C⁷⁴: Yeah.

T⁷⁵: That's the sign of the healthy you—what I want to work with.
You and me against that unhealthy part that says you have
to hurt yourself, you have to get somebody to beat you, you
have to do all these irrational things.

C⁷⁶: I'm in agreement. It's just that I might not be able to give
enough right away.

T⁷⁷: I understand that you have been through quite a bit of hell,
from what you have told me so far. And I am assuming that
getting you to function in ways that are more satisfying for
you is going to take some effort, maybe a hell of a lot of
effort—hard work on your part. I am not expecting miracles.
But if you are really ready to do some hard work, to adopt
some different practices, different from those you have
adopted in the past, and you are really ready to commit yourself to this, and you and I work together as a team, then
we can put some distance between you and your problem.
I want you and I working together. Does this make sense
to you?

C⁷⁸: Yeah. One of the things I want to accomplish is—well, this
thing about punishment is all tangled up and connected with
sex.

T⁷⁹: Um-hm. Well, would you like to do some reading?

C⁸⁰: Yes.

T⁸¹: You may like to start with Ellis & Harper's *Guide to Rational
Living*, then.

C⁸²: Okay.

Dr. Ard's recommendation that the client do some reading as a
supplement to her sessions with him is another typical method of
RET. Because the theory states that people can be *taught* to understand and change their thinking, RET employs many different kinds
of teaching techniques, including bibliotherapy. At the Consultation
Center of the Institute for Advanced Study in Rational Psychotherapy in New York City, we give each new client a package of
reprints that briefly state some of the main principles of RET. We

also recommend strongly that each client purchase a paperback copy of *A Guide to Rational Living* (Ellis & Harper, 1970) and that he ultimately read several of the other main RET texts, such as *How to Live with a Neurotic* (Ellis, 1969a), *Reason and Emotion in Psychotherapy* (Ellis, 1962), *How to Prevent Your Child from Becoming a Neurotic Adult* (Ellis, Wolfe, and Moseley, 1966), *Sex Without Guilt* (Ellis, 1970), and *The Art and Science of Love* (Ellis, 1969b). Although controlled studies of the effectiveness of this type of bibliotherapy have not yet been done, clinical reports indicate that it both hastens and intensifies the therapeutic process in many instances.

T[83]: It might be helpful, then, if we could get some orientation as to how you feel about sex and guilt, and start looking at some of your assumptions—start working on them.

C[84]: It doesn't surprise me that I feel guilty about sex, because of what happened right off the bat with this guy who committed suicide.

T[85]: But sex doesn't always have to be associated with guilt and bad feelings, does it?

C[86]: I realize this.

T[87]: Sex can be enjoyable and a good part of life, integrated in a satisfying way in your life and not involving beatings or punishment or bad feelings; is that possible?

C[88]: Yes, but it kind of has to.

T[89]: You assume.

C[90]: It's been my experience.

T[91]: I can understand that. Is it possible, though, that you could think of sex in a different context?

C[92]: Yeah, if I find somebody that I really dig.

T[93]: You could change your ideas about sex, then.

C[94]: Yes, but I just don't know how to go about it.

At this point Dr. Ard interrupted the session somewhat to tell the client about another of his clients, an alcoholic woman, who also had severe sexual problems and who was very guilty about having relations with men. In spite of her severe handicaps and problems, he was able to show her how to combat her guilt and how to become so liberal sexually that she was able to go out by herself to bars and other public places, to pick up male companions, and to have sex relations with them if she cared to do so. She ultimately found a steady lover and later married him. The client showed great interest in this story and was apparently affected by it, in that she began to think that she, too, could be helped to overcome her sexual guilt and self-punishment.

This method of using stories, fables, events in the lives of other clients, personal incidents from the life of the therapist, and other material of this sort is frequently used in RET to make certain points clearer and to indicate to clients that they, too, can overcome their handicaps just as others have been helped to do so.

T⁹⁵: This means changing your assumptions about yourself, punishment and sex, and men—the interrelationship of all these factors.

C⁹⁶: I think I can do it but it might take some time and you might get fed up with me.

T⁹⁷: Has that happened with other therapists?

C⁹⁸: The people at the hospital got pissed off at me.

T⁹⁹: Why so?

C¹⁰⁰: They felt that if I had the willpower I could do it.

T¹⁰¹: What do you think about that?

C¹⁰²: I don't think that just locking a person up in a place is going to help them change their ideas. The reason shock treatment didn't work for me was that I considered it a punishment. I had about six or seven series of them (with about eighteen to twenty-seven in a series). I swallowed some razor blades, and they had to operate on me to get them out. They had to do that three times in four months. They put me in a maximum security ward, but I did it again just to prove to them that they couldn't stop me from doing it.

T¹⁰³: You proved it, didn't you?

C¹⁰⁴: Yeah, rather painfully so.

T¹⁰⁵: Well, now, I hear you saying that you are giving yourself an awfully bad time and doing a variety of things that are really self-defeating for you, and have been doing them for several years—

C¹⁰⁶: Since I was twelve. I only started it because I couldn't get to my mother. I was getting tired of my father saying I was rotten like my mother, and no good. Until this year I was not going to have any kids because I just knew I would beat them up like my mother did. I kept having dreams that I was beating a child. And I would get sexual pleasure out of it. That really bugged me, you know? Because it just proved to me that I was just like my mother. I mean to me it proved that I was just like my mother.

T^{107}: You think it proved you were no damned good, huh?

C^{108}: Well, yeah.

T^{109}: But it doesn't, does it, really? Can you see that, now?

C^{110}: When I want to, I can scrape up a lot of patience.

T^{111}: So there are a lot of good things in you, too.

C^{112}: But it scares me to get angry because I just think I could kill somebody or something. I use to dream I was getting beaten by some guy with a black and silver belt until I got some guy to do it, then I didn't dream about it anymore. I used to get sexual pleasure out of that dream, too.

T^{113}: Are you telling me—do I hear this right, that you want to get to the day, someday, when you won't need razor blades, or black and silver belts, beatings, etc.?

C^{114}: Yeah; if nothing else, it's a damned nuisance, you know. And I don't want to hang around with that kind of a crowd (the kind of guys who will do that sort of thing). As far as razor blades are concerned, it's a bloody mess to clean up. Not everybody in society is going to understand, and you are going to get rejected a lot.

T^{115}: And maybe be put back in the hospital again?

C^{116}: Yeah. And I don't believe in starting out on something unless you really want to do something about it.

The remainder of this session is taken up with arrangements being made for the client to be transported regularly to the sessions and to arrange for them financially. The therapist, in response T^{111}, makes something of an RET error. For his pointing out to the client that "there are a lot of good things in you, too" implies that she cannot prove that she is no damned good *because* of these good things. This is technically correct, since she obviously cannot be *no* good if she has *some* good in her. In RET, however, we try to show individuals that they are not worthless or of no value to themselves *even* if they have no "good" or "worthwhile" traits. Because the goal of their lives would better be not *rating* themselves at all as being either "worthwhile" or "worthless," but merely *enjoying* their existences. The therapist, more elegantly, therefore, could have pointed out to the client that she *does* have some good, efficient, or strong *traits* but that she'd better not rate or judge her *self* by these traits. *She* is neither good nor bad, even though her individual characteristics may be measurable.

Dr. Ard also chooses not to deal, at this point, with the client's statement that she gets so angry that she thinks she could kill somebody or something. Perhaps he does so because he knows that the session is near its close. Normally, however, a rational-emotive therapist would quickly pick up on a client's feelings of rage and show her how she creates these feelings herself by irrationally *demanding* or *dictating* that others behave the way she wants them to behave, and that she would benefit herself by disputing these irrational demands.

Although this first session has presented to the client little specific evidence of her irrational ideas and how to combat them, it has induced a highly disturbed individual to open up about herself, shown her that she is needlessly self-condemning, and got her to agree to collaborate with the therapist in an empirical and logic-based attempt to solve her problem.

SECOND SESSION

During the second session, the therapist continues to work with the client along lines similar to those he employed during the first session and particularly tries to get her to change some of her negative, punitive ideas about herself. Here is an excerpt from this session:

T[1]: I'm saying that you have some stupid reasons for doing many of the things that you've done in your life. Now my job, as I hear it, is to help you to see that what you've been telling yourself as reasons for doing them are stupid reasons, and to help you see for yourself that there are better ways of running your life. Does that make sense to you?

C[2]: Yes.

T[3]: That means that you're going to have to give up some of your previous ways of thinking, because they're self-defeating for you. Now, at the beginning you may not see that. Because as you say, for example, the belt bit, the "black and silver," does bring some pleasure. But in so far as you get beat up by it, that's not a good thing. The same thing about the razor blade. In so far as you punish yourself, and you *want* punishment, that makes some sense. But it's *really* self-defeating for you. And I want you to see that, not because I say it, but because it's true—whether I'm alive or dead—that if you go through life the way you have been in the past, you're only hurting yourself. And we've got to get you to *question* some of your assumptions and *change* them. Now that's easy for me to say; it's hard to get you to do.

C⁴: But you see, all the evidence I have tells me that I *deserve* it.

T⁵: That's what we're gonna have to question! And we're gonna only have to accept as evidence what is logical, clear, rational—not just because you have a *feeling*.

C⁶: Yes, but isn't it because I've contributed to someone's suicide?

T⁷: That's *not* justification for all the misery you've given yourself. No, no!

T⁸: Yes, but they put people in prison for life.

C⁹: Yes, but not for getting other people to commit suicide. Let's look at that one minute. If a person commits suicide, many people in his life could say that they are involved with him. But if I understand suicide, it means that by definition *he* chooses that. Now if you pulled a gun on him and shot him, that's murder. But murder is not the same as suicide. If he takes a gun and shoots *himself* because you said something to him, you are still not to *blame* for his death. Even though you said, "You know, I think you're a crumb, and you ought to kill yourself!" and he then goes and shoots himself, you're still not to blame.

In RET, the therapist teaches long-range instead of short-range hedonism: that even though the client enjoys, in the short-run, punishing herself, in the long run she is acting foolishly. He also teaches that feelings do not constitute evidence for beliefs or facts. The client *feels* that she deserves punishment for her past misdeeds, but this feeling hardly proves (*a*) that it is a *fact* she has done badly or (*b*) that she *should* or *must* punish herself for her "bad" act.

The rational-emotive therapist also tries to help the client see that *telling* someone to shoot himself does not actually cause him to commit suicide. He still *chooses* to heed the so-called suicide-impelling statement. Moreover, even if the client were truly responsible for another's suicide or significantly contributed to it, that client would not be to blame—meaning, condemnable or rotten *as a person*—for this wrong deed.

Technically, the therapist makes some mistakes, from the standpoint of rational-emotive philosophy, in response T[5], where he says: "That's what we're gonna have to question! And we're gonna only have to accept as evidence what is logical, clear, rational—not just because you have a *feeling*." For his "gonna have to question" and "gonna only have to accept as evidence" are imperative, absolute statements that themselves could help create anxiety in the client. For if she *has* to question or *has* to accept as evidence what is logical, and she actually does not do what she *has* to, she will almost certainly condemn herself for her horrible errors. Dr. Ard could have more accurately pointed out to her that "*it would be better* if you questioned your assumption" and "*it would be much more desirable* if you accept as evidence what is logical, clear, rational." Then, if she does badly, she will tend merely to feel sorry rather than self-condemning. I have made this same error of using "have to," "should," "got to," and so on, with clients and in my early writings (including *A Guide to Rational Living*). But these days I am more careful and rarely goof in this respect!

THIRD SESSION

During the third session, the therapist continues to show the client that her self-punishing tendencies stem from her religious and other judgmental ideas and that she can change these ideas and thereby stop punishing herself, sexually and otherwise. A significant excerpt from this third session follows:

C[1]: So I'm beginning to think that if they [the early Christian fathers] could be so wrong then— You're right, I have been questioning some of these, you know, beliefs.

T[2]: So you don't have to blame yourself and get into all this punishment kick just because of some of the religious teachings you've been taught in the past.

C³: Well, so far I've been working on trying to convince myself that maybe everything I believe is not true.

T⁴: You mean in regard to religion?

C⁵: Yeah. And if I can do that, then—you know, then I can feel free to do other things. As far as religion, I do believe there is a God. But if he's the kind of a God that they've convinced me so thoroughly exists and presented to me, then—then the hell with it!

T⁶: Um-hm. It sounds to me like you've made some progress in this regard!

C⁷: I hope so! Because I'll be a lot freer if I can.

T⁸: Um-hm.

C⁹: It's still with me. But I'm working on it!

T¹⁰: Good!

When the rational-emotive therapist encounters a client whose dysfunctional behavior clearly seems to be related to her dogmatic religious beliefs, he may try to get her to modify her beliefs and still be somewhat religious, or to change her beliefs radically and to surrender her religion. If, for example, she devoutly believes that her religion demands that she kill others who are irreligious, he may try to get her to become differently religious or nonreligious. In this case, the client seems to be maintaining a basic, somewhat vague belief in God, but to be giving up the damning aspects of the particular God in whom she used to believe. This may well be a satisfactory solution to her problem of self-punishment.

Later in the session, Dr. Ard discusses the client's relations with the latest boyfriend.

T¹¹: Can you do it [have sex relations] with Jack without being beaten?

C¹²: I've never done it with Jack. I don't think Jack would give it to me, either.

T¹³: Give what to you now?

C¹⁴: He'd give me sex.

T¹⁵: He'd give you sex?

C¹⁶: He would! I think he—he would! Well, if he's going to take me to Los Angeles for a week, I mean—it's kinda obvious that he would. Because he wouldn't be—

T^{17}:   Think you could have sex with Jack without being beaten?

C^{18}:   I hope I can. I hope that by the time I get around to it I—I—think I can picture—I can picture him— I can tell, you know—you can tell how gentle a guy's going to be by just, say, the way he kisses or the way he holds your hand or something.

T^{19}:   Um-hm.

C^{20}:   And Jack is very, very gentle. He's just kind of a groove. Really!

T^{21}:   So you might be able to have sex with him and enjoy it, and have orgasm with him sometime, without ever having to resort to black and silver belt beatings?

C^{22}:   I kinda think so. Because I can picture it in my mind. And—

T^{23}:   Isn't it better to picture that than to picture being beaten by black and silver belts?

C^{24}:   Yeah, man. It's a groove!

T^{25}:   Well, if you continue to think that you've got to pay for some sin that you *assume* you've committed, that you *assume* you should be beaten for, then you'll resort to "black and silver" again.

C^{26}:   I guess so!

T^{27}:   And if you don't want to be beaten again, the way to avoid it is to question your assumptions that you have committed these sins, which you *should* be punished for.

C^{28}:   Well, I—Okay, I've been questioning mostly beliefs—that anything I've been told has been true. And I've pretty well come to the conclusion that maybe it hasn't. And I've also been thinking about what you were saying about people not being sinners but merely doing wrong acts.

T^{29}:   Um-hm.

C^{30}:   Doing wrong acts. And that makes sense. You know—

T^{31}:   Um-hm. So you can goof from time to time, but you don't have to blame yourself for your sins.

C^{32}:   Yeah, but I've goofed plenty! Hah!

T^{33}:   But you don't deserve the kind of punishment you've gotten for yourself. That right?

C^{34}:   Well, I've been accustomed to it! Though—

T^{35}:   I realize that—

C^{36}:   I didn't have to go out and *get* it, from the day I was born. I mean I—

T³⁷: Just because your mother beat you up, though, does that mean
       that you have to be beaten the rest of your life?
C³⁸: Um-hm. Um-hm. Well, I don't know.
T³⁹: You said, for example, that your family taught you some reli-
       gious things, which you're now beginning to question.
C⁴⁰: Yeah.
T⁴¹: It is possible that they also did some other things to you which
       you now could begin to question?
C⁴²: Oh, sure!

Dr. Ard keeps showing the client that she may well be able to
change her self-defeating sexual pattern if she changes her self-
damning assumptions. Even though she may have strongly learned
from her family to defame herself, she could question their beliefs
about her, just as she is now beginning to question the religious
beliefs they taught her. In RET, the therapist takes almost every
opportunity to show the client that her disturbed behavior is belief-
caused and that she has the ability to change her beliefs.

TENTH SESSION

The intervening sessions between the third and the last (tenth)
session, the therapist used various techniques that are somewhat
unique to rational therapy—namely, confrontation, confutation, de-
indoctrination, reeducation, and homework assignments. Some examples of these may be seen in the excerpts from the first, second,
third, and tenth sessions.

The basic cause of this young woman's problems seems to reside
in her unquestioned philosophic and religious assumptions, which
she had heretofore never examined critically. The therapist works
directly and actively at getting her to challenge and question her
basic assumptions and to substitute less self-defeating ideas to enable her to live a more satisfying, more rational life.

C¹: A friend read me the books of Matthew and Mark, to check
       it out, and there are some contradictions there.
T²: A few.
C³: Yeah, yeah. Like where it said Judas gave back the silver.
       In Acts it said he went and bought some land with it.
T⁴: He couldn't do both, could he?

C⁵: No, I guess not. I've almost decided that all Christianity is a form of mass hypnotism.

T⁶: That's quite a bit different from what you have believed for a long time, isn't it?

C⁷: Yeah. I've almost decided that there is no hell.

T⁸: If there really was no hell, then you wouldn't have to worry about going there, would you?

C⁹: No.

T¹⁰: It might be worth your while to check that out real good, wouldn't it?

C¹¹: Yeah. All the churches have a different concept of hell. And they all claim that they come up with scripture to prove their concept is right.

T¹²: And that shows you that they can't all be right, doesn't it? Your logic is good: they can't all be right. And as a matter of fact, they may all be wrong.

C¹³: No.

T¹⁴: There may be no hell at all. Is that possible?

C¹⁵: Yeah, that's possible.

T¹⁶: In which case your worry about going to hell would be unnecessary, wouldn't it?

C¹⁷: Yeah, if there were none.

T¹⁸: And all that punishment jazz would have to go by the boards, wouldn't it?

C¹⁹: Yeah. If I got to believe that there was no hell, then there wouldn't be any fear of hell.

T²⁰: And you wouldn't have to punish yourself anymore, or hire those guys to punish you with those black and silver belts anymore, would you?

C²¹: No. I went through a period of a couple of days when I felt almost free from hell, and I didn't desire to be punished.

T²²: Well! Congratulations! That has been a long, hard road getting there, hasn't it?

C²³: Yeah.

T²⁴: You don't really need it, do you?

C²⁵: No.

T²⁶: That would be a great sense of relief to you to know that you don't really need it anymore; you don't have to have beatings, you don't have to punish yourself.

C²⁷: Yeah. True.

T²⁸: And you can live a good life without worrying about whether
        the streets are paved with gold or burning with fire, or what-
        ever that hereafter is supposed to have—those presuppositions
        that the Christians ask that you believe on faith alone.

C²⁹: Yeah. How's come, if we are supposed to believe on faith alone,
        that God gave us a mind that would ask questions? You know,
        he gives you this mind so that you can explore things and
        then is all pushed out of shape when you can't accept them
        on faith.

T³⁰: You are using your mind to think with and any idea about
        religion that says that such a God would object to your using
        your mind that you do have, is a pretty sad idea, isn't it?

C³¹: Why did he give it to you if he didn't intend for you to use
        it?

T³²: Maybe he didn't give you anything; maybe the whole story
        is made up. Did you ever think about the story of Genesis,
        where he is supposed to have said don't eat of that tree in
        the Garden of Eden, and when he came and saw that they
        had eaten, he said "Where are you, Adam?" Isn't God supposed
        to be omnipotent? Doesn't he know where everybody is? How
        come he is asking where Adam is?

C³³: Because he wants to make him suffer by making him come
        out and face him.

T³⁴: Yes. As a matter of fact, that God of the Old Testament urged
        people to go out and kill all the men, women, and children
        in certain villages.

C³⁵: Yeah, right.

T³⁶: Is that the kind of God you want to believe in?

C³⁷: No.

T³⁸: And yet that is the same God who is writing down in his
        book every thought or fantasy you have, you say, according
        to what you have been taught. Why not say that that is a
        vicious idea, and I don't believe in such stories?

C³⁹: And how's come the very first thing every religion attacks
        is sex?

T⁴⁰: There you are.

C⁴¹: I am afraid I will fail at sex.

T⁴²: You tell yourself all sorts of garbage, don't you? If you tell yourself you are going to be a failure in a sex relationship, what better way is there to insure that you will be a "failure"? There is no better way, is there? If you doubt your ability to function—if you say, "Oh, I'm going to do something wrong," "I'm going to make the wrong move," or "I'm not going to do the thing right"—then you pretty well insure that that is, indeed, what you are going to do, by worrying about it. Or, "He won't like this about me." Whereas, if you said, "I'm going to do the best I can; I'm going to try to be rational and sensible about this," then that would probably be a healthier attitude, wouldn't it?

C^{43}: Yeah, it would be.

T^{44}: If you have to ask yourself, "Would God like this? Would he like this act, or that movement?" that would really foul you up, wouldn't it?

C^{45}: Yeah.

T^{46}: But if you are willing to look at the consequences of your act from the point of view of what effect it is going to have on you, and forget about whether God is writing it down in his book or looking over your shoulder, that latter idea is a vicious idea, isn't it?

C^{47}: Yeah.

Dr. Ard does not hesitate, in the RET method, to directly dispute and question some of the client's basic religious ideologies. Thus, in T^{32}, he continues to attack the whole idea that the God of the Old Testament really exists and is all-powerful; and in T^{46}, he points out that it is a vicious, self-defeating notion to believe that God is spying on people and writing down, for future retribution, their errors. From his efforts in this respect during previous sessions, the client is already seriously questioning her self-punitive, religiously oriented beliefs; after she brings up the subject, he pursues it further with her and strongly tries to induce her to challenge her previously held dogmas.

The rational-emotive therapist is firmly disputatious and attacking in these important respects because (a) he believes that the client often can benefit from having straighter thinking pointed out to her; (b) he wants to show her, by precise examples, that her irrational ideas do cause and influence her emotional reactions, and that if she changes the former she will also significantly change the latter;

and (c) he keeps teaching her a specific empirico-logical method of challenging any of her present or subsequent inconsistent, self-sabotaging philosophies, so that she will ultimately be able to use this method herself and not require his or any other therapist's help. Because of his attacking position, the RET therapist is often accused of trying to convince the client of his own ideas and therefore of being authoritarian. Actually, as consistently shown in this case, he attempts to help the client see how *her* ideas do not hold water when empirically and logically analyzed and how, if she sticks with them, she will continue to harm herself. He continually asks her to think about her own ideologies, to check them herself, to figure out how invalid they are in their own right and not because *he* says that they are. If she merely accepts *his* word that they are mistaken and harmful, she may then suggestively feel better; but he would not agree that she actually was better, for she would still be unthinking, highly suggestible, and poorly perceiving. She would also still be overly dependent on him or on others.

After helping the client challenge her religious ideas, Dr. Ard does not hesitate to bring up, once again, her sexual philosophies. He does not necessarily wait, as most psychoanalytic or client-centered therapists would do, for her spontaneously to come back to this issue. In the interest of saving her time and trouble, and getting to the source of her major irrational ideas efficiently, he again raises the question of her sexual notions and tries to show her how they are integrally connected with her misleading religious suppositions.

T[48]:   What do you think about punishing yourself to have some sex? Is that a question we can look at now? Have I got this right? In the past, implicit in what you have done, you think that it is all right to have sex or an orgasm *after* you have been beaten.

C[49]:   Yeah. Well, it makes it all right.

T[50]:   How does it make it all right?

C[51]:   I guess by paying for the wrong you are going to do.

T[52]:   In advance, so to speak.

C[53]:   Yeah, right.

T[54]:   So you pay for this "bad deed: sex" by being punished beforehand.

C[55]:   Right.

T[56]:   Like a little kid saying, in effect, I am going to play over the fence where I am not supposed to, so spank me first so I can go enjoy myself, right?

C⁵⁷: Yeah.

T⁵⁸: And yet, we are saying that if you decide it is really all right to go and play over the fence, then you don't have to be punished.

C⁵⁹: Right.

T⁶⁰: Is that applicable to your case, right now? To say that you don't have to punish yourself with black and silver belts in order to have enjoyable sex experiences?

C⁶¹: I don't know.

T⁶²: You said in this letter you left with me last time that when you are unhappy, you go to some God and talk to him and feel better; then you praise him for making you feel better, after his making you unhappy to begin with. Isn't that the same kind of thinking you have been doing on this sex bit and the beatings? That is, you are assuming that you should be punished, because sex is bad, and therefore you punish yourself first so that you can have the sex. How about questioning the assumption made at the beginning, that you have to punish yourself because sex is bad? If sex is not bad, then you don't have to punish yourself for having it, do you?

C⁶³: But the Bible speaks of fornication, adultery, and this and that.

T⁶⁴: I thought we were going to try and question that.

C⁶⁵: Oh, yeah, well—yeah, okay.

T⁶⁶: You said in this letter that there is something wrong with the idea of going to a God and talking to him, and he makes you feel better, when he is the guy who made you feel bad to begin with. Is that right?

C⁶⁷: Yeah.

T⁶⁸: You are saying, "God says sex is bad"; therefore anyone who indulges in it should be punished. Then you say, okay, I'll punish myself first, then I can have some sex (it will balance the books).

C⁶⁹: Yeah.

T⁷⁰: But maybe you ought to question what you assume without question: that sex is bad and God is against it. Maybe you don't even have to worry about that. Maybe sex is just natural and normal, and you don't have to worry.

C⁷¹: Yeah. In the churches they even think that masturbation is bad.

T⁷²: Do you think it is bad?

C⁷³: I was taught it was bad. God gave us sexual emotions and feelings, and then if you do something about it, it is bad. That doesn't make sense because he gave them to you to begin with.

T⁷⁴: Right. That is like giving you a mind and then saying "Don't eat of the tree of knowledge," isn't it?

C⁷⁵: Yeah.

T⁷⁶: He did that too, supposedly, according to the Bible. And maybe in both cases we shouldn't believe either of those stories. How about that?

C⁷⁷: Yeah. You know Paul, in the Bible?

T⁷⁸: Um-hm.

C⁷⁹: Well, I think he was against a lot of things anyway.

T⁸⁰: He sure was, wasn't he? He was a very sick man.

C⁸¹: Like I think he despised women.

T⁸²: Yes, and yet he has probably influenced more Christians than perhaps any other man in the Bible. He influenced a great many Christians to believe that women are kind of bad, didn't he?

C⁸³: Yes.

T⁸⁴: And yet, in our culture, we base so much of our thinking on Christianity, and that puts women in a second-class citizenship, all because of Paul. That's pretty sick, isn't it?

C⁸⁵: Yes.

T⁸⁶: And if Paul was kind of off his rocker—

C⁸⁷: I think that bolt of lightning that hit him on the way to Damascus must have done something to him.

T⁸⁸: And so we should not believe what a man like that says; is that a fair conclusion? That is, if we ask how should we treat our women then we certainly shouldn't ask a man like Paul who has such a low opinion of them.

C⁸⁹: Yeah, right.

T⁹⁰: We ought to at least treat them as equals, as worthwhile human beings, and not beat them like gongs or drums. And yet you have a sort of philosophy that you should be beaten before you can have sex, that you should be punished. That is a sort of twisted, sick idea that we could trace back to Paul, couldn't we?

C[91]: Yeah, I guess so.

T[92]: And you are believing it when a man like Paul believed it, and yet you just told me you think he was kind of sick.

C[93]: Oh, yeah.

T[94]: Maybe we can dispense with Paul's beliefs about women and punishment and sex and marriage. And you decide what kind of philosophy of life you want to have on the basis of what works out best for you, what the consequences are for you.

T[95]: Paul was the author of that famous statement, "It is better to marry than to burn." That's a pretty sick way to look at marriage, isn't it?

C[96]: Yeah.

Going ruthlessly on with his attempt to help the client dispute her self-punishing religious philosophy, the therapist does not hesitate to point out, in quite a heretical manner, that St. Paul was "a very sick man." He quotes chapter and verse to back this hypothesis; and he shows how the antisexual Christian philosophy, which the client has clung to for many years, directly stems, in all probability, from Paul's disturbed attitudes toward human sexuality. He takes the opportunity again, as is common in RET, to indicate that the client's goal would better be to acquire a philosophy of life connected with what works out best for her. Whereas much that goes on in psychotherapy is quite Establishment-centered, in that the therapist is helping the client adjust to the kind of society in which she accidentally was reared and to give up a good amount of her individuality in order to be accepted in that society, RET tends to be more truly client-centered, in that the therapist tries to help the client discover what she really wants to do, whether or not she receives considerable social approval for her acts, and to help her undefeatingly achieve her goals. The rational-emotive therapist fully realizes that, because she normally chooses to live in society, the client would better be socially as well as individually interested and should try to achieve individuality-groupness, or what Hans S. Falck (1969) describes as the "I-G effect." But because the client is usually too socially conforming and too little individually oriented, he tends to stress the latter rather than the former.

C⁹⁷: Somewhere he [St. Paul] said that if you masturbate, you
       would be left with a reprobate mind. I thought, well, gee—I
       masturbate, now what in the hell does "reprobate" mean? So
       I went and looked it up. 'Cause if I'm going to have a reprobate
       mind, at least I want to know what kind it is.

T⁹⁸: What did you find out?

C⁹⁹: It means corrupt, hopelessly bad and depraved, condemned.

T¹⁰⁰: And so once again we have that vicious circle, haven't we?

C¹⁰¹: Yeah.

T¹⁰²: But you are *not* depraved or a reprobate or all bad like that,
       because we can question the assumption that started the whole
       thing.

C¹⁰³: Yeah.

T¹⁰⁴: I would like to give you some "homework" assignments: do
       some writing like you did in this letter, that is, some thinking
       about why you feel guilty, why you think you ought to punish
       yourself; and then begin to examine and question your as-
       sumptions that lead you to feel guilty and think you need
       to be punished. If you would write some of those things out,
       I think it might help both of us get real clear about it. You
       would be clear in your own mind, having worked it out on
       paper, so to speak; would that help?

C¹⁰⁵: Um-hm.

T¹⁰⁶: Would you like to do that for next time?

C¹⁰⁷: Yeah.

T¹⁰⁸: You did it somewhat in this letter you wrote to your friend,
       but I am interested in your thinking it through for yourself.
       What follows from following your philosophy, which is the
       basic Christian philosophy of life?

C¹⁰⁹: Um-hm.

T¹¹⁰: That you should be punished for being a bad girl; that you
       ought to be punished for having sex; and as I recall, you have
       even said that you ought to be punished for even having fan-
       tasies.

C¹¹¹: Oh, yeah, because—let's see—

T¹¹²: Jesus was supposed to have said, "The thought is as bad as
       the deed."

C¹¹³: Yeah, right.

T¹¹⁴: That is another vicious idea, isn't it?

C^{115}:   Yeah, it is kind of a vicious idea, because there is nothing wrong with thinking, I guess, but he said there was.

Dr. Ard gets around to one of the main aspects of RET: assigning a specific homework task to the client. In this instance, he asks her to work out on paper some of her assumptions about guilt and self-punishment, and then to question these assumptions. Often, the rational-emotive therapist gives activity or motoric assignments as well. Thus, he may have this client deliberately engage in "forbidden" or "guilt-provoking" sex behavior, to show her what her specific beliefs are when she does so and to demonstrate that, by taking such risks, she does not have to make herself feel terribly guilty. Or he may have her deliberately refrain from all sex activity, to show her the logical consequences of her antisexual philosophy.

The specific homework assignment that he gives (or has the client give herself or asks her therapy group to give her) is partly designed to change her motoric patterns of behavior: to get her to do something, for example, that she thinks she "can't" do, and to help her become habituated to doing it easily and enjoyably. But it is largely designed to help change her thinking: to show her, in one way or another, that risk-taking is not catastrophic, that she has specific ideas motivating her disturbed behavior, that she can change these ideas, and so on.

T^{116}:   He said so; does that make it so?
C^{117}:   "Whatsoever a man thinketh in his heart, that shall he do," or something like that.
T^{118}:   So you can't even think about robbing a bank. Or passing a bakery shop, you can't even think about having a chocolate cake you see in the window. You are a sinner, hm? That is a pretty sad way of thinking, isn't it?
C^{119}:   Well—
T^{120}:   Even if you walk on down the street [and think of stealing but] don't steal anything. I don't see that you are such a terrible human being.
C^{121}:   Actually, it seems like it would be a compliment to the bakery.
T^{122}:   Why, certainly. Did you ever think about a married man walking down the street, and he sees a pretty girl going down the street; if the thought occurs to him, "There's a pretty girl," isn't that natural and normal and healthy, really?

C¹²³: Well, yeah.

T¹²⁴: Despite the fact that Jesus said he has committed adultery in his heart. I say that's just too damned bad. I am sorry Jesus felt that way, but it is mentally not very healthy to think that every time you have a thought you should be blamed and punished for it, even if it is a natural, normal, healthy thought—

C¹²⁵: Hey! Well, how come it doesn't work the other way, then? If you think something good, you have already done it?

T¹²⁶: It doesn't work that way either, does it? Do I get credit in the good book for having thought about giving a million to some charity but never actually doing it?

C¹²⁷: No.

T¹²⁸: Right. That shows you how foolish it is, doesn't it, really?

C¹²⁹: Mmmm.

T¹³⁰: He is docking you for all the bad thoughts but not giving you any credit for the good. You can't win in that system, can you?

C¹³¹: No. I guess not.

T¹³²: One other reason for getting rid of that system—one good reason for dumping the whole system. Does that make sense to you?

C¹³³: Yeah.

* * *

T¹³⁴: If you did some reading and thinking about your own philosophy, I am sure you could come up with a better philosophy than the Christian philosophy, couldn't you?

C¹³⁵: Well, yeah.

* * *

T¹³⁶: We could talk forever on how many angels can dance on a pinhead, and there is not much way of resolving that question since we don't know what size angels there are. But do you know that Christians have debated those kinds of questions endlessly?

C¹³⁷: Really?

T¹³⁸: Yes. *But don't take my word for it. Check it out.*

C¹³⁹: Oh, wow! A lot of good it is going to do you if you find out the answer!

T¹⁴⁰: I use that as an illustration of some of the absurd things religious people get into when they are trying to resolve issues that are unresolvable. So that is why I am saying to you: you don't have to resolve these issues—just dump the whole load.

C¹⁴¹: Oooh.

T¹⁴²: You don't have to spend any time trying to find out how many angels can dance on a pinhead because it is a *meaningless* question to begin with.

C¹⁴³: Yeah; I don't see the importance of it, anyway.

Dr. Ard uses several methods that are commonly employed in RET: (a) He shows how the antisexual Christian philosophy, which he deliberately takes to extremes, is utterly self-contradictory, impractical, and absurd. (b) He points out that it is actually natural and desirable to think and act the way the antisexual philosophy says it is unnatural and undesirable to act. (c) He prods the client into bringing up an excellent logical point that she has thought out herself: namely, that if mere *thoughts* or *fantasies* are punishable, they are also logically rewardable; but that actually the Christian philosophy does not acknowledge their rewardability. (d) He indicates that the philosophy that the client swears by is one with which she can't possibly win. (e) He encourages the client to rethink her ideological position and to come up with a better, less defeating set of values. (f) He explicitly tells the client, once again, *"But don't take my word for it. Check it out."* (g) He notes how metaphysical and definitional the client's whole philosophy is: that it asks foolish questions and thereby gets foolish answers. (h) He encourages the client to stand apart from her own value system, to weigh it more objectively, and perhaps dump the system entirely.

T¹⁴⁴: I am going to offer you the idea that the same thing is true as to whether it is a sin—mortal, venial, or otherwise—if you masturbate, or whether you fornicate or not, or whether God cares about your fantasies (positive or negative). Let's put all that stuff in the garbage can, and let the garbage man take it away and you not worry about it anymore; then you could go on to live a happy, healthy, normal life. And you wouldn't hurt anybody intentionally, I'm sure, would you?

C¹⁴⁵: No.

T[146]:   You don't have to hire anybody to hurt you anymore. And
          you don't have to cut yourself with razors anymore.

C[147]:   No. I hope so. Another thing I do that I think would go if
          I could straighten all this out—you know how some kids carry
          a blanket, their security blanket? Well, I carry razor blades
          around with me, everywhere I go.

T[148]:   Let's see if I understand that. You carry these razor blades
          around with you so you can punish yourself by cutting yourself
          anytime you want to?

C[149]:   Yeah, right.

T[150]:   And we are saying that if you can get rid of this neurotic
          need to punish yourself, then you don't have to carry razor
          blades.

C[151]:   Yeah, yeah.

T[152]:   When you get an idea in the future that you want to punish
          yourself, what can you do instead of cutting yourself? Can
          you think of some things you could do? What alternatives
          can you think of? Say, next week you felt like you ought to
          punish yourself, and you happen to have a razor in your bag,
          what could you think—instead of what you used to think—that
          would prevent you from cutting yourself again? What could
          you think that would help you throw that razor blade in the
          garbage?

C[153]:   That I don't need to suffer anymore, maybe.

T[154]:   Yeah. You don't need to suffer anymore. And no *maybe*—
          period. You don't need to suffer anymore, period.

The therapist tries to show the client what she can do in the future
when she is "overwhelmed" by the idea that she should cut herself:
namely, that she doesn't need to suffer anymore. He could have,
more specifically, shown her the A-B-C's of RET:

At point A, the *activating event* occurs when she makes some
error or performs worse than she would like to perform. At point
C, the emotional *consequence* is that she feels guilty and is impelled
to cut and punish herself. Instead, however, of thinking that A must
lead to C, she could stop and ask herself, "What am I telling myself,
at point B, my *belief system*, to make me feel self-punishing at point
C?"

Her answer would then normally be: "First, I am telling myself
a *rational belief* (rB): 'How unfortunate for me to have made that

error; I wish I hadn't made it.' But that would only lead, if I rigorously stuck to it, to a *rational consequence*: appropriate feelings of sorrow, regret, and annoyance at my own foolish behavior. Since I am actually getting a very *irrational consequence* (feelings of guilt and the urge to cut myself up), I must be telling myself an *irrational belief* (iB), such as 'How *awful* for me to have made that error. I *should* not have made it! What a louse I am for doing what I should not have done. I must condemn and punish myself!' "

The client could then be shown by the therapist exactly how to *dispute*, at point D, her *irrational belief*, by challenging herself as follows: "Why is it awful for me to have made that error? Where is the evidence that I *should* not have made it? Even if it was quite wrong of me to make it, why am I a louse for doing this wrong thing? What is the reason that I have to condemn and punish myself for acting badly?"

She would then tend to experience, at point E, the cognitive *effect* of believing (*a*) that it is not awful, but only inconvenient and unfortunate, for her to make errors; (*b*) that there is no evidence that she *should not* be fallible and make errors; (*c*) that she is never a louse or a worthless individual, even if she does things quite wrongly; and (*d*) that there is no reason why she ever has to condemn herself as a human being, even when her acts are heinous, or why she need punish herself for doing these acts—though there are good reasons why she'd better accept the wrongness of her deeds and make future efforts to correct them. She would also tend to experience, along with these cognitive effects, the behavioral or emotional effects of feeling considerably less anxious, less guilty, and less self-punitive.

The therapist, by helping the client to see that "I don't need to suffer anymore, maybe," has probably induced her, vaguely and by shorthand statements to herself, to quickly undergo this A-B-C-D-E self-deconditioning process of RET. If further sessions had materialized, he could have persuaded the client to go through the more longhand process many times, and more effectively depropagandize herself and immunize herself against future recurrence of guilt and self-punitiveness.

T[155]: If you could read the Bible critically, it might be good for you—that is, to question it. Read it like you would any other book. And say, "What did he say? What did he mean? Is it true? And so what?"

C156: Yeah. Like in Matthew, Jesus did a stupid thing. He cursed a tree because it didn't have any fruit on it, and it was not the season for the fig tree to have any fruit, anyway. So he cursed the poor tree when it wasn't even made to have fruit then.

T157: That is pretty stupid on his part, isn't it?

C158: Yeah. And the time he cast the devils into the swine, and those guys got pissed off at him? Well, I would too, because they were their whole herd, you know; he destroyed the guys' herd.

T159: And it wasn't the pigs' fault, was it?

C160: No. And I think it was selfish, too, because he destroyed some guys' ways that they lived on.

T161: And yet millions of people follow his every word, thought, and deed, as if he is God's own son; and he does stupid things like that.

C162: In John is the only book where he says he is the savior, and if it was that important, why didn't they put it in all the rest of them?

T163: Why, indeed? It sounds to me like you are beginning to question, beginning to think, beginning to use your mind.

C164: Yeah.

T165: In good, critical ways, for any book you read, including the Bible.

C166: Yeah. And they found a man's bones that was over thirty thousand years old.

T167: Despite the story in the Bible that the world is only four to six thousand years old.

C168: Yeah.

T169: The answer to that which I have heard some Christians give is that the devil must have planted those bones to confuse us.

C170: Oh, wow!

T171: Those kinds of answers ought to convince you that you don't have to worry about the Christian view of man anymore. Then you don't have to worry about hurting yourself anymore.

C172: Wow! The devil planted the bones there to confuse us! How did he make bones to begin with?

T[173]: That's like the angels on a pinhead, isn't it? Not worth really discussing because there is no point to it.

C[174]: Yeah. There are people starving in the streets, and these people waste their time trying to decide how many angels can dance on a pinhead.

T[175]: Well, I see our time has gotten away from us. When would you like to get together again?

C[176]: In about two weeks.

T[177]: Okay. Same time?

C[178]: Yeah.

It certainly would appear, from the closing passages of this session, that Dr. Ard's original goal has been at least somewhat achieved: that the client is beginning to think for herself, and not merely parrot any views that he may have given her. He agrees and in response T[155] onward, adds to her anti-biblical views. But it seems as if *she* is making an effort to gather information in this respect and to think things through. So she appears to be successfully carrying out one of the main goals of RET: to have the client replace conventional, dogmatic beliefs with more individualized, open-minded attitudes.

Because of the impossibility of her making satisfactory arrangements (because of her physical handicap) to continue the sessions, this tenth interview proved to be her last. It had been previously agreed, moreover, that she would not have many sessions altogether; and it appeared to her that she had already made highly satisfactory progress; so therapy was, at least for the time, terminated. While it can hardly be said that the client was completely cured, she certainly seemed to benefit appreciably from the ten sessions she had with the therapist. The material just presented may help show what can be accomplished with an individual who seemed, at the start, to be almost hopeless. By pursuing rational-emotive therapy in an active, direct manner, the therapist helped this client to make some significant progress in a short period of time.

CHAPTER 3

Rational-Emotive Therapy with a Culturally Deprived Teen-Ager

H. JON GEIS, Ph.D.

The client in these sessions is a seventeen-year-old high school student who comes from a lower-class home in New York City. He is of Rumanian extraction and lives alone with his mother. His father, brother, and sister died after the family came to the United States, largely as a result of the extremely poor socioeconomic conditions in which the family lived. He was referred to Dr. Geis, who was then a supervisor of counselors in training at New York University, by his high school guidance counselor, who had worked with him for some time and had been unable to get beyond temporary support. In giving the presenting problems over the phone, the guidance counselor merely told Dr. Geis that the boy was "suicidal, perfectionistic, and felt low all the time."

An unusually long block of time—over an hour and a quarter—was available for the first session, though RET is frequently done (especially by Dr. Geis and myself) in half-hour sessions. Consequently, the therapist used the first half of the first session to get a good deal more information about the client than is often done in this kind of a case. During this part of the session, he discovered that the client is, in his own words, a worrier who feels that he has to get at least 90 on any test, or else he is a failure; he is a junior in high school but has almost no friends; he speaks only Rumanian at home because of his mother's poor command of English; he has never had a date with a girl; he does not miss nor mourn for his father, who was a "drill sergeant" and beat him severely when he was a child; he finds his mother to be very nervous, angry, and overly-restrictive; he frequently daydreams about being a great success but fears that he will end up as a Bowery bum; and he does not admit to having any serious problems. In his response C[108], he

46

says, "I guess I'm no problem!" Dr. Geis, feeling that he has more
than enough information on the client by now and that it is safe
to confront him with some basic issues, picks him up at this point.

FIRST SESSION

T¹: Is that right?

C²: I guess I made—that's the way—that's the way, I think
       it—(*raises voice*) it appears to you.

T³: I think you've got plenty of problems. I think they're all solv-
       able, too.

C⁴: (*Pause*) Mr. Nolte told me—everybody has those problems.

T⁵: No—well, everybody has some problems, but they don't have
       the ones you have—you've got them in a fairly intense
       form—and you're overcoming yourself to some extent. You
       know, your emotions are pretty intense right now. Everybody
       doesn't have exactly these problems and this intensity. But
       problems occur like this. These are psychological problems,
       and psychological problems have to do with the way you think.
       And the way you think is not like a skin problem, or it's
       not like being physically disabled and not having a leg, or
       something. You can change the way you think, so you don't
       have these kinds of problems any more. Now, my work is,
       Mr. Nolte must have told you—I'm supervisor of the counsel-
       ors down here. I'm a psychologist, and I do work for a lot
       of hospitals. I do essentially what a psychiatrist does. And
       I think you need this kind of help. I think you're giving your-
       self a pain in the ass about a lot of things you don't know
       how to find your way out of. I can thoroughly understand
       what it feels like, and I think you can find your way out.
       It happens that I have some time, once a week, or more if
       necessary, and I'll be glad to see you if you'd like to get
       working on this.

C⁶: It's my only way out. (*Laughs*) Yeah, I want to—sure, see
       somebody—that's all.

T⁷: Yeah.

C⁸: So I can say—'cause I can't just—can't just go—go to anybody
       else, and tell them about it.

T⁹: Well, you can, but they're not likely to give you much help, 'cause they don't know what's up on this either.

C¹⁰: (*Mumbles*) I'd be—I'd be damn afraid if I did and I—I'd feel like—like ten fools.

T¹¹: Which is part of your problem.

C¹²: Yes.

T¹³: 'Cause you think you're a piece of shit, and you've got to prove to them differently.

C¹⁴: I'm glad you understand that. (*Laughs*)

T¹⁵: That—in that way you're not much different from most people, 'cause a lot of people think that they've got to prove that they're not shits instead of starting out with—

C¹⁶: I'm afraid they do.

T¹⁷: —assuming they *are* okay, just to—

C¹⁸: I started to prove it indirectly by getting a high average and—

T¹⁹: Yeah, but see, your mistake is that you believe you're a piece of shit in the first place, and then you try to prove you're not.

C²⁰: How? (*Laughs*)

T²¹: Well, it's a matter of the way you describe yourself, see; let's suppose, for example, you flunk this term. Let's suppose you do, okay?

C²²: Yeah, and I don't know what I'll do. I'd probably—I don't know what. I'd just—just sink to the ground and forget it. (*Laughs*)

T²³: Yeah, well, someone else might say, "God, I flunked. I'd better get going and try something different, handle it in a different way." You'd sink yourself to the ground *because* you'd say to yourself. "Ah hah, that means I'm a no good piece of—"

C²⁴: I think my first time—

T²⁵: Yeah, yeah. But I'm saying, see, that this is just more evidence of the way you're giving yourself a hard time, because you're saying to yourself something like, "If I fail, that proves I'm no damn good."

C²⁶: (*Grunt*)

T²⁷: And I'm saying to you, you start out with the assumption "I'm no good; I'm no damn good unless I can do very, very well." (*Pause*) You see, so that if someone says "The moon is made of green cheese—it's made of green cheese unless you go out and run around the block in four seconds." It's just as idiotic, you see. The burden of proof is on the person who asserts it in the first place. You're asserting something that's very nutty. You're asserting that you're a piece of shit as your basic premise; and then you're saying to yourself, "Well, I'm a piece of shit unless I get very, very high grades." And since you, like everybody else, don't want to see yourself as a piece of shit, you work your ass off to get high grades.

C[28]: Um-hm.

T[29]: You know the story of the millionaire who makes one million, two million, and—

C[30]: Yes.

T[31]: Not twenty million is enough. Why? Because he's always got to prove to himself that he's not a piece of shit by making another million. But it's not making a million that's going to solve it. It's changing his idea of himself. 'Cause there is no such thing as a person being a piece of shit or a worthless person. People wrongly make mistakes—

C[32]: Well. (*Mumbles*) Who wouldn't give a damn.

T[33]: But who in the fuck needs to give a damn for you. What the hell do I care whether anybody gives a damn? If you die, you die. You're assuming that it's going to be horrible if people don't give a damn—which most of them don't anyway, because most of them don't know you, as far as that goes. So it's tough, you ain't got anybody. You can live very nicely for the rest of your life if you never talk to another person, you know damn well. But you believe you've got to have some kind of swinging relationship with people who understand you and all that kind of thing—which would be very nice, don't get me wrong. I think that's nice. I think that getting along with people is very nice, you could learn to do it without question. But you're putting yourself in the hole because you believe you need it. So it's touch shit if you fail a course. So you don't have people you can talk to who understand you. It's partly that way because you keep away from them.

C³⁴: Oh, really, you're at one extreme or the other, either at the bottom or at the top of it. It still don't have no way. (*Laughs*)

T³⁵: Sure.

C³⁶: It still (*mumbles, laughs*)—

T³⁷: Comes out the wrong way.

C³⁸: I understand that.

T³⁹: Sure, yeah, and you're beating yourself over the head with that psychological baseball bat. You're making problems for yourself. I want to show you how to unscramble them. You see? But when you stop making the problems for yourself, then things begin to swing more easily, and you have people if you *want* people. But you don't need people as you think you do, and you don't need to succeed in school—which you obviously can do, but you think you *need* to do, you see. And you *need* to do it because you think "I'm no goddamn good unless I do."

C⁴⁰: That's right. That's—that's the bag.

T⁴¹: Yeah, that's right. And that's bullshit because it's an arbitrary definition you've set up. What if I said to you, "Look, you're no damn good, unless you can run around the block in four seconds." That would be silly, wouldn't it? Would that make you no damn good? It would only make you no damn good in *my view*, you see? Now what if you said that to yourself, "I'm no damn good unless I can run around the block in four seconds"?

C⁴²: It would really be that way.

T⁴³: Hm?

C⁴⁴: It would really be that way for me, if I said it to myself.

T⁴⁵: That's right. But it's idiotic, isn't it?

C⁴⁶: Yeah.

T⁴⁷: Because—well, what does "no damn good" mean anyway? "No damn good" is a value judgment of your worth. You say, "I'm worthwhile as a person if I can do this or this or this." But let's suppose you had a son, seventeen years old, and you said to him, "Son, you're no damn good if you don't get 93s or above." Would you say it to him?

C⁴⁸: No.

T[49]: Would you believe it—that he would be no damn good if he didn't succeed?

C[50]: No.

T[51]: Well, how can you believe it about yourself?

C[52]: (*Laughs*) I don't *know*.

T[53]: Well, I know. This is what you learn from your family—you said your father was pretty kookie, and your mother to some extent misunderstands some of those things. And you learn this from them like most other kids do. Now you've got to unlearn it, that's all.

C[54]: How?

T[55]: By examining it, by being more aware of it, and by questioning it just the way I'm questioning you. Use the kinds of questions I'm throwing at you. I'm asking for evidence about these things. This is the type of thinking you have to learn to do for yourself to get rid of these. Let's suppose you believe that black cats brought bad luck. It's a superstition. The kinds of things you believe are like this superstition. The kinds of things you believe are like this superstition. So I would say to you, "All right, let's suppose you and I talk about black cats bringing you bad luck." And you say, "Well, I know, Mr. Geis, I know they don't really bring you bad luck, but somehow I feel they do." What this means is that you seemingly do believe it. You see? And so what we do, we talk about it; you think about it. You go outside, and you look at black cats for a week or two. You think about it some more, and we talk about it some more, and you ask yourself, "Hell, could it *really* bring bad luck?" And then you go up and pat a black cat on the head, and after a while, your fear is gone, because you don't believe that bullshit, you see? You thought your way out of it, and you have the experience. This is the same kind of thing. Now, maybe, you'll never get completely over some of this. Most likely you can get over a hell of a lot of it, enough so that you can live a very normal life and be happy and continue to strive for the things you want to strive for. You can continue to work very hard to get good grades and all the rest of it if you want to. But you won't *need* to. You won't be scared to death that you're going to flip your top or do something like that if you don't get good grades.

Mr. Nolte said something about your talking about killing yourself.

C[56]:   Yes.

Several important facets of RET are demonstrated in the foregoing passages:

1. Dr. Geis frankly tells the client, in T[3] and T[5], that he has severe emotional problems on which he had better work. This kind of confrontation is common in RET. After the therapist has determined that the client can take it, he frequently shows him—sometimes quoting chapter and verse from his own statements—that he has more disturbances than he may think he has, and that although he is privileged to do nothing whatever about these, it would be far better if he did work hard against them. At the same time, he usually shows the client that his problems are quite solvable—*if* he wants to do the work to understand and uproot them. He is therefore supportive as well as confrontational, and consequently little traumatization of the client results.

2. Dr. Geis tells the client, in T[13] and the next few responses, that he thinks he's "a piece of shit" and that he has to prove otherwise to those with whom he comes into contact. Mind you, the boy has not said anything of the sort, up to this point, about himself— that he considers himself terribly inadequate or worthless. But because of his perfectionistic demands on himself and because of his anxiety and depression, the therapist can easily deduce that he thinks he's some kind of rotter. He therefore takes a chance on calling this to the boy's attention—mainly in the interest of efficiency and brevity. If his "shot in the dark"—really, his shot in the light of RET theory—does not work, the therapist will not be nonplussed but will merely try another tactic. If evidence presents itself, he may even revise his hypothesis that the client thinks he's "a shit." But almost always this kind of a highly educated guess works, and the client responds confirmingly and seems to be grateful that the therapist has understood him so well.

3. Dr. Geis takes a hard RET line, in T[33] and tries to show the boy that he definitely does not need others' approval, though he might very sensibly want to have this approval. He deliberately takes his fear of disapproval to extremes and indicates that if *nobody* loved him he would not have to be utterly miserable (though he would normally be quite deprived and saddened). He makes the classical

RET distinction between an individual's *wants* and his presumed *needs*; and he strongly implies that if the boy will surrender his needs, he will become more efficient at getting what he wants—people's approval. This is one of the main "selling points" of RET: that if the client will work hard to retranslate his needs into wants, he will then usually become much more effective at actually getting many of them fulfilled.

4. Having successfully taken a chance at confronting the client with some of his basic problems, Dr. Geis feels safe, in T[55], in questioning him about his talk of suicide—which the therapist only knows, at this point, through the referring source. In this respect, RET is often a most *probing* kind of therapy—partly because the therapist feels that it would be valuable if the client fully and openly acknowledged his real feelings, including his most negative ones, and partly because he also feels that no matter what material is brought out, it can usually be effectually handled with RET methods. Other kinds of confrontational methods, especially those used in encounter groups and Synanon-type groups, are often quite effective in inducing clients to bring out their deepest feelings and problems, too (Yablonsky, 1965). But RET offers much more than ventilation of emotions in this respect; it also offers problem-solving methods that may well help to change or eradicate destructive emotions (Ellis, 1969a, 1971b).

T[57]: How long have you been thinking about this?

C[58]: Oh, during the summer.

T[59]: Um-hm.

C[60]: That's when I had—had the time to think about a lot of things. I—I don't know. Sometimes I would seem to, so I would be so depressed. I don't know what reason or what thought. Just feel so damn out of place and what. So—so it's that.

T[61]: How's it lately? You think of this, too?

C[62]: Not too lately.

T[63]: Um-hm. (*Pause*) You think you can really do it?

C[64]: No, I don't think I have the nerve or—but if I were—(*inaudible*) would be existing, and it would be intensified. I guess that would be the only way out.

T[65]: Um-hm. It always—with a situation like this, it's this way—the way you're getting very depressed. You're not thinking very clearly; your judgment's not good. You've been thinking about the stuff before, and you think about it again. You could do something impulsively, see. I don't think you have particularly to worry about it now—that is, in your present state. I don't think you would have gone further, and help was around the corner, right around the corner. But I think your problems are quite solvable, quite solvable.

C⁶⁶: I hope so.

T⁶⁷: Well—

C⁶⁸: I don't know how the life will be. I can always (*inaudible*) stop living.

T⁶⁹: What the hell—why do it now? Why not give it a try to solve it?

C⁷⁰: That's—that's a good way of (*laughs*) looking at it.

T⁷¹: Sure, anybody can do that little thing. Hemingway did it when he was sixty-some years old, presumably because he had cancer. Yeah, with *that*, I might want to.

C⁷²: Yeah, but I don't know how the life will be, how the sky will look, how the sun will—how the sun will look if I get—if I take myself out of the hole like I'm doing now. I don't know what I'm stepping into.

T⁷³: You know what you're stepping into. You're stepping into being *yourself* with lots of problems. I had a client—

C⁷⁴: How—how's that?

T⁷⁵: Yeah.

C⁷⁶: What's that like?

T⁷⁷: I had a client who sometimes just had to go on faith, because lots of other people are screaming in the world. And (*laughs*) it's not unreasonable that you could learn to be that way, too. I have seen lots of people work on this kind of thing—I had a client last year whom I was working with who said after one session, "You know, sometimes I begin to think it's a pretty shitty world." And I said, "I'll tell you a secret. It *is* a pretty shitty world." A war is pretty shitty in a lot of ways. They're killing guys over in Vietnam on both sides, and people are being raped and houses burned and all this kind of stuff. Okay, that's not a good war or a good world!

C⁷⁸: What are we going to do about it?

T[79]: You've got to protest. You've got to do something about yourself. I mean you're a person. Now, as I said to this client, "Look, your problem is not to have a shitty view about the world. Your problem is to get the best things in life for yourself. And as long as you say, "Oh, what a shitty world," and you take a shitty view, and have shitty glasses on, of course you're going to see only a shitty world. Now there are people who have a good time in life, who make a swinging thing out for themselves or at least don't give themselves the pain in the ass you're giving yourself.

C[80]: Um-hm.

T[81]: So your problem is, not to look at things in a shitty way, but to go on after the good things in life for yourself. Get as much as you can out of it. And there ain't no more. Recognize that a lot of it is shitty. But look—leave the shit to other people. You try to get what you can, which is what you're doing, of course. But, see, this is the difference. You could compare your—your situation right now with a river full of logs, let's say, running down to the mill.

C[82]: Um-hm.

T[83]: The logs are floating down, except they're jammed up. It's a good river full of logs, except they're jammed up. What we've got to do is get the logs that are jamming it up out of the way so it can flow right along, or you can be at a standstill. That's the way you can be yourself—(*Pauses, groping for name*)

C[84]: Robert G!

T[85]: Robert G!

C[86]: Right.

T[87]: Okay. Well, how do you pronounce it?

C[88]: Gulanovitch.

T[89]: Gulanovitch. Would you rather I called you "G" or Gulanovitch?

C[90]: Robert G.

T[91]: Okay.

C[92]: It's so much more easier.

T[93]: All right, you can be Robert G. And this means getting some of the nutty ideas out of your being and that sort of thing; and, then it's the world that it always was. See, the world doesn't give a shit how you feel. The sun's got to come up tomorrow whether you're here or not—and even whether you like it or not. I may like it, or I may not. That's tough shit! It's going to come up whether I like it or not. And the war in Vietnam is going to go on, a little while longer at least, whether I like it or not. So my problem is to square myself away, to not be upset about this stuff. By intelligent thinking, and going after the good things that I can get, in order to meet my responsibilities. And that's all there is in life—period. With regard to the everyday business of living, it's pretty tough sometimes. You have to work all hours of the night sometimes. Maybe you can't get off tonight, or maybe you haven't got a girl friend, or whatever the hell it is. So, tough! What are you going to do, cry about it? Or make plans, so you can get what you want? See, in a way it's a common sense thing. In another way, it takes some pretty good thinking and some learning. You've got some nutty ideas that you've picked up along the way without questioning. What you've got to do is unlearn them and replace them with sensible ideas. I've a lot of clients who get well whether they are willing to work or not; but if you're willing to work, you'll get better a lot faster.

C[94]:   I'll work on everything.

T[95]:   I would think you would.

C[96]:   I don't have any way out except to work on it! (*Laughs*)

Dr. Geis's responses, in T[81], T[83], and T[93], are the kind of statements that often get rational-emotive therapy and those that practice it into trouble, since it is easy for the client or anyone else to misconstrue them. What he is really explaining to the boy is that he (and anyone else) actually can enjoy his own life a good deal even though life itself, or the environment in which it is presently lived, is pretty shitty. But he is not encouraging him to be irresponsible, short-rangedly hedonistic, asocial, or antisocial. For the RET philosophy overlaps significantly with the slogan that Reinhold Niebuhr coined and that Alcoholics Anonymous uses: give me the power to change what I can change, the serenity to accept what I cannot, and the wisdom to know the difference between the two. Once, through the use of

RET, the individual has attained a state of nondisturbance or "unupsetness," he is then able to go back to the poor conditions that exist in his life and to work very hard, if he chooses to do so, at changing them. Dr. Geis, therefore, is *not* counseling Robert G. to ignore the shitty world in which he lives and to give up all endeavors to reconstruct it. He is counseling him, instead, not to *demand* that the world be better—and thereby to put himself in a position where he may be able to better it.

T⁹⁷: Yeah, and you can notice results pretty quickly too—some of them. Let's get back to the fact that you think you're a shit, because you're a failure. You're a shit, because you don't get good grades or top grades. Now you don't get good grades or top grades. What's the evidence that you're a shit? (*Pause*) Well, it's my turn. But it does seem to stem from what you *think*.

C⁹⁸: (*Laughs*). Well, well, there are seven million volumes in the New York Public Library. And if I don't master at least a hundred, it's just—this isn't—this isn't reality. I'm just thinking—

T⁹⁹: Yeah.

C¹⁰⁰: —the way I want to stress it. If I don't master a hundred, and there is so much knowledge in this one hundred books— And even if I do, there're still six million, nine hundred thousand something—

T¹⁰¹: Yeah, you can never get it all.

C¹⁰²: You can't get it all, and you can't get half of it, and you can't get one fourth of it—

T¹⁰³: Right!

C¹⁰⁴: And you're having a hell of a time getting a hundredth of it, a hundred books mastered. And—you think if you do get this, and then go to the second hundred, it's—

T¹⁰⁵: I'm asking you, "Do you have evidence that you're a shit if you don't get it?"

C¹⁰⁶: Yes. And look—a million other people read a hundred volumes, and if they do it, why can't I? And if I can do it, then why can't I do two hundred?

T¹⁰⁷: You can.

C^{108}: And—I'm afraid I can't.

T^{109}: You don't *have* to, though. See, this is the point! And you believe you have to, or you're going to be a shit. Isn't this true? (*Pause*) Okay, now what's the evidence for this belief? Again, we're back to the moon made of green cheese. I can say that I can hear little Martians, but if there isn't any evidence, you'd better not accept it. You'd better get rid of this idea. It's interfering with your life—this notion of knowing everything.

C^{110}: Well, I gave the evidence. I always thought the evidence was—well, you know it. Then I sup—I'm *supposed* to know it. I mean if—

T^{111}: Says who?

C^{112}: Says me. That's the fact. It's—

T^{113}: Well, but who are you to say—

C^{114}: I don't know. Explain it.

T^{115}: Well, you'd better start trying. You see, you picked this belief up somewhere along the line because of some kind of propaganda you got from somewhere, like the rest of our people get. It's in our culture, this kind of bullshit. To get ourselves healthy again, we've got to start thinking our way through this crap. Now, you're saying, "I'm a shit if I don't read two hundred books." Well, I'm saying, unless there's some evidence that you're going to be a shit, that you can prove that you're going to be a shit, you'd better give up this idea. 'Cause you're the one who's saying it, who's obsessed with this idea.

C^{116}: I'm proving it in my—myself.

T^{117}: You're not *proving* it. You're *asserting* it. You're *saying* it's the case.

C^{118}: Yes, I'm *asserting*, and I'm taking that as proof, I guess.

T^{119}: Yes, that's exactly right. You are. You see, the real fact is that there *is* no evidence. Because this—this is not the kind of statement that you can *have* any evidence for. Because it's a value, a moral value; what someone's worth. That's what we really mean by "shit." You're a worthless piece of shit or something—or you're a worthwhile guy. Look at this: If I say you're a worthwhile guy, that doesn't make you a worthwhile guy. If I say this is a desk and you're a human being, those are true statements. But if I say you're worthwhile, all I'm really saying is that I *think* you're worthwhile, you're a valuable guy, you're a nice guy. But this doesn't make it so. What if I say to you, "Robert G., you're an automobile"? Does this make you an automobile? Even if you get down on your knees and drink gas and chug along, does that make you an automobile? No, of course not. So if I say to you, "You're a worthless piece of shit, Robert G.," it doesn't make you a worthless piece of shit either. You feel that way because you *think* that way. You can't possibly have a feeling like this unless you have some idea about yourself.

C¹²⁰: I tried to make it my own way. I've—I tried to do thinking my own way, to shut out what you think, or what he thinks, what she thinks, what—

T¹²¹: Yeah, yeah, but the problem is what *you* think, you see.

C¹²²: And I tried to make it what I think, and I made it wrong.

T¹²³: Right. You did. You made it wrong. Now we're—

C¹²⁴: (*Mumbles*) I made—

T¹²⁵: Yeah. Now, I'm saying you've got to get rid of this nutty idea that *you* have.

C¹²⁶: All right, what do I substitute?

T¹²⁷: You substitute the notion that you are worthwhile, *whether or not* you get good grades, *whether or not* you read two hundred books, *whether or not* anybody else likes you. Because that's what worth is. It's something that does *not* depend on something else. The minute you say, "I'm worthwhile when I get high grades," you put yourself in a box, because the minute you don't get high grades, guess who you are? And what do you *think* about yourself? You're obviously bright 'cause you can understand a lot of this stuff, you know—which is kind of complex. Now you've got to rethink. I'm asking you for evidence, and you haven't given me any evidence. And I know it, 'cause you're in a box, 'cause there *is* no evidence, you see.

C¹²⁸: Um-hm. Well—(*Voice trailing off*)

T¹²⁹: And so the question is, how can you go on thinking this idiotic jazz about yourself without the evidence, particularly when you screw yourself up? Nobody ever found out how you were screwing yourself up, of course. That's what I'm doing now.

C¹³⁰: (*Laughs*) Well, it's not going to hurt me. (*Laughs*) It's supposed to make—benefit me.

T¹³¹: *You're* supposed to benefit *you* 'cause—

C¹³²: I'm supposed to help me help myself?

T¹³³: Yeah, that's right.

C¹³⁴: Um-hm.

T¹³⁵: And just the way I'm giving you the idea that you could have come to yourself—that you screw yourself up by the way you think—by the same token, you give yourself all the goodies by the way you think, too. You can *make* yourself feel good.

C¹³⁶: Um-hm. I guess that's true. (*Laughs*)

T¹³⁷: —I defy you to get angry at me right now without *thinking* something.

C¹³⁸: What do you mean?

T¹³⁹: You can't get angry at me or have some kind of emotion or get depressed or anything unless you've got some idea behind it. There are no such things as just emotions floating around. They come from ideas and nonsense.

C¹⁴⁰: Um-hm.

C¹⁴¹: So I'm trying to show you that you will feel better when you get your concepts and ideas straightened out.

C¹⁴²: Um-hm.

T¹⁴³: You see, one of these is that you would always be a piece of shit *unless*—

C¹⁴⁴: Um-hm.

T¹⁴⁵: And I don't give a shit who says it, no matter if it is all the teachers or all your friends. 'Cause they think this, too: they're shits, and you're a shit if you don't do well in school. The society thinks it, but I don't care if they think that. They are wrong—they're simply wrong. And this is one of the biggest problems in the American culture—the problem you present. This is one of the main things I'm trying to get through our counselors' heads in working with young people—last year and this year again. The minute you attach your personal worth to something outside yourself or to some condition, you put yourself in a box, 'cause the minute that condition is not met, you feel lousy, and you're depressed. You say, "Oh, how terrible, what a worthless guy I am."

C[146]: All right, so I'm a good guy all the time. You're a good guy.
You think of yourself as a good guy—

T[147]: 'Cause I am intrinsically worthwhile, yeah.

Dr. Geis emphasizes, in T[115], T[127], and T[145], what I now call the less elegant approach to helping the individual feel that he is not worthless, is not a shit. That is to say, he shows the boy that he is only a turd by his own arbitrary definition and that there isn't (nor ever really can be) any empirical, scientifically-based *evidence* to back that hypothesis. Human worth, he insists, does not depend on the person's reading many books, getting good grades, winning other people's approval, or anything else. The individual is "good" simply because he exists—because he is intrinsically worthwhile (Hartman, 1959, 1967; Tillich, 1953).

This is a pragmatically sensible standard of human worth— because it works. But, as I have shown elsewhere in this volume and in a number of other publications (Ellis, 1968, 1971a, 1971b, in press a, in press c; Ellis and Gullo, 1971), it is philosophically inelegant and would better be replaced by the idea that humans are not really ratable at all, that they are therefore neither good nor bad, and that they would best discontinue all forms of deifying and devilifying themselves (or awarding themselves "ego-strength" and "turd-hood"). Even RET therapists, however, who today use this more elegant approach with their clients, as I usually do, would have to decide whether it would be wise to attempt to do so with a relatively young, unsophisticated client such as Robert G. He might well not be able, as yet, to achieve this abstract level of thinking. Consequently, if he is helped merely to accept himself as "good" because of his aliveness, and in that manner to stop rating himself as "bad," this may be the best solution feasible in his case (and in many similar instances).

C[148]: You never want to be that—that—that level.

T[149]: Now, wait a minute! I'm not talking about not wanting to succeed. I'm very ambitious to succeed myself. I'm writing a book, a book I'm half working on; I've got eleven articles going; I'm doing all sorts of things; and I want to do lots of things. I—

C[150]: And you're not putting yourself in the box?

T[151]: No. You know why? Because I don't think I'm a shit if I don't succeed.

C[152]: Um-hm.

T[153]: But *you* do. That's the difference, you see. But if you can go ahead [with wants] and start with the same things, you'll in fact be more likely to attain them.

C[154]: Um-hm.

T[155]: So you free yourself.

C[156]: It sounds—sounds easy.

T[157]: It is simple. But it takes some retraining, you see. 'Cause your thoughts, particularly the ones you're not aware of, often have been all in this sort of direction. So it's going to take some working on, but it isn't that hard.

C[158]: Where do I start?

T[159]: Well, you start by thinking; but think it over a lot. Take notes, if you want, on this stuff.

C[160]: I've thought about it already.

T[161]: That's all right. I could suggest a book you should get. Now, if you're going to spend money on the book, I won't charge you anything for this session. 'Cause this is—this would be part of our work down here [at the New York University guidance clinic].

C[162]: What book?

T[163]: Well, I'd suggest to you a book with a lot of these ideas in it. If you've got any money, you can come to hear some lectures. Matter of fact, you're welcome to hear a lecture I'm giving at the university here on Monday on doing therapy with yourself. This is psychotherapy or analysis or whatever you want to call it.

C[164]: (*Laughs*) I love the way you put it. (*Laughs*) I don't know. It's—nobody ever got to me this—this deep in my life. (*Laughs*)

T[165]: Well, you're off in the winning then.

C[166]: —on Monday?

T[167]: You don't have to come—I'm just saying that this is available, 'cause if you and I are going to work together and I'm going to help you, I want you to work on this and do some thinking. If you've got money for a book, I can send you uptown to the Institute for Rational Living, where you can pick it up.

And you might get some information there about some of the courses and lectures. I won't expect you to take a course at the Institute, but I'm going to be lecturing, and some other people are going to be lecturing—psychologists and psychiatrists. But if you want to get involved in straightening out your thinking, you see, we talk healthy talk and teach healthy thinking. So a few months of getting involved in this kind of thinking, and you'd be significantly better. In—well—you'll probably notice in about a few weeks. And you probably feel better today—

C168: Yeah, I think I do.

T169: —because you're thinking a little straighter. But in a couple of weeks, if we work together, you'll feel significantly better. And then you'll have to tackle the hard work of getting at some of the things you haven't been aware of before that are real habits. These are some—all of these ideas lie in your mind, so to speak, just like habits. And you've got to work on them and get rid of them. Like the fear of girls. We've got to get you over that—take your ass out, and get you having experiences with girls—

C170: Well, I met a girl who somewhere (*inaudible*)—that's it. (*Laughs*)

T171: What happened?

C172: I can't get close. I don't know how to approach—

T173: You can't

C174: I don't know how to talk.

T175: So you learn.

C176: Would you, from a book?

T177: From a book and getting practice. You can learn how to play baseball like a major leaguer from a book. You can learn to drive an automobile or repair an automobile from a book, partly.

C178: Hm?

T179: And that's just like this. That's what we would do. We'll talk about the ideas and what your experiences are, and then it's up to you to go on and just give 'em a try. You don't have to be very successful. All I want you to do is start getting involved, you see. Like when you sit down to study, I'd like you to start listening to what you're saying to yourself about

"Oh, I've got to get this grade," and all this sort of thing. More important, listen to what you hear yourself say to yourself. 'Cause 90 percent of what people say to themselves—

C¹⁸⁰: All right, I really could listen to myself.

T¹⁸¹: —90 percent of what you say, you probably don't hear. You bought something; you're going home; you probably say, "Oh, I should take that subway. I'll go over there, and I'll do something." You don't hear what you're saying half the time.

C¹⁸²: Um-hm.

T¹⁸³: See, now we want to get you more sensitive to hearing what's going on.

C¹⁸⁴: All right, I'm going to listen to what I'm telling myself.

T¹⁸⁵: You find out the major thing you're telling yourself and ask yourself, "Is it true? What's the evidence? What's so terrible about that?"

C¹⁸⁶: Right or wrong?

T¹⁸⁷: Yeah. And let's say, you say to yourself, "Oh God, if I go—if I ask this girl for a date, if she says no, what's she going to do? Well, she might not like it. Well, so what if she doesn't like it?" See, you can be challenging these ideas you have. 'Cause you've got certain assumptions now that things are gonna be terrible and horrible.

C¹⁸⁸: Um-hm.

T¹⁸⁹: Now you've got these assumptions. And there ain't a damn thing that's terrible and horrible in life in itself. Sure, you can name the atom bomb or say that somebody with a baseball bat's gonna hit you on the head. These you can get legitimately afraid of, see? I was just talking to my students a couple of hours ago about the war crisis three years ago when we thought Manhattan Island might be bombed. It's a wonder how I talked myself out of 96 or 97 percent of my anxieties. I first got very anxious, but then I said, "What the hell's going on here? So I'm going to die sometime, you know. Why should I go out half-cocked and waste a life, avoid having a ball, or something, or get scared just because I'm very anxious? I'll get rid of the anxiety and do things rationally." So I heard what I was saying; "I think it will be so terrible if I die, in the building there's no place to run," and all these things. I said, "Shit! If there's no place to run, so I die! So it's close to forty years earlier than I expected, so what!" So I didn't get anxious anymore. I was able to go about doing some work. And you know you can do this. You can learn how to do it.

C¹⁹⁰: All right. (*Laughs*) When do I come?

T¹⁹¹: Well, when *can* you come?

C¹⁹²: Uh-mm, Saturday? Uh-mm, Saturdays.

T¹⁹³: Any other time—in case we have to set it up for some other time? Saturday I think will be okay as far as I can see now.

C¹⁹⁴: No possibility of Sunday?

T¹⁹⁵: No.

C¹⁹⁶: Uh.

T¹⁹⁷: Eventually I perhaps could see you at home; but I can't right now because I'm moving into my new place. But it may be more appropriate here, and Saturday I have to be here. One of the students is, and the counselors are working. So—

C¹⁹⁸: Hey, Saturdays are all right.

T¹⁹⁹: Okay.

C²⁰⁰: As long as I have some time (*pause*) I—I just piece out my time so I have time here and have time to study, weekends. Just—just look in books and grab a bite, and that's it. Weekend—that's the weekend.

T²⁰¹: Are you working now? Making any money?

C²⁰²: Oh, in school I am. I might be a neighborhood Youth Corpsman, and I'm—I'm doing clerical work.

T²⁰³: You're making money for it?

C²⁰⁴: Yes.

T²⁰⁵: Yeah. 'Cause I'd like you to get this book. And I'll write out for you where to go, and you just tell them I sent you, and they'll fix you up. Do you have the money for the book, and could you get up there [to the Institute for Rational Living] this afternoon?

C²⁰⁶: No, not this afternoon, I don't think so.

T²⁰⁷: Well, after school Monday or something. Whenever you can.

C²⁰⁸: Yes.

T²⁰⁹: I'd like you to do a little reading in this book, just on things that are of interest to you. It's a reference book. It's not something you read once and put down. But it'll discuss a lot of these ideas that you and I have talked about, plus some other ones which may be helpful.

C²¹⁰: (*Silence*)

T²¹¹: Maybe you'd better call first because they may not have a copy on hand. I talked to the secretary yesterday. Tell her that you're seeing me for psychotherapy and that I asked you to ask her if they'd give you one of their copies, 'cause I want you to have it as soon as possible.

C²¹²: (*Silence*)

T²¹³: Now, what do you think you could be doing this week to work on your problems? What would you like to do? 'Cause in this kind of work, we expect you to do some thinking and some practice and try to tackle some problems a little bit, so after a while they get easier and easier. If we just talk over everything and you never try to tackle them, why, it's going to be a long, slow process. So what do you think you could do—call it homework?

C²¹⁴: Um, talk to the girl. (*Laughs*) And I made that—I made my mind up to do that last night.

T²¹⁵: Um-hm.

C²¹⁶: I could—call her up tomorrow—and see if I could see her Tuesday. Tuesday is a holiday.

T²¹⁷: Um-hm.

C²¹⁸: That's sort of auto-psychotherapy, I guess.

T²¹⁹: Self-saving therapy?

C²²⁰: Um.

T²²¹: Any chance you'd be interested in or available to come to this lecture I'm giving Monday, 'cause I'm—

C²²²: Well, what time is it on Monday?

T²²³: It's—six—ten minutes after six. Gonna be in this building.

C²²⁴: Oh good, as long as it's not on a school day.

T²²⁵: Okay. I don't know if we'd be able to—

C²²⁶: Psychologists have always interested me.

T²²⁷: Maybe you'll be one some day.

C²²⁸: (*Laughing*) Oh, no!

The closing part of this first session with Dr. Geis and Robert G. is notable for the use of several other methods that are commonly employed in RET:

1. In T¹⁶¹, the therapist highly recommends that the client purchase

and read one of the main self-help texts of RET: *A Guide to Rational Living* (Ellis and Harper, 1970). He is so eager for the client to read this book that he even suggests that he will arrange with the clinic under whose auspices he is working to charge the client no fee for the first session if he purchases a copy of the book. As mentioned in my comment on some of the other counseling cases in this book, this is a frequent practice in RET. Clients are assigned reading material to supplement the therapy sessions, and it is generally found that considerable amounts of therapist and client time and energy are thus saved.

2. A little more unusually, Dr. Geis also suggests that the boy may find it helpful to attend some of his talks at the university or his courses at the Institute for Rational Living in New York City. Often, especially in rural areas of the United States, such talks and courses are not available. But in larger cities, therapists and their colleagues may give public presentations on RET or related topics, and these are often found to be quite helpful to clients or ex-clients. The Institute for Rational Living also distributes some recorded talks that can be similarly employed by clients.

3. It is notable that, in response C[164], the client remarks that "nobody ever got to me this deep in my life." Even though he has had several sessions with his high school guidance counselor, he recognizes that Dr. Geis, in a single session, has reached him on a much deeper level. This is not merely because the therapist has directly probed and asked him about intimate details of his feelings that no one has previously inquired about, but mainly, probably, because Dr. Geis has explained to Robert G. exactly what he has been thinking to create some of his most self-defeating feelings and precisely what he can do to change them. This is a frequent finding in RET: that even when the therapist does not use dramatic experiential, cathartic, physical, existential, or encountering methods of "opening up" the client, his didactic talk with this client is on such a deeply insightful and philosophically attacking level that the client experiences profound feelings about himself that he sometimes has never previously known in his life. This is not to say that the "releasing" methods of Janov (1971), Jourard (1968), Perls (1969), Reich (1949), Schutz (1967), and others do not work; for in some respects they do. But it is to point out that there are more ways than one of skinning a cat, and that explanatory, teaching, and rational methods of discourse may not only "open up" many individuals within a short period of time, but may also give them

methods and ideas with which to work against many of their most
self-sabotaging emotions.

4. Dr. Geis briefly shows Robert G., in response T^{185}, how to zero
in on any irrational idea, such as the notion that he is a worthless
individual, and to dispute and challenge it, especially by asking himself, "Where is the evidence that it's true?" and how to challenge
his own catastrophizing by asking himself, when something really
goes wrong in his life, "What is so terrible about that?" In subsequent sessions, of course, he is prepared to present more details
about these RET challenging methods.

5. In typical RET procedure, Dr. Geis sees that Robert gets a
specific homework assignment. He induces Robert to give himself
this assignment—to talk to the girl whom he has previously mentioned—and to try to make a date with her. If the client had not
suggested this homework assignment himself, the therapist would
have in all probability suggested something similar to it. The object
is to get the client, as soon as possible, to do something that he
has hitherto been afraid to do, and either to help him overcome
his anxiety about it in short order or else to help him zero in on
the concrete beliefs he is telling himself to create and maintain
this anxiety.

All told, this lengthy session with Robert G. has been replete with
RET techniques, especially from the middle of the session onward.
Once Dr. Geis knows enough about Robert, he swiftly focuses on
what he thinks are the client's central problems and philosophies,
tries to get him to understand them and do some counter-conditioning thinking about them, and assigns him some in vivo desensitizing
homework to help him tackle them.

SECOND SESSION

T^1:   Well, how did things go this week?

C^2:   All mixed. I tried what you said, and I guess there were
        results.

T^3:   We don't expect a 100 percent or even 2 percent—it is the
        trying—

C^4:   There were results.

T^5:   What happened?

C^6:   I don't know where to start—

T^7:   Well, we had the girl, and we had the school—

C⁸: Yes, we had the girl and the school problems. (*Laughs*) Well, one thing, I think I had better tell you this first. I tried thinking, as a matter of fact, the same day that I saw you—last Saturday—I went home and I thought—and I sank into one of my moods—

T⁹: You sank your*self* into one of your moods.

C¹⁰: I sank myself, and I started writing, and it is ridiculous; and I wanted to show it to you. I'll read it to you. I wanted to show it to you on Monday. I started copying notes from what you were saying.

T¹¹: On the lecture?

C¹²: Yes, I was interested.

T¹³: Did you get anything out of it, by the way?

C¹⁴: Yes, I liked it very much. I admire how you just keep talking. Reason is coming out of it; it is not just blah, blah, blah—

T¹⁵: There is no reason at all why some day you can't do that.

C¹⁶: I don't know why I persist in saying to myself, "Gee, I will never get that high."

T¹⁷: Because you have been doing that for about seventeen years, and you don't get rid of a habit like that overnight. You can't be right-handed when you have been left-handed all these years. (*Laughs*) People—

C¹⁸: Okay, now you are going to laugh. You will probably jump up and hit the ceiling—

T¹⁹: That is your assumption—

C²⁰: Yes, and because I think what I just said is ridiculous, I am sinking into a depressing mood. (*Reads*): "The radio is playing a concert; there is a feeling of going around in circles, no beginning, no ending. This is the way I feel. And I am constantly trying to make up my mind to do something, but I can't make up my mind. I get up and walk from one end of the wall to the other. I sit down; there is a desire for action, and I want to sleep. I am breathing and I am drowning; I am sleeping and I am awake; I am blind and I can see, night and day. This is the way I feel."

T²¹: Hm, hm. Yes.

C²²: (*Reads*): "There is a vision, but it has no meaning. There are a million words, which are behind a concrete wall which want to be free, which want to express their meaning, which want to express my feeling, but they cannot do so. I listen, but I am deaf. I speak, but I am dumb."

T[23]: Now what did you do with all that when you put it down? Did you challenge it at all, or ask yourself questions about it?

C[24]: No, the next day, I read it and I said, "What the hell is all this? I can't interpret it."

T[25]: No, what I mean, when it was going on, did you do anything with it, or just sit on the floor and write this stuff down?

C[26]: I just let it flow—

T[27]: Remember, when we talked about being aware of this stuff. And I think this is a good step toward being aware of it—by asking yourself questions about it. Did you do any of that—try any of that?

C[28]: Yeah, I said, "What is this? I can't interpret it." I said, "What is it? What is it I have put down?"

Very actively and directively, Dr. Geis keeps after the client during the first part of this second session. First, he indicates (in response T[3]) that he doesn't expect Robert G. to achieve anything like 100 percent results. Then, in response T[9], he points out that the client sank *himself* into one of his moods—rather than, as the client puts it, he passively sank into a mood. Thirdly, in response T[17], Dr. Geis shows the client that he has become habituated, for almost the last seventeen years, to thinking and acting in a certain dysfunctional manner, and that therefore it will take some amount of time before he significantly changes. Most importantly, in T[27], he gets after Robert G. about asking himself questions when he feels moody, to determine what he is telling himself to create his moods.

Although the client may seem to be spontaneously talking and directing the session himself, it is clear that the therapist is actually leading him into certain specific directions and is making something out of a good many things that he brings up. In RET, the client's own materials, particularly his feelings (at point C), are constantly used; but the therapist does not hesitate to give clear-cut interpretations, reassurances, directions, and so on in regard to these materials. Moreover, as does Dr. Geis, he keeps actively pushing the client to bring out certain information, and to change his thinking and action when they appear to be disadvantageous.

T²⁹: Wait, you said, "I am drowning," and the immediate question would be, "Am I *really* drowning?"

C³⁰: I said, "I am breathing and I am drowning."

T³¹: All right, "I am breathing and I am drowning. Am I *really* breathing and am I drowning?" And the answer would be, "I am breathing, but I am not drowning." Because the reality is that you are *not* drowning.

C³²: The reality?

T³³: Yes, this is what we want to bring home.

C³⁴: · But that is—is the illusion that I am having.

T³⁵: You are going to keep having it until you start questioning it and bringing the reality more and more home.

C³⁶: Yeah, I understand that—

T³⁷: Now, what I am saying is, why didn't you question it a little bit? This is what we want you to start doing. If you remember, in the lecture I talked a lot about the questions that you can ask yourself: "What is so terrible about that? What is the evidence of all that?" Yes, what's the *evidence* for your drowning?

C³⁸: I didn't establish any evidence, but I just thought—

T³⁹: You didn't try to think, did you?

C⁴⁰: No, I didn't try questioning that hard.

T⁴¹: Did you try a little bit?

C⁴²: I guess I tried a little bit, and I thought it was ridiculous. I threw it away. I threw it on the desk—

T⁴³: I do think it is ridiculous, some of these ideas—but *you* are not ridiculous. And what you were thinking, when you thought it was ridiculous, is, "This ridiculous stuff means that *I* am a shit-head or a ridiculous guy."

C⁴⁴: Yeah, going back to turning myself into a polycratic Martian—

T⁴⁵: As we saw last week, there's no such thing as a ridiculous *person*. People do *act* ridiculously sometimes, and some of your ideas are clearly "nutty" ideas, and so are some other people's ideas "nutty" at times. You are not a "nutty" *guy*.

In responses T⁴³ and T⁴⁵ Dr. Geis again takes the opportunity to indicate that although the client has some ridiculous ideas, he is not ridiculous; and that although people's ideas are often "nutty," they are not "nutty" guys. This is standard procedure in RET: to help the client, time and again, to differentiate between his behavior's not being exemplary and his being a bad person. Because human beings seem to be strongly predisposed to rate themselves along with their behavior, the therapist keeps showing them how to do otherwise.

C⁴⁶: What should I do?

T⁴⁷: What do you think you should do?

C⁴⁸: Well, I try listening to myself. I think I did a lot of that—especially last night—

T⁴⁹: In getting a lot of material, do you mean, or did something happen last week?

C⁵⁰: Well, especially last night—I went to the Institute; I met a girl—

T⁵¹: Is this the same girl? What's her name?

C⁵²: Marcia.

T⁵³: So we can talk about her and I will know. Yeah. So we won't mix her up with the other girls.

C⁵⁴: There are no other girls.

T⁵⁵: There may be—

C⁵⁶: There are none—

T⁵⁷: There may be later on—

C⁵⁸: Oh, later on—but this is the present. Well, I will start from last week. It was on a Friday—last—either Sunday or Monday night—maybe it was Saturday—I called her up and I asked her if I could see her—on Tuesday because Tuesday was no school. And she explained to me that she was in the midst of a huge program. She was studying a lot. She had—which I do not know anything about—a "sweet sixteen" party—whatever that means. I never—

T⁵⁹: I imagine she has turned sixteen—

C⁶⁰: Yes, that is what I imagine also. I don't know anything about parties. And she is a business manager for a paper in Queens and a school paper, and she is having a meeting and all that. I understood all this, and I told her that I understood this. I said, "Anytime during the week, if you want to go out to a movie, a theater, anything you want to see, let's do something." And she said that she would really like to oblige me, but she does not enjoy going out, and it is not her policy, really, to go out. She says she tried it before, and she really does not want to do it.

T61: It could be true or it could be untrue; there are two possibilities—

C62: Yes. All right, I made a deal to meet her at the Institute on Friday. She would go along with this.

T63: Did you have to persuade her, or did she readily agree?

C64: She did readily agree—that I would meet her at the Institute on Friday.

T65: Maybe she is not too disinterested—she may be interested then. This may be true that she doesn't like going out. She's had—

C66: She's showed me her verification that she is a business manager—

T67: In other words, she is not trying to get rid of you particularly.

C68: No, I have a feeling that she is not trying to do that. And honest to goodness, the truth is that I am more involved with her, with that particular individual—

T69: It sounds like you are.

C70: Yeah, I just never had the chance to get involved with another person this deeply. It certainly is not deep—

T71: That's right. It certainly is better than being at home, since you do have a date with her.

C72: Yes it seems like I never could get to her. So she said that she had a party, and she goes out with her own friends. Not too often, but she usually goes with much closer friends.

T73: But you were still persistent at getting her to go out with you—

C74: Yeah, but she still persists in saying that she doesn't go out too much. Once in a while, with a friend. And I said, "Well, can't I be your friend?" I don't know if that is good to say, that. "I am your friend," I said. "Can't I be your friend?" And she said, "I would like to oblige you," and so we made a date at the Institute.

T75: It's better than nothing.

C76: Yes—thank God!

T77: What do you mean, "Thank God," like the world is going to fall? There you go—

C[78]: Am I turning colors?

T[79]: No, your assumption is you are. That is part of your nuttiness, that the world is going to fall if you don't get this girl—

C[80]: So I hung up the phone. This was a phone on the street. I wouldn't dream of telling my mother who I am calling; I do not want her to know anyway. And I just started walking in one direction. I walked for about ten blocks before I knew where I was ending up—

T[81]: You were walking with her?

C[82]: I was walking alone. She was at home.

T[83]: After you made the appointment at the Institute?

C[84]: Yes.

T[85]: You stuck in though—

C[86]: Yes—

T[87]: But, you didn't give up. "I am sorry I called—"

C[88]: I had that point in mind. I got my two bits in, but I felt so bad because she said that she wouldn't want to go out. I really felt, "Oh, boy, the world is going up—she really doesn't want to go out with me—"

T[89]: "That would be horrible—"

C[90]: "She really doesn't like me. She would like to oblige me with words—keep on going around—"

T[91]: Condescending on her part. "I will take care of you a little bit, help you a little bit." Not as if she is intrinsically interested in going out with you?

C[92]: Yes, I understand, that part of condescending. Well, I started walking in one direction for about ten blocks. I looked at the moon. It was night, and it was cold, and I didn't feel the cold. I started walking back home to sleep, went to sleep. Couldn't sleep half the night because "She doesn't like me. Maybe I was rude." In fact, I apologized to her on the phone. I said, "If I in any way make you feel silly, or have insulted you in any way—" And she said "Nothing of the sort."

The remainder of the second session continues in much the same manner as this first part, with steady attempts by Dr. Geis to induce Robert G. to give up his catastrophizing, self-condemning thinking and to take more chances at doing what he would really like to do in life. The third, fourth, and fifth sessions continue in much the same vein. These sessions seem to have paid off quite well, since in the sixth session the client shows some distinct progress.

SIXTH SESSION

T[1]: How're things going?

C[2]: Many different ways. (*Laughs*) Well—it's always hard to start. For instance, I know one thing is for sure, I have a lot of confidence.

T[3]: Confidence?

C[4]: Yeah. I find myself jumping up and sputtering mad in the classroom and telling everybody what I'm thinking, and I don't care whether they like it or not. I just want to get my two cents in.

T[5]: Are you physically asserting yourself, or are you doing that plus being angry, or what?

C[6]: No. Just asserting myself, even deliberately, whatever that means. (*Laughs*)

T[7]: Um-hm. Not being angry or anything like that?

C[8]: No. Sometimes.

T[9]: The reason I say that is because sometimes when people jump up and say things, it could be self-defeating, because it could get you into trouble. On the other hand, if you're just speaking your piece and it's really not going to go against you except that some people may not like it, well, then—

C[10]: Yeah. A lot of them don't like it.

T[11]: What do you say, for example?

C[12]: Well, I usually jump up in my hygiene class. I don't like hygiene anyway. I get 97s and 98s in the subject, and I don't even look in the book, and it's—the only good thing about it is the conversation. So sometimes I add more information to the class, or I don't agree with somebody else, or sometimes we go off on a tangent. And I'm never afraid to speak up, somehow. (*Laughs*)

T[13]: What would you say that before you would have been afraid to say?

C[14]: What I thought. Right off the dot.

T¹⁵: Um-hm. Like what? What's an example of something you said yesterday, or the day before, or Friday, last Thursday, something like that?

C¹⁶: Well, just today we were talking about narcotics addiction, and the teacher—and everybody raised their hands—asked, "What is narcotics addiction? How does it affect us?" And everybody seemed to jump up and say that it had a physiological effect on us; and they kept saying the body needs—it affects the body, and nobody looked at the mind, for crying out loud. And I said I thought it was a psychological effect mostly, a great deal. Because, of course, it's hard to get on the needle or what do you call it—however they call it—become a junky. And suddenly you stop and say, "I'm not going to take any more, 'cause it's going to affect the mind one way or another." And it does affect the mind, I think—the need for it. It is not only physiological, but psychological.

T¹⁷: So you said it?

C¹⁸: Yeah.

T¹⁹: And you would have been afraid before, you think—

C²⁰: Yes, because I would have thought that I wouldn't know what I was talking about, and to a certain extent I'm not sure I know. Well, I do.

T²¹: It's not horrible, even if you don't know.

C²²: Yes, it's not horrible. Right!

T²³: So you've got much more confidence. Good!

C²⁴: However that's going to help. I don't know.

T²⁵: Well, yes, you do.

C²⁶: I just don't see confidence. It's important to me, I suppose; but it's growing to have less importance to me. I want something else out of it.

T²⁷: Out of what?

C²⁸: Well, not out of confidence. I hope these sessions are helping me to get more different aspects of reality; looking at reality and picking out what I'm most interested in. It's the critical thinking and picking out of phrases of irrationality. That's what I'm most interested in.

T²⁹: Well, I would put confidence in this kind of framework. I'd say that confidence—what most people call confidence—is feeling so good that you're not so much afraid any more. Of course, that's not exactly what you're saying; but I want to give you a couple of other ways to think about what most people think confidence is: "I can only buckle up my courage and feel better and cover up the fear I really feel." I think confidence includes, in the first place, a realistic appraisal of your abilities that are involved in a situation; secondly, a willingness to take a leap and be involved with those abilities in a situation, because you're not going to give yourself any fear-inducing bullshit, like "oh, it will be terrible—"

C³⁰: "What if I fail?"

T³¹: Right! It's realistic. You know, a lot of people can have confidence that they could jump over the moon; but they can't. Or they think they know exactly what this topic is all about, but they really may not know. Like you partly suggested, you may not know. But what's so important are two things: realistically knowing that there's no crime in speaking; secondly, not inducing fear in yourself. And when you're not afraid, you can go right ahead and say what you think. And when you feel wrong, you learn why you're wrong, if you check up on it. If you're right, so much the better. That will give you some pluses in somebody's book.

C³²: Well, what I was most afraid of before was speaking out. Because I always thought, "Gee, I don't know too much about anything." And I always said to myself, "So I won't say a word. Gee, I'm not certain on this anyway." Only in my English class—like last time when I wasn't seeing you—I really spoke up. Somehow I spoke up in English, because I guess I had to, you know, read compositions in front of the classroom. That was the only time I spoke up before, in the past. I've always had the idea that I didn't know too much, or enough, or average about anything, or better. Yet I always knew a little bit above average about anything.

T³³: You know we have lots of graduate students, people twice your age and more, who are the same way when you get them in a class situation.

C³⁴: I've actually thought about it, and I said to myself, "Of course, you don't know 100 percent about this subject—about hygiene. Or better yet, you don't know 100 percent of this book. You don't know 100 percent of it, and you don't care. You don't have to knock yourself about it." Let's take a different subject, like medicine. There must be a hell of a lot of medical students who have finished college and finished graduate school, medical school, and—what do you call it?—internship; and they are doing graduate work and trying to get their Ph.D.'s. "And there's got to be some kind of doubt, no matter what man is in what field," I've said to myself; "he has to have some doubt, about his field, that he doesn't know something."

T³⁵: Of course, the fact is not whether he has some doubt, but that he doesn't know everything in his field.

C³⁶: Yes. There's always something new, and there's always something that no matter how good you are, you don't know.

T³⁷: Right.

C³⁸: And see, I'm over here floundering in the pool like a fish.

T³⁹: Only knowing 99 percent or 73 percent. Why should you have to know 100 percent anyway? Or 90 percent or 80, just to speak out?

C⁴⁰: That's true. Nothing is in my way—nothing is going to stop me from trying to know more.

T⁴¹: But before you didn't just *like* to—you *needed* to.

C⁴²: It was most ridiculous before. I always looked at it, and I worried about it. And I just worried and worried; and instead of doing something about it, I just worried and didn't do anything about it, as if I was doing something in worrying.

T⁴³: Well, you were like most people, it's true. That's the way people tend to behave. But the notion you mentioned—"I didn't know enough"—is the same notion that a lot of our graduate students tell themselves. And when I talk with them, this is what they tell me, "I don't know enough to contribute," which, in most instances, covers the idea and is the screen for the basic fear that they are going to expose themself, and that would be horrible. Not that they just do not know enough.

C⁴⁴: Bullshit! Yeah!

T⁴⁵: Yes. But, look, a lot of people don't know enough, and they don't mind speaking at all. But others hang in the back and say, "I don't know enough." Well, the problem isn't not knowing enough, it's what they think about not knowing enough.

"If I speak and they don't see, then I'm really a worthless son of a bitch, or something like that. And that would be horrible!"

The client is obviously doing quite well, especially in asserting himself; but Dr. Geis wants to make sure that he really is being assertive rather than, in addition, hostile. For one of the main goals of RET is to help people differentiate between actively going after what they want to get out of life and trying to conquer others or do them in. But Robert G. really seems to be saying what he wants and holding his own ground, in the classroom illustration he gives (in C[16]), and not mainly to be trying to lord it over others.

The therapist, in T[3] and T[15], takes the opportunity again to show the client that he doesn't have to do well in order to speak up. In much of this present session, the boy is trying to indicate that having confidence in oneself, through knowing what to do and doing it, is the great goal one should seek in life. But Dr. Geis keeps gently but firmly contending that this is all very well, but that it merely constitutes achievement-confidence or work-confidence rather than self-confidence. Self-confidence (or self-acceptance) is gained when the individual is willing to take risks and assert himself whether or not he is pretty sure that he is going to succeed (Ellis, 1962).

C[46]: Gee, you made me feel so good last week. (*Laughs*) I went home almost intoxicated, I felt so good. I sat down and started writing. I used the method they taught me at the Memory Institute where you draw a circle. For anything you want to recall, you draw a circle and put the most important thing you want into the circle. And you draw rays like the sun, and you put on those rays various facts; and one fact strangely enough leads to another. They call that "psychological association" at the Institute. It's just a tendency for one thing to lead to another. And I started—I almost recalled every word we—that passed through us last week. I wrote it down, something like two thousand words; some of my own I stuck in, but I tried to recall as much as I could. I got about three sheets packed with words.

T[47]: What made you feel so good last week?

C[48]: Well, especially when you made reference to the taffy I thought I needed—that really cleared the way a lot. If it didn't clear the irrational thoughts 100 percent away, it cleared at least 85 or 90 percent of them away.

T[49]: How do you mean?

C[50]: How I was a little baby, and I always wanted something; and if I didn't get it, I would cry. I wouldn't look at reality and say to myself, "All right, it's hard to get. Why should I stay here and sulk, when I could be out and trying to get it." Before I was a little baby; and I cried if I didn't get what I thought I needed.

T[51]: In your own way, you cried. Not necessarily with tears, but you pounded your fists on the floor, psychologically.

C[52]: Yes.

T[53]: Which is really, in summing it up, a protest against reality. Saying, "Oh, how horrible it's this way! It's horrible. I can't get what I want!" Rather than trying to get what you want and accepting the grim reality that's going on.

The statement made by Dr. Geis in the previous session, which apparently was taken to heart by Robert G. and proved to be very helpful to him, was a point that is commonly made in RET: namely, that most of the things that people say they absolutely must have, or *need* are really pieces of taffy that they *want*; and that when they are "terribly frustrated" and upset about this frustration, they are like little babies who are crying for their taffy. In using this argument, and showing the client that he practically never really needs what he wants, RET might be called the original "Reality Therapy"—for many years before William Glasser (1965) brought out his first writings on reality therapy, rational-emotive practitioners were showing clients that they'd damn well better stop wailing and whining about what they cannot have in life and would better accept reality, no matter how grim it may be. This, of course, was also emphasized many years previously by Epictetus (Hadas, 1964), Alfred Adler (1927, 1929, 1931), and Bertrand Russell (1950).

Another thing that has apparently helped the client appreciably (as he indicates in response C[46]) is that he has not only listened carefully to the therapist and gone to hear him talk outside of therapy, but has also spontaneously done his own written homework assignments by writing down the gist of the helpful material he has thereby been learning and going over his written material several times. Here again is some evidence that bibliotherapy and homework are important parts of psychotherapy, when properly employed.

C⁵⁴: Well, I sat down on Sunday, and I wrote down something about no matter what's going to happen, I'm always going to have to pay the piper. I'm always going to have to confront problems. I'm going to have to produce solutions, no matter what. If I fail or if I don't, I'm always going to have to do something like that, no matter what; and it's the most ridiculous thing in the world to worry about how I'm going to make out on the next test. If I fail, I'm going to be horrible, and I'll be worthless. And anxiety is almost—is actually one obstacle in the path, which obstructs the way I want to get to my goal. In other words, there is the goal and there is me, and in between me and the goal are fear, worry, and anxiety.

T⁵⁵: Which you have been creating for yourself.

C⁵⁶: Yes. Irrationally. And in creating these obstacles, I've wasted a lot of energy, and by the time I get through that—I hack away from that to get at the goal, I'm all exhausted. And that's how I came here. Remember I said I had a lot of pressure, and I felt just—you know. I got there—I got to the 93 average, but I felt like hell, because I had to weigh all this.

T⁵⁷: And even after you get through all your craziness and finally reach the goal, you're sort of pooped out, and it hardly makes it worthwhile anymore. If you had to do that for all the 93s in your life, you wouldn't live very long.

C⁵⁸: No (laughing), I don't think so. And I don't know, does it sound reasonable to you what I'm saying about the obstacles?

T⁵⁹: Quite. I understand exactly what you're saying. It's a good description of it.

C⁶⁰: Because it's a hell of a lot of junk in between what I want and the path that I have to travel to get what I want.

T⁶¹: Yes.

C⁶²: And I could do away with all this because, in the first place, it means creating; and instead I can save all that energy to travel in that path to the goal. That was the real insight—I don't know in what terms you could say—what steps of progress you could classify it in. I don't know how to describe it. I just never had the thought before, and it seems so logical to me. And it's so easy; I don't have to break my head trying to build up mountains of fear and anxiety. And that's what gets me; I was always building it up, and I can't see that.

Why was I doing that? Why was I telling myself—why was I creating for myself fear and anxiety and all this worry and hardship? And, really, it was a strain on me that way.

T⁶³: Yes. When people say, "Well, how can I get rid of all this stuff—how can I change? It will be very difficult to change," we often say, "But we wonder how you can keep all that, 'cause it's more difficult to keep telling yourself all that crap." Actually, in some ways, it's very easy—because you get in a rut, and you keep going in the same way; and you have, like, psychological blinders on, and you don't know any other ideas. Nobody confronts you with different ideas, and you don't confront yourself with different ideas. You never stop to think out what you have started to do. You've done a great deal of it within the last few weeks, which I've started you off on. Nobody said "Whoa, take a look, ask yourself sensible questions. Is it really true that failure is so horrible, that it 'makes me a lousy no-good shit?' " Nobody ever said, and you never said to yourself, "Is it really true? What's the evidence?"

The client's responses, C⁶⁰ and C⁶², and Dr. Geis's follow-up on them, T⁶³, show how valuable insight can often be achieved in RET without the use of classical psychodynamic methods that are supposed to produce this kind of insight, such as free association, probing into the client's past, dream analysis, analysis of the transference relationship between the therapist and client, and so on. Robert G. now sees that he has ostensibly wanted certain goals, up to now, such as success; but instead of spending most of his time and energy trying to achieve these goals, he has actually utilized them in creating—yes, creating—anxiety and various forms of defenses against this anxiety. Now he sees that "I don't have to break my head trying to build up mountains of fear and anxiety," and that he can instead turn to his originally desired achievements.

Dr. Geis correctly points out that these significant insights that Robert G. is now acquiring mainly stem from the simple fact that he never before challenged, or even thought of challenging, his anxiety-creating ideas (especially the idea that it would be awful if he failed). Once the therapist showed him how to do this, he has been doing quite a bit of such challenging—and therefore he is now achieving a whole chain of important insights.

C⁶⁴: Well, maybe that's what you're trying to get at. Maybe you're trying to find out why people tell themselves these things.

T⁶⁵: Well, we know lots of reasons why they do.

C⁶⁶: Well, then you know it?

T⁶⁷: Yes. But it's not so important why they begin to do it—only to diagnose why they continue to do themselves in, to show them what they do, and to show them how not to do it—which is what I've been doing with you.

C⁶⁸: Um.

T⁶⁹: There are lots of very understandable reasons why people get into this kind of a rut.

C⁷⁰: Curious to know what—when it's going to leave me—how far will I go?

T⁷¹: Well, you take the chains off you; then you go as far as your values and your abilities take you.

C⁷²: But—I remember you once said that we should know our goals; we should know our limits, our capacities.

T⁷³: Well, you should be as realistic as you possibly can about the world and yourself. If you haven't got a certain aptitude, it's best to be realistic with yourself and recognize it and focus on the aptitude that you have got or the things you can get. Otherwise, of course, you decide to take the one chance in a hundred where you can get something without planning. And often goals—including, in particular, vocational goals, which seem very real to a person your age when getting near to getting out of high school and planning for college and so forth—are unrealistic. You can't begin to make sense of and define a vocational goal until you have certain kinds of experiences, until you get older. Some people decide their vocational goals early, some people later. Not until late adolescence do most fellas begin to define theirs pretty clearly. Even then, it may not be for some time. But it's very desirable to have goals. It's very desirable to be fully aware of your own values, to know what you want. But you'll be changing as you grow older, to some extent, and you can't always know these things fully. It's very desirable to know them as fully as you can. Hardly necessary, though, to a happy existence.

C⁷⁴: Hardly necessary to a happy existence.

T⁷⁵: It's not necessary to have firm goals all the time.

C⁷⁶: Not necessary.

T⁷⁷: Not necessary, no. Well, you tell me. Is it necessary, do you think? Firm, fixed goals?

C⁷⁸: But if you did, would that bring confidence?

T⁷⁹: No. It depends on what your goals are. I mean, if you have goals, you may be shaking yourself up about them; "Oh God, will I get there or not?"

C⁸⁰: Well, supposing you set a group of goals, which you know are within your aptitude?

T⁸¹: All right. You can have two fellas—let's say two fellas who are aspiring to medical school, to being a doctor, just the way you at present apparently are. You have two fellas, both who clearly set goals. One fella is giving himself a real hard time about it and is really full of what you were before, like "Oh God, it will be terrible if I fail! I've *got* to do this, I've got to do that," so nervous that he's not studying very well. The other guy has the same fixed goals, but he's much more realistic about it and is much more rational in the way he goes about things, and he doesn't give himself this same kind of crap. And so he just goes slugging it right along. He is more likely to do a good job getting there, you see, and to use all the potential he's got—all the aptitude and intelligence and energy he's got in getting to the goal, because he's not going to be so nervous and so tense and worry so much and focus on irrelevant things. So it's not really the goals in themselves. Although in one way, knowing a goal fairly clearly is good for very nervous people. If one knows the goal—one's got a goal and got a fix on it—maybe he's going to be a little less nervous. Like, if you know where the enemy's coming from, you're going to be a little less nervous than if you don't know where they're coming from. But those are guys who are somewhat upset and irrational in the first place.

C⁸²: What's always impressed me when I've looked on a man, a middle-aged person or an old person who's been successful or is successful in life—he has a big company or something—he's successful—what always strikes me is the way that he—the confidence he has in himself. He's sort of—he knows what he's doing all the time almost. At least, he *seems* like he knows what he's doing. Even that is important, and it seems that he's been through all this—am I right? Has he been through all this crap that I've been going through?

T[83]: No. A lot of these guys can function very well in their jobs. Let's take a job for example—could be at home or somewhere else, but most often it's the job. For example, the high financiers, Wall Street. I don't know any personally that I can think of offhand, but I can bet that a lot of them are pretty neurotic guys in some ways, and a lot of them have lousy home lives and get depressed fairly often. But they can function on the job because they have a clear sense of what they're doing. For them the job is an adaptation and a way of shutting out and hammering away a lot of the anxieties they create in other ways. You see? So it depends upon the adaptation. I would say a person is going to do best and function all around in a good, well-adjusted way to the extent that he is rid of his irrational ideas.

C[84]: Most of these guys have learned to get rid of these irrational ideas?

T[85]: Yes, to some extent some of them have had certain experiences and gradually changed their beliefs as a result of these experiences. But some of them have some of the nuttiest ideas; some of them still believe that failure is horrible—the guy who kills himself, for example, when his business collapses. Other guys have three businesses that collapse, and they say, "That's the way it goes; I'll try to build another one. And if I can't build another one, and I'm too old, well, that's just the way it goes. I wish I had succeeded, but I don't have to. I'll try and do the best I can."

C[86]: But he doesn't give himself hell for failing.

T[87]: That's right.

In responses C[72] to T[85], Dr. Geis is giving Robert G. some practical vocational counseling, but included in this counseling is a hardheaded rational-emotive philosophy. First, he lets Robert know that he'd better be realistic about the goals he chooses, and that he may not be able to pick adequate vocational choices until he has gained some more experience. Secondly, he indicates that clear-cut goals are desirable but that even more important is the individual's determination but *not necessity* to achieve them. Thirdly, he points out that many seemingly "successful" businessmen still have basically irrational attitudes and are covering up their anxieties with their successes rather than looking at and undermining the belief systems behind these anxieties. Fourthly, he once more tries to teach Robert that failure is not catastrophic and that a rational person can go on from a great failing enterprise either to build another and another or to philosophically accept the fact that he is no longer able to succeed.

Dr. Geis's vocational counseling, in this respect, is typical of the way that the rational-emotive therapist usually handles practical problems. He does not hesitate to give information and even advice about such problems, but he puts them within an RET framework, so that he is doing much more than that. He is invariably more interested in the client's basic value systems and how they may irrationally interfere with his functioning and his happiness than he is with merely helping him to solve practical vocational, sex, family, or other problems.

C[88]: I've been doing that all along. I haven't failed. I'm still—

T[89]: You might as well have!

C[90]: I'm not now, but I was. A great deal.

T[91]: And that's the surer thing that would have led you to failure, not to mention blowing your brains out. Something like that, that you were plotting around a long time.

C[92]: Um-hm. (*Pause*) Come to think of it, I thought of it this week—blowing my brains out. Now, I examined it, and I said, "It's really out of this world. It's crazy; it's just not rational. There's all the chances in the world. There's a big future ahead, and no matter what you do, you're still going to be a part of it and something. If you fail or not, you can always try again." But then—but for just three seconds, or five seconds, I reveled in the idea of suicide. Is that the right word?

T[93]: You toyed with it because it felt safe?

C[94]: Yes. Somehow. But then I snapped out of it right away. I just didn't—it seemed rational at first; it seemed glorious. Then I thought, "What the hell am I thinking about? Let's forget about that!"

T[95]: Why did it seem glorious?

C[96]: I don't know. It seemed like that's a nice door to open, a door behind which you don't know what's going to happen.

T⁹⁷: Sure you do. (*Pause*)

C⁹⁸: Sure I do?

T⁹⁹: Sure, you know what's going to happen if you blow your brains out. You won't be here anymore.

C¹⁰⁰: Well, of course, yes, but the door which I open—which behind the door— All right, I know that I won't have to go through what I have been going through or what I might go through in the future.

T¹⁰¹: Yes. You still may be unwilling to put out some of the effort to do some of these things. You still may have some of these—

C¹⁰²: (*Interrupting*) For crying out loud. I'm—I'm—I'm determined to put out the effort! (*Sighs*)

T¹⁰³: Yes, I bet you are. You see, sometimes people who are sort of determined, at the same time sometimes they tend to give up easily. I don't think this is at all true of you or likely to happen. I'm not suggesting that. I'm suggesting that you have a residual belief. You still believe a little bit some of the things you used to believe.

C¹⁰⁴: I want to eradicate all those beliefs.

T¹⁰⁵: Well, I think you can; and if you only end up with 1 percent of your former beliefs, you're going to just have to lump it. That's the way the ball bounces. Just be human like the rest of us. You can't have it all. Because you've got to be fallible. You make a mistake, Robert, demanding that you have no irrational beliefs, just the way you demanded before you've got to have all great grades.

C¹⁰⁶: Declaration.

T¹⁰⁷: Yes. It's the same kind of jazz. So I think you ought to really try your hardest to get rid of as much as you can. And when it gets to the point where you can't get rid of any more, just do the best you can.

C¹⁰⁸: It will be very little to get rid of.

T¹⁰⁹: That's right.

Robert G. shows that he still, from time to time, has very crazy thoughts, such as suicidal ideas. Dr. Geis is hardly thrown by this seeming setback and, in fact, insists on discussing it after Robert seems to be willing to slough it off. He makes two important points,

which are again typical of RET: (1) Robert can easily have two sets
of beliefs simultaneously, a rational and an irrational set. Although
he seems to be becoming more and more rational, he still also believes, at least a little, some of the senseless things he used to believe.
This is not unusual, but is only to be expected. (2) There is no point
in Robert's demanding that he be completely free of irrationalities.
He will always be a fallible human; and, as such, can again be expected to have silly ideas. If he insists on having *no* irrationalities,
that idea itself is silly—and will perfectionistically tend to drive
him into feelings of anxiety. Therefore, he'd better accept himself
with his irrationalities, while at the same time trying to minimize
them.

One of the main difficulties in RET is the client's using the system
perfectionistically and condemning himself for not being perfectly
rational, not improving rapidly enough, still having "shameful"
symptoms, and so on. Dr. Geis prophylactically tries to counter this
tendency in Robert.

C[110]: (*Laughs*) I'm going to miss (*laughing*) seeing you. I don't get
a chance much to talk to too many people at all like you.

T[111]: Well, what do you mean? You like me to share your ideas
or feelings?

C[112]: Yes. To share the ideas and get rational, educated answers.
I mean something which can make me think. Also, something
that any street walker would answer, "Don't bug me." And
I know I wouldn't want to bug you with too many more problems, but—

T[113]: Well, you don't bug me with problems. You ought to stop
thinking you do. This is my job. Now, I don't let things outside
me bug me. I bug myself whenever I do. I don't bug myself
very often at all. Patients have twenty problems or one problem, it's all the same. But you'll run into educated people,
if you seek them out and talk with them. But you won't run
into a lot of people who share these ideas. Because these ideas
are developed around a psychological framework, and I'm a
psychologist, and I've been around these ideas a fair amount
of time.

C[114]: That's what fascinates me. I can talk to somebody like that,
and I always wanted—I always wanted to. As a matter of
fact, I was always interested in the knowledge, and I guess

I needed it also real bad. I did. But I'm sorry, I probably won't need it too much in the future.

T[115]: Why would you be sorry? You mean because you wouldn't have someone to talk with like me? Well, that may just be the way the ball bounces. And I'm sure you could live. You could seek out people. There are a number of associations that are in town, for example, and you could drop in once in a while, of course, to say hello. But there are a number of organizations where people gather to share these kinds of interests, these rational interests. Some of them [the people] are kind of irrational, but they're there to get more rational.

C[116]: That's tautological.

T[117]: Hm?

C[118]: That's tautological.

T[119]: Well, you could join the Philosophy Club, for example.

C[120]: Trying to do so—hope so. I can—I will somehow. I'll get into one of those clubs. Not just anything—something.

T[121]: Why don't you start one?

C[122]: What are you bringing out in me now? (*Laughing*) My originality, my initiative?

T[123]: Well, I was thinking, there may not be anything like this in your school going on, or with your associates. This is one way for you to get along with some people whom you would be interested in talking with.

C[124]: In my school, very few people—it's very hard—oh, because about 80 percent of them that walk around my school are like simian morons and—

T[125]: But you don't need 80 percent.

C[126]: Yes, I know I don't. As a matter of fact, it would be good if I find people.

T[127]: But it doesn't even have to be a group from your school. There must be five guys somewhere. And you don't exactly overflow with friends—you could stand a few friends. That's something you could get working on.

C[128]: No, I don't have a lot of friends.

T[129]: You don't have any friends, really, do you? You told me that the first time we talked.

C[130]: No real friends, in a sense.

T[131]: Close, but never friends.

C[132]: Not at all. Well, what'll I do? Look for friends? Try to get
        friendly?

T[133]: What will you advise your seventeen-year-old son, Robert?

C[134]: "Go out and conquer the world." Or—I don't know.

T[135]: That's not helping him very much. Or maybe you don't
        know—as a father, you don't know.

C[136]: That's the way the ball bounces?

T[137]: Well, you tell me.

C[138]: Well, I could do something about it.

T[139]: What if you wanted to get an automobile, and you didn't know
        where to get it, or you didn't have any money? What would
        you do?

C[140]: Ask someone, that's all.

C[141]: You'd get in action some way, wouldn't you? What if you
        wanted a girl friend?

C[142]: (*Laughs*) No, I really don't know anything about girls.

T[143]: What if you wanted to talk with interesting people? What
        if you wanted to learn about something? What would you do?
        Sit on your can and just moan?

C[144]: No. I know what to do when I want to learn something.

T[145]: Or say I don't know?

C[146]: No. I know. I don't know which one you're referring to—the
        automobile, the friend, or the learning.

T[147]: It's all the same.

C[148]: It's all the same. (*Pause*) Go out and try to learn how.

T[149]: Yes. There're really only two alternatives: to go after it or
        not go after it—unless you can think of another one. I can't
        think of it.

C[150]: Oh, well—you say there are two things; maybe you think mak-
        ing a few more friends would help?

T[151]: Well, I seriously think that, in the first place, friends are
        enjoyable for many people.

C[152]: Well, I consider them—they take up a lot of time.

T[153]: Secondly, you've got to—you haven't got a lot of practice or
        experience at this, and this is an error in your personality
        that you could stand to know, particularly if you're going to
        work with people in the future—be a doctor. You're going
        to have to learn about how you're going to make friends—how
        to have friends sometimes. But you're entitled to be friendless

and to be by yourself. There's no law says you have to. I'm thinking of Robert as just a guy getting the maximum out of life. And we can often get more out of life if we have some friends than if we don't have friends. It's not an infallible principle, but you've been a loner all your life, I gather, so it's an area you can try out in any case. You don't have to eat octopus or squid either, but if someone says, "Well, it may be enjoyable," you kind of owe it to yourself to at least give it a try and see what's going on with octopus or squid, unless you're prejudiced to begin with.

C[154]: Prejudiced?

T[155]: Yes, against squid.

C[156]: And octopus?

T[157]: And you told me you'd like to have some friends besides.

C[158]: Yes. Did I?

T[159]: Yes.

C[160]: I'm trapped on all sides, ain't I?

T[161]: You don't really have to be. I'm not raising it because you have to be.

C[162]: Oh, I'm not worried about it. That's good, isn't it? (*Laughs*)

T[163]: Yes, that's good.

C[164]: Well, (1), if I have friends, it will help develop my personality. I'll get more out of life. (2), I don't have friends. (3), What'll I do to get friends? (4), Go out and make friends.

T[165]: Not bad.

C[166]: It's not a masterpiece of deduction, but it's hard to think of.

T[167]: That's a little different from what you told your son, Robert, a few minutes ago. "I don't know, Son."

C[168]: (*Silence*)

T[169]: Now, you've really got to distinguish between knowing what you might do and having to do it. You don't have to do anything, you know, but it's real useful to think things out and see what the options are.

C[170]: Yes. That's what I like, to think things out. I've been intending to do a lot more of that. (*Pause*) I'll always remember what you said during the lecture, "What distinguishes man from the animal is his ability to utilize symbols, to put together, to recognize and remember symbols." And I started thinking about that, and I suppose the more intelligent the person is, the more ability he has of remembering symbols and recognizing and putting them together and using them.

T¹⁷¹: It's one of the common definitions of intelligence, yes.

C¹⁷²: Well, I don't know. It seems what I want to say is too crude. How do I attempt at becoming more, more adroit at utilizing symbols and remembering and then trying to—you know, I don't know if this is going to help. Is it—

T¹⁷³: (*Inaudible*)—a book to use symbols—to think more clearly and to clear up our speech and thinking to the point where we're most efficient and clear and concise.

C¹⁷⁴: I don't know if there's a straightforward answer.

T¹⁷⁵: Well, you tell me. Would you?

C¹⁷⁶: Go out and think. Of course, read and try to—well, think. That's all I can think of. *Think.*

T¹⁷⁷: And try to develop your use of words. Be very sensitive, and try to listen and be very aware of what other people are saying and the way you're using words and the logic involved. Yes, work on this. I used to carry around a vocabulary-builder book when I was your age. I never worked through the whole thing, but I worked through part of it, and to some extent it helped. I paid attention to the use of words, and I tried writing for a spell, and other sorts of things.

C¹⁷⁸: Yes. I'm doing the same thing. I have one hundred different kinds of vocabulary books at home, and I have a scholarship class where we're studying words and I guess—

T¹⁷⁹: Yes. You seem to have a pretty good vocabulary.

C¹⁸⁰: That comes, as a matter of fact—that reminds me of the mathematical part. I'm not good about that. I'm going to do something about that this summer. I'm going to improve myself by getting into a mathematical course or something like that on the mathematical part. If I could score highly, at least average on the SAT [Scholastic Aptitude Test], the official SAT. The PSAT was on Saturday. And a funny thing happened when I took the PSAT. I looked at it, and a verbal part came first, and the mathematical part came second; I looked at the verbal part, and I was going to start on the verbal part—I know I'm good at the verbal. I knew I was good, because I just know; and I don't know how to describe it, but when I took it, I was a little nervous. And I was trying to beat down the nervousness, and I asked myself, "Why am I nervous now? I'm good at this." But there seemed always to be gaps—gaps of a little bit of fear. But I got through with it, I finished the verbal part. But when I got to the mathematical part, something funny happened. I said to myself, "Well, gee, I'm not good at math, so I won't beat myself. I'll really take it easy." And I started doing the math, and I saw I was doing the problems mentally, and I wasn't even bothering figuring out the problems on paper, with paper and pencil, and it was so easy at first, I just had eradicated any fear or anxiety about math.

T¹⁸¹: You didn't over-focus on it to begin with. You just took it as it came.

C¹⁸²: Yes, and I found I was doing problems naturally; and I looked at the problems, and, gee, that answer—just common sense tells you that's the answer. I just took it, 'cause, "So what if I fail, if I get a 200?" 200 is the lowest mark.

T¹⁸³: Putting this in a very tactful way—and this is a very common problem, Robert—people screw themselves up on exams because they focus too much on how well they're doing, rather than on *what* they're doing. And you here were focusing on what you were doing, because you didn't need to focus on how well you were doing.

C¹⁸⁴: Because I knew. I wasn't doing very well at first.

T¹⁸⁵: Well, also, you said "What the hell!" You had the general orientation, "Oh, it's not a horrible thing if I should fail."

C¹⁸⁶: But on the verbal part, where I knew I was going to do good, I also got a little nervous.

T¹⁸⁷: And what would you say you were telling yourself then?

C¹⁸⁸: Well, I was trying really hard—really trying hard to question—tell myself, "All right, so what if I don't do well on this test. This test isn't going to count anyway."

T¹⁸⁹: Yes. But that implies that you were trying to challenge what kind of assumption, though?

C¹⁹⁰: I can't remember the assumption.

T¹⁹¹: Well, if you're saying to yourself, "Look, Robert, it doesn't count too much, don't worry about it."

C¹⁹²: "Gee, I know this one. Oh God, come back to me! I'll go to the next one, and the next, but I'm still worried about this one here. What am I worried for? Hell, I'll come back to it, so what. If I can't come back to it, so what?" That's what I was telling myself.

T^{193}: "Oh, it will be horrible if I can't get it! And oh, I've got to get it! I need to get it!"

C^{194}: Yes. In the first place, I know I didn't get every one of them. So what's so horrible about this one?

T^{195}: Just a *little* worry never hurt anybody. Yes, but you apparently needed to do well on everything, and you were probably not challenging this assumption.

C^{196}: Yes. I tried to do well on everything.

T^{197}: Well, don't stop *trying* to do well, and *desiring* it, *preferring* it. Striving is fine. *Needing* to do well is, of course, a different color.

C^{198}: Or maybe I was fearing that I wouldn't do well.

T^{199}: Yes, but the fear is related to the need.

C^{200}: Um-hm. Then, was I really saying that I *needed* to do well?

T^{201}: "Oh, my God! I've *got* to do well! I've *got* to get it!" Something like that. According to your assumption.

C^{202}: I'm focusing more on *that* than on the material.

T^{203}: Yes. Remember about a week or so ago, we talked about your general orientation. I think it was last week, when you were going through the week kind of testing yourself. It was my belief that you had a general orientation, where you made yourself have the general view—where you've *got* to do this, you've *got* to get that, you've *got* to do that. Remember? And it would be the same kind of thing.

C^{204}: I said, in a sense, that we do need to pass this, to get y's in order to get to z's. We do need y's to get to z's. And then I questioned you on that, and you explained. Well, I *do* need to do well on this exam in order to get on the next.

T^{205}: When your platoon is bedded down for the night in enemy territory, no one has to say to you, "Look, keep an eye out for the enemy." So you're on guard all the time, and you're not always saying to yourself, "Oh, my God, I've got to keep my eye out for the enemy, gotta keep my eye out for the enemy, gotta keep my eye out for the enemy!" You don't say that all the time—you may say it once in a while to yourself;

but it's your general assumption, and you're watchful. You see. In the same way it would be your assumption that fills you full of tension—you got to get this, you gotta do that, you gotta hurry or else it's going to be horrible. Or maybe, then, "I gotta get all these. Now that I'm good, I should be able to get a lot of these because I'm good. Because it would be very nice if I got all these, it means I've got to get a lot of these!"

C^{206}: (Laughs) I got to—I do need to, in a sense, looking at it realistically, but I don't need it—

T^{207}: To get to y. That is, to get to college or things like that. That's what. But if we can show you, as we have, how y or z, or whatever the hell we're talking about—college, that particular college, that particular high grade—isn't so all-important. You can live without it. Then that need becomes an impersonal thing, and it's not all-important for you. And here, like I said, you're so much more likely to get it because you give yourself lots less of a hard time, and you crawl out of a mess.

C^{208}: Yes, and I was really surprised because I was going through. I didn't finish it, but I saw it was very easy.

T^{209}: Let's say you took the PSAT last spring. What would your reaction have been? Or even five weeks ago, six weeks ago, before you first came in [for these therapy sessions]?

C^{210}: Um. "What did I do? Gee, I wonder what I got on the test. Oh boy, I know I did really bad on it. One really bugged me. Gee, I didn't get that one right."

T^{211}: Do you think you would have performed the same way on the test? You might have; do you think you would have?

C^{212}: No, I think that test, if it were last spring, would have been much lower.

T^{213}: If it were what, did you say?

C^{214}: If it was last spring. If I were to take the test last spring, it would have been much lower, I think.

T^{215}: Why?

C^{216}: Because I had all that junk in my head then, floating around.

T^{217}: Well, how would that have interfered? I'm trying to get you to spell it out.

C[218]:   Well, instead of focusing on the material like you said, I'd
         have to focus upon the dust particles of irrationality and that
         would actually hinder my end results of the test.

T[219]:   Putting it simply, I would say you'd be upsetting yourself
         so much you couldn't do so well.

C[220]:   Right.

T[221]:   Including focusing on other things. When people upset them-
         selves, they focus on what they're upsetting themselves about,
         rather than on the material they should be working with.
         (*Pause*)

C[222]:   Well, what do I focus on now?

T[223]:   Well, what's for this week? What are you going to do to try
         to improve a little bit more or reinforce what you've already
         done? This may be a good part of what you'd be doing for
         a while now, reinforcing what you have achieved, as far as
         thinking clearly and disturbing yourself less. You want to
         consolidate and practice and practice some more, and after
         a while it'll just be a normal part of you.

C[224]:   It's sort of an implication that there are more steps to climb.

T[225]:   Well, in a sense of cementing some of these things you learned
         and working on the last of them and working on new areas,
         like maybe the friends, the girls, the fear that's projected in
         meeting her, the study habits or whatever.

C[226]:   Study habits. I'm going to get into my midterms next week,
         and out of a forty-eight-hour weekend, if I can get twenty
         hours of that weekend—that's twenty—that's close to a whole
         school week.

T[227]:   Is it realistic to plan to do that? Could you do it, you think?

C[228]:   I think I can do it. In a weekend I've done twelve hours, and
         I don't think I killed myself. So I know it's the midterms
         that's important—so what if I fail one?—that's not going to
         be horrible. Why should I worry about it when I have a week-
         end? If I can, I'll try and put as many hours as I can.

T[229]:   How about this week, up until that time? Are you studying
         all along?

C[230]:   Well, it is next week.

T[231]:   A week from now? Are you studying this week?

C[232]:   Yes. I'm going to have a test Thursday in English, and I have a few bits of homework to do, and I study my chemistry. I'll work it out.

T²³³: So you don't have to leave all your studying for the weekend?

C²³⁴: Yes, I'll try to get some in the week. Mostly the weekend reviewing; I prefer to reinforce a few facts here and there.

T²³⁵: Yes, that's your time to go over a lot of these factors and things. You're still doing a lot of studying during the week as you go along, normal studying.

C²³⁶: Oh yes. Nearly all homework, of course. I think they're going to consider the homework for this week very little. So that gives me more time to pitch in more. I never do too well on the midterms. I always come in very grand on the finals, but on the midterms I never do too well. Now I should do much better, because now I have a plan of action.

T²³⁷: Well, then do you want to come in on Saturday or do you want to put it off, or what.

C²³⁸: No, I don't want to put it off.

T²³⁹: You mean you'd rather come in Saturday than a week later, something like that.

C²⁴⁰: I don't know. I guess you've been seeing me too much anyway.

T²⁴¹: Well, if you think I could be helpful to you if you come Saturday, come on in as far as I'm concerned.

C²⁴²: I'll take a chance and miss a week.

.T²⁴³: All right.

C²⁴⁴: See what the outcome will be.

T²⁴⁵: Then I'll see you a week from this coming Saturday—12:00.

In the closing section of this sixth session, several things occur that are again typical of the RET approach:

1. In C¹¹⁰ and C¹¹², Robert G. indicates that he realizes that he is getting better and that the sessions with Dr. Geis will soon be at an end. He knows that he is going to miss seeing the therapist—not because he merely likes him, loves him, or finds him a substitute father, but because he greatly enjoys talking with him intellectually and ideologically. This could, of course, be interpreted, in psychodynamic terms, as his really being attached to the therapist emotionally; but it is doubtful whether that is true.

Many clients are somewhat disappointed in classic RET procedures, which may include a minimum of warm relating between therapist and client, because they describe the therapist as being "cold," "unemotional," or not sufficiently interested in them personally. But many other clients, such as Robert G., greatly enjoy RET because they want intellectual stimulation and the adventure of learning about themselves and others, and find this sort of thing highly "emotionally" gratifying. For the first type of client, RET can be mixed with a warmer approach—and it frequently is, especially with clients who are ultra-vulnerable, depressed, and suicidal. But it generally tends to be much less "warm" than other kinds of therapeutic relationships, because so much time is spent (as in Dr. Geis's sessions with Robert G.) in the therapist's teaching, explaining, and giving information to the client that, in spite of his real interest in helping the client, great gobs of warmth are largely precluded. Besides, the therapist wants to make pretty sure that the client improves for the right and not the wrong reasons: because he sees that he can think differently and act more efficiently *himself*, and not because he has faith in the therapist's (and, by extension, other people's) caring for him and thereby ensuring his being "worthwhile."

2. Although he is not exceptionally loving to Robert G., Dr. Geis—as, for example, in his response, T[115]—keeps urging him not only to work at getting over his emotional problems but to enhance his potential for happy living. For, as I have been emphasizing throughout this book, what we call psychotherapy (or what I prefer to call emotional education) has at least two main facets: first, the individual's overcoming his severe disturbances by thinking and acting much more efficiently; and second, his learning how to enjoy himself more as he has increased time and energy to do so, partly because he is no longer too absorbed in emoting dysfunctionally.

Dr. Geis, therefore, tries to show Robert that he could widen his scope of interests and friendships—in addition to becoming less anxious and depressed. Here again, his interest in Robert could be construed as helping him by relationship methods; and client-centered and relationship theorists, such as Carl Rogers (1961) and C. H. Patterson (1969), would probably say that his empathic, warm attitude toward Robert is the essence of the help he is giving the client. A close reading of the sessions included here, however, will show that Dr. Geis is far more didactic than empathic—which is exactly what Raskin (1965, 1966) found in a study comparing excerpts from one of my own psychotherapy sessions to one by Carl Rogers, and to those of several other psychoanalytically-oriented and experientially-oriented therapists. In fact, the professional raters of the therapy protocols whom Dr. Raskin employed in his study wrongly (at least in my estimation) found that I showed relatively little "unconditional positive regard" for my client—probably because they confused this kind of regard with personal warmth. I think it would be fairly evident to any unbiased observer that both Dr. Geis and I, in the protocols included in this volume, show considerable "unconditional positive regard" for our clients—meaning, that we fully accept them with their failings, do not condemn them no matter how execrable their behavior is, and consistently try to help them with their emotional problems and in regard to their achieving their fuller potentials for personality growth and enjoyment. But we do so largely through didactic rationality rather than through warm relating.

3. In response T[181], Dr. Geis gives Robert a chance to think out things for himself and to feed back to him some of the things he is figuring out. There can be a temptation by RET therapists merely to feed the client information and straight thinking, and not to check whether he is beginning to do it for himself. Consequently, the therapist would better stop from time to time and see whether the client really is thinking differently, and not merely agreeing too easily and conformingly with what the therapist is saying. RET would preferably become a kind of Socratic dialogue (Diaz-Guerrera, 1959; Sahakian, 1969) rather than primarily a lecture series.

4. In responses C[180] and C[182], Robert shows that he is now able to use RET principles even when he is under severe pressure, as when he is taking an examination and may well do poorly on it. When he anti-catastrophizes and accepts the fact that if he gets the worst possible mark, 200, on the math part of the Scholastic Aptitude Test, he is still not a worm or a no-goodnik, he finds (as innumerable people do, using this technique) that he is actually able to do much better than he ever did before on a similar test. This is exactly the result that Dr. Geis is trying to achieve with his client: to get him to change his attitude toward failing, at point B (his belief system) and therefore to be able to return concentratingly to point A (the activating event, the math test) and to do much better on it than he would do if he were catastrophizing about failing.

5. In response T[183], Dr. Geis shows Robert a point that RET therapists frequently make to their clients (Ellis, 1962; Ellis and Harper, 1970): namely, that if they focus on how well they're doing instead of on what they're doing, they will almost always do poorly on any kind of test, audition, public speech, or other performance. This is not merely because they are catastrophizing and potentially putting

themselves down, and thereby creating interfering anxiety. It is also because of the general psychological phenomenon of inter-ference or diversion. If an individual is partly concerned with (1) "What steps shall I take to solve this problem?" and partly concerned with (2) "It will be awful if I fail to solve this problem well!" it is highly unlikely that he will be as effective in his solutions as he would be if he were almost entirely concerned with the first of these steps. For his thinking will be so diverted, diffuse, and on-off that he will, at best, be spending about half his time and energy focusing on the problem-solving; and his efficiency will thereby be importantly reduced. Psychotherapists who look for in-volved, overcomplex, "psychodynamic" explanations for poor prob-lem-solving usually forget this simple and obvious finding of experi-mental psychologists. RET practitioners, keeping this point in mind, frequently point it out to their clients, first, to show these individuals what is really going on; second, to give them an incentive to change their thinking-catastrophizing patterns; and third, to indicate how they can refocus on the essence of the problem to be solved instead of on what they will be "worth" as humans if they fail to solve it.

6. In response T^{195}, Dr. Geis tells Robert that just a *little* worry never hurt anybody. More precisely, he could have indicated that concern—the belief that "It would be better if I succeeded, and therefore I will do my best to work at succeeding"—is much different in its effect on the client's performance than worry or anxiety—the belief, "I have to succeed, because I am a pretty worthless individual if I don't!" In response T^{205}, Dr. Geis makes this point clearer, where he indicates that even when an individual is in dangerous territory, he'd better not keep telling himself, "Oh, my God, I've got to keep my eye out for the enemy!"—for then he will make himself overcon-cerned, catastrophizing, and hence less effective in protecting him-self.

7. In response T^{217}, Dr. Geis, once again in a typical RET fashion, tries to get the client to be more specific in spelling out what he means by his insight that "I had all that junk in my head then, floating around." One of the main effective aspects of RET is that it is rarely content with the client's vaguely and imprecisely seeing what bothers him and what he'd better do about it. For most clients, in fact, "know" that they are disturbed and, often, precisely how they are disturbed. They also often "know" what to do about this, even though they may not actually do anything about it. One of the chief reasons for their inactivity is that their "knowledge" is

too general and unoperationally defined. For the individual to tell himself, "Yes, I am neurotic (or phobic); now I must stop being neurotic (or phobic)" is almost useless. But if he can be taught to tell himself, much more clearly and operationally, "I am afraid to ride in buses because I think I might feel faint and would be viewed as an ass by the other passengers, and that would be terrible!" he can then much more concretely see what he'd better do to change his major belief (that it would be terrible if others thought him an ass), and thereby interrupt his phobia-producing thinking. In this respect, RET is one of the most clear-cut, definite systems of showing the client how to define his symptoms, what he does to bring them about, and how he can change them.

After the close of this sixth session, Robert G. had a few more sessions with Dr. Geis and then felt that he was able to get along without further therapy. His final session occurred more than five years ago, and in check-up reports he has indicated that he is doing well in school, is much less perfectionistic than he was, has been having a reasonably good social life, and in some ways is extending the personal gains that he was able to make during three months of psychotherapy. There seems to be little doubt, as a result of his sessions with Dr. Geis, that he has gained considerably and that RET can be quite effective with teen-agers from lower socioeconomic backgrounds and from exceptionally unconstructive home environments. Dr. Geis has also been able to use RET with a good many other youngsters, many of them black and Puerto Rican, from ghetto areas and with intellectual and educational attainments considerably below that of Robert G. Although it would better be frankly admitted than this method of therapy by no means works as well with this type of individual as it does with middle-class, highly educated ones, it still seems to be a far better method of choice with the former than virtually any of the other contemporary modes of psychological treatment.

CHAPTER 4

A Young Male
Who Is Afraid of Becoming
a Fixed Homosexual

ALBERT ELLIS, Ph.D.

The client in this case is a twenty-six-year-old male who is a commercial artist. He has graduated from college, is doing well at his work, and has a steady girl friend with whom he has excellent sex and other relations. Nonetheless, he is terribly afraid of becoming a homosexual and is obsessed with the idea that he may turn into one. He is somewhat typical of many males who have little or no real homosexual urges but are so afraid that they may become exclusive or "real" homosexuals and that they might thereby lose all their "masculinity" that they become seriously disturbed and think incessantly about the great "danger" that faces them. They usually have a very low estimation of themselves and, after awhile, are hardly able to function in any other aspect of their lives.

FIRST SESSION

T¹: What's the main thing that's bothering you?

C²: I have a fear of turning homosexual—a *real* fear of it!

T³: A fear of *becoming* a homosexual?

C⁴: Yeah.

T⁵: Because "*if* I became a homosexual—," what?

C⁶: I don't know. It really gets me down. It gets me to a point where I'm doubting every day. I do doubt everything, anyway.

T⁷: Yes. But let's get back to—answer the question: "If I were a homosexual, what would that make me?"

C⁸: (*Pause*) I don't know.

T⁹: Yes, you do! Now, I can give *you* the answer to the question. But let's see if you can get it.

C[10]:   (*Pause*) Less than a person?

T[11]:   Yes. Quite obviously, you're saying: "I'm bad *enough*. But if I were homosexual, that would make me a *total* shit!"

C[12]:   That's right.

T[13]:   Now, why did you just say you don't know?

C[14]:   Just taking a guess at it, that's all. It's—it's just that the fear really gets me down! I don't know why.

T[15]:   (*Laughing*) Well, you just *gave* the reason why! Suppose you were saying the same thing about—we'll just say—stealing: You hadn't stolen anything, but you *thought* of stealing something. And you said, "*If* I stole, I would be a thorough shit!" Just suppose that. Then, how much would you then start thinking about stealing?

C[16]:   (*Silence*)

T[17]:   If you believed that: "If I stole it, I would be a thorough shit!"—would you think of it often? occasionally?

C[18]:   I'd think of it often.

T[19]:   That's right! As soon as you say, "If so-and-so happens, I would be a thorough shit!" you'll get *obsessed* with so-and-so. And the reason you're getting obsessed with homosexuality is this nutty belief, "If I *were* a homosexual, I would be a total shit!" Now, look at that belief for a moment. And let's admit that if you were a homosexual, it would have real disadvantages. Let's assume *that*. But why would you be a thorough shit if you were a homosexual? Let's suppose you gave up girls completely, and you just screwed guys. Now, why would you be a thorough shit?

C[20]:   (*Mumbles incoherently; is obviously having trouble finding an answer*)

T[21]:   Think about it for a moment.

C[22]:   (*Pause*) Let me explain one thing.

T[23]:   Yeah.

C[24]:   I went to the group—

T[25]:   To the what?

C[26]:   Six months ago—about five months ago—I went to the Staten Island County Therapy.

T[27]:   What's that—a clinic?

C[28]:   Yeah.

T[29]:   Right.

C³⁰: And after about five visits, the man says, "Don't bother me. Believe me, you're heterosexual—don't worry about it."

T³¹: Yeah.

C³²: He says—"There's nothing to worry about. Look, the only problem you have is getting along with people." So he put me into group therapy. And the group therapist wanted to see me alone for awhile and—he did.

T³³: And what was *his* view?

C³⁴: I don't know. He just *sat* there.

T³⁵: Oh, I see. He didn't say anything to you.

C³⁶: No.

T³⁷: How long did you see him?

C³⁸: Oh, about six times.

T³⁹: And did you also continue in group? Or just see him?

C⁴⁰: I continued in group. I didn't—I really don't think I need the group. I'm hard to make friends with, admittedly. But once I do make friends with a person, I can get along very well.

T⁴¹: So you got little out of it because he didn't say anything? Is that right?

C⁴²: No. The Center is closed.

T⁴³: Why is it closed?

C⁴⁴: It just closed down. I don't know.

T⁴⁵: Oh, it went out of business. Was it a county center? Who operated it?

C⁴⁶: No, it was a private center. Look, I became obsessed: "You *might* be a homosexual." I became obsessed with the fear.

T⁴⁷: Right! For the reasons I gave you before—which both therapists seem to have ignored.

C⁴⁸: Yeah.

T⁴⁹: See, the first one was correct. You're *not* a homosexual. You *could* become one; but the chances are you won't. But he didn't explain to you why you are upset.

C⁵⁰: No—I realize that. And that's why I'm here.

T⁵¹: But the reason you're obsessed is the same reason you'd be obsessed with anything. I see people who are obsessed with five thousand different things. But in every single case, just about, I can track it down; and they're saying, "*If* I were so-and-so—" For example, "if I got up and made a public speech and fell on my face, I'd be a shit!"—"If I went to school and failed, I'd be a shit!"—"If I tried for a better job and failed, I'd be a shit!" Now, you're doing the same thing about homosexuality: "If I ever *did* fail heterosexually and become a homosexual, I'd be an utter worm!" Now that will obsess you with homosexuality.

C[52]: And that obsession brings me to doubt myself.

T[53]: Well—no. It's part of your general obsession. Your real obsession is: "If (1) I failed at something big, like heterosexuality, and (2) other people didn't like me—they really didn't like me—then I'd be no damned good!" Now, as a *subheading* under that, you've got the homosexuality. Your general fear is of being worthless—isn't it?

C[54]: Yeah.

T[55]: And you don't only have it in the homosexual area—that's only dramatic and outstanding. What are you working at, at present?

C[56]: I'm a commercial artist.

T[57]: Now, how do you feel about that, when you work at it?

C[58]: Well, I made supervising artist. But I really didn't feel it was good *enough*. And I just keep going on and on—

T[59]: Oh. You see: "I made supervising artist, but if I'm not *outstanding*, I'm a shit!" Is that what you're really saying?

C[60]: (*Silence*)

T[61]: Think about it, now. Don't agree because I said so. Isn't it something like that?

C[62]: (*Pause*) I'll go along with it. Because I doubt just *everything*!

T[63]: Right! But why does anybody doubt everything? Suppose I introduce you to another guy and—I can show you guys who have Ph.D's, who have M.D.'s, who are outstanding painters or sculptors, and they feel the same way as you. And some of them have got reputations in their field; they're doing well. They still think they're shits. Now, why do you think they do?

C[64]: (*Pause*)

T[65]: There's one main reason for shithood. Now what do you think it is?

C[66]: (*Pause*) Their goals are set too high?

T[67]: Exactly! They're not saying, "I'd *like* to succeed." They're saying, "I've *got* to! I need an *absolute guarantee* that I *always* will succeed. And since there's always a good chance I won't, I'm no damned good!"

C[68]:   They're foolish for that.

T[69]:   Right. But you're believing that, aren't you?

C[70]:   (*Pause*) Yes, I am.

T[71]:   Now the problem is: How are you going to give up that crap?

Although I, as the therapist, know very little about the client, I size him up quickly and decide to take a chance, on the basis of RET theory, and to try to get at one of the main cores of his problem quickly: his terrible feelings of inadequacy or shithood. I assume, because of his longstanding obsession and his not responding at all well to previous therapy, that he rigidly holds on to his ideas of how awful it would be for him to be a homosexual in particular and a weakling or an incompetent in general; and I make an attempt to show the client, almost immediately, what he is doing to cause his central upsetness and what he presumably can do about understanding and changing himself. Because I believe that I know right from the beginning what is basically irrational about the client's premises, I start getting at them in his third response, and even insist in my fifth and sixth responses, on bringing these prime irrationalities to the client's attention. I know fully that I may be barking up the wrong tree, and am prepared to back down later if I turn out to be mistaken. But I know, on the basis of considerable prior evidence, that there is an excellent chance that I may be right; and I want, by taking that chance, to try to save the client a great deal of time and pain. So I not only immediately try to educate him about his own magical beliefs in wormhood and its connection with his fear of homosexuality, but I also try to show him how human beings, in general, easily think the way he does and how so many of them, no matter what their abilities and talents, wind up by hating themselves because of this type of crooked thinking. I am thus exceptionally educational in the first minutes of this first session—just as, presumably, any good teacher would be.

C[72]:   (*Pause*) I mean, I—I sit there and I try to prove what a homosexual is. Then I try to prove what a heterosexual is. And then I try to prove what *I* am. And to try to prove what *you* are, as a person—

T⁷³: Yeah?

C⁷⁴: —is very hard to do.

T⁷⁵: Because there *is* no way of doing it—except by some *definition*: "that if I were completely heterosexual, or if I were a *great* supervising artist, or if I were an Adonis, *then* I'd be a good guy!" That's the only way you can *prove* yourself: by some arbitrary definition of accomplishment.

C⁷⁶: Yeah, I kept, like—in the other therapy, I kept using the words *abnormal* and *homosexual*.

T⁷⁷: Meaning—but what you mean is, "*If* I were abnormal—if everybody is normal but me—I'm no good!" Is that what you mean?

C⁷⁸: Yeah, I do mean that.

T⁷⁹: But let's suppose that, now. Let's just suppose that. Let's suppose that ninety-nine out of one hundred guys are normal—which is not true, but we'll deliberately suppose it—and they all are screwing girls and having a ball and marrying and having children; and you're the one out of a hundred who can't do that, who really is homosexual. All you can do is go after boys, and you can't make it at all with girls. You're impotent; you just can't make it with girls. We'll deliberately assume that. Therefore, *statistically* you're abnormal. Right? 'Cause you're one out of a hundred, and they can do things that you can't do. Now, why would you be a no-goodnik? Not why would you be abnormal—we're just assuming that you would be; now, why would you be a no-goodnik *if* that were so: you were the one out of a hundred who couldn't make it heterosexually?

C⁸⁰: Well—maybe fear of loneliness.

T⁸¹: That's why it would be *inconvenient*: because they'd get along with girls, and you wouldn't. So therefore you might be lonely. Though that's not true either: you might have a lot of homosexual guys. But let's suppose you're lonely. Now, why would you be a *louse* because you're lonely? Not why would you be failing? Because we're assuming you'd be failing. They're succeeding heterosexually; you're not. Now why would you be a louse?

C⁸²: For not falling in with what they're doing.

T⁸³: But that's a definition! Now let's suppose the opposite, incidentally—that ninety-nine out of one hundred guys just
about made it with girls—they got a girl here and they got
a girl there, and they sort of succeeded—but you were *outstanding*, and you really were very good-looking and bright
and sexy, and girls just fell all over you. And you screwed
one after another, and they kept calling you up, wanting more.
Now that would be *abnormal*, statistically. Right?

C⁸⁴: (*Pause*) It would be.

T⁸⁵: Why wouldn't you be a shit *then*? You'd be one out of a
hundred!

C⁸⁶: So I'm going by the use of a definition?

T⁸⁷: That's right! "That I have to be *super*good. Then I'm okay.
But if I'm superbad—one out of a hundred on the bad side—
then I'm a louse!" That's your definition. See? Now, is a definition—does a definition prove anything about a fact? Because
it is a definition; and if you want to feel you're a shit, you
can feel you're a shit. But does it really prove you *are* a shit?—
if you can only get there by definition?

C⁸⁸: I dunno.

T⁸⁹: Because it can really get absurd. I, for example, could say:
"I'm a tuba." And you say, "You're a tuba? Well, how did
you become a tuba? Prove it!" And I say, "Well, I'm going
around *oomp-oomp-oomp-bah*. Therefore I'm a tuba!" Now, does
that prove I'm a tuba?

C⁹⁰: No.

T⁹¹: What does it prove? It does prove something. What?

C⁹²: That you're not one. You may want *to be* one—

T⁹³: Yes, that I *think* I am a tuba. That's what it proves. Because
if I'm going to go around acting like a tuba, whether I am
or not, I think I am a tuba. But it never proves I *am*, you
see. Therefore, if you go around acting as if you are a shit,
it doesn't prove you *are* one; but it does prove that you *think*
you are. And *that's* the story of your life! "If I'm not *at least*
as good as others, and preferably much better, I *define myself
as* an utter lowlifer! A skunk!" Right?

C⁹⁴: Yes, that's true.

T⁹⁵: All right. Now, if that's so, how could you become a non-shit?

C[96]: By recognizing what I have. Or what I am.

T[97]: Recognizing—but let's suppose the worst: you recognize what you are. But we'll go back to the previous hypothesis: you really are the one out of a hundred who is homosexual, while the other ninety-nine are straight. Would you then be a shit?

C[98]: (*Long pause*) Yeah.

T[99]: Why would you be?

C[100]: (*Pause*)

T[101]: Not, why would you *think* you were? But why would you actually *be* a shit if you were the one out of one hundred who couldn't make it with girls and the other ninety-nine could?

C[102]: (*Long pause; silence*)

T[103]: You haven't proved it to me yet! *Why* would you be no good? Worthless?

C[104]: (*Long pause*) Because I'm not.

T[105]: You're not what?

C[106]: I'm not part—of the ninety-nine.

T[107]: "I'm not part and I should—"

C[108]: I should be!

T[109]: Why? Why *should* you be?

C[110]: Because of what I am.

T[111]: Look! If you really are homosexual, you are a homosexual. Now, why should you be *non*homosexual if you're really homosexual? That doesn't make sense!

C[112]: (*Long pause; silence*)

T[113]: See what a bind you're in?

C[114]: Yeah.

T[115]: You're taking the sane statement, "It would be *desirable* to be heterosexual, if I were gay," and you're translating it into, "Therefore, I *should* be." Isn't that what you're doing?

C[116]: Yeah.

T[117]: But does that make sense? It doesn't!

C[118]: If I were the one out of ninety-nine percent—

T[119]: Yeah; and we're assuming that's undesirable.

C[120]: I should be heterosexual.

T[121]: Why? You haven't given me any reason yet. "Because I'm abnormal, I should be normal." Now *why*?

C[122]: Because homosexuality is described as being abnormal.

T[123]: Granting that (1) it's abnormal, and (2) it's undesirable, we're assuming that. Now, why *should* you be normal and desirable? Not "Why is it *nice* to be?"

C[124]: Because I *want* to be!

T[125]: That doesn't equal *should*. You might *want* to have a million dollars. You might *want* to be the greatest supervising artist that ever lived. Most of us do. Now, does that mean you *should* be, because you *want* to be? No, you see you're saying, "I *should* get what I want. I *should* be most desirable!" Not "I *want* to be"—that's perfectly sane. But "I've *got* to be what I *want* to be!" Now, does that make sense?

C[126]: In other words, I'm pushing up against it. I'm—I'm expressing my wants against what my desires, what my—

T[127]: You're making your wants into necessities—not desires. Which they are! "I *want* a million dollars; therefore I *should* have it. And I don't have it; therefore I'm a shit!" "I *want* to be straight, right now I'm gay"—we're just assuming that you were. "Therefore, I'm a shit!" Now, do those things *follow*?

C[128]: (*Pause*) No, they don't follow.

T[129]: So your shithood doesn't come from your desire. It comes from your demand: "I *must* be normal; I *must* do the right thing. I've *got* to!" And as long as you have any demands, you're going to be anxious. As I tell my clients all the time: if you *demand* that "I *must have* a dollar in my pocket, at least a dollar, at all times," what's going to happen when you don't have the dollar?

C[130]: You're gonna feel all out of place without it.

T[131]: You're gonna feel terribly anxious. Now suppose you *do* have the dollar. You're saying, "I've gotta absolutely have that dollar, at least a dollar at all times!" And you have it; you have exactly a dollar in your pocket. How are you then going to feel?

C[132]: That you've gotta have more.

T[133]: You'll still feel anxious. Because you'll need the guarantee that you'll *always* have a dollar; you can't have a guarantee. So even if you're 100 percent straight, and you're saying to yourself "I've got to be straight; I must be straight; it's necessary that I be straight," you'll be anxious. Because you have

no guarantee that you'll always be straight. Twenty years
from now, you might become gay!

C[134]: That's what scares me.

T[135]: "Because I've *got to* be!" Now suppose you were saying, "I'd
like to have a dollar in my pocket at all times; I'd very much
like to have it, but it's just a *like*." And you don't have a
dollar; you've got ninety cents. How are you going to feel?

C[136]: Well, ninety cents will have to suffice.

T[137]: Yeah. "It's too bad I don't have a full dollar. I'll try to get
ten cents more, since I'd like to have a dollar. But if I don't,
I don't. And if I do have a dollar, and I'd *like* to have one,
then I'll be pretty happy." Right? The *like* to have a dollar
or *like* to be straight is vastly different from *got to*, isn't it?

C[138]: One is a *demand*, and one is expressing a *wish*.

T[139]: That's right. And *you* really don't have wishes. You translate
all your major wishes into demands: "I've *got* to be a great
supervising artist. I've *got* to be absolutely straight. I've *got*
to do well in various other areas." Now, isn't that what you
invariably do?

C[140]: Yeah, I do, do that. I transform all my wishes into—into demands.

T[141]: Now how can you be nonanxious, if you do that?

C[142]: Yeah.

I, as the therapist, keep belaboring a single point here, until I
am fairly sure that the client is getting it. For this is one of the
main cores of RET: to show the client that his anxieties are *not*
caused by his failing to achieve some goal that he wishes to achieve,
but by his *demanding* that he achieve it. I feel, with practically
all my clients, that if I can get over to them this single point, especially in one of the early sessions, that I have given them something
of almost inestimable value: namely, the idea that *they* create their
anxieties and other upsets, and that they almost invariably do so
by a single major irrational idea: the idea that they *must have* or
need what they want. If they see this, then no matter *what* they
are anxious, guilty, depressed, or angry about, they have a simple
way of quickly discovering the *real* cause of their disordered emotion—their own demandingness—and of starting to challenge and
attack it right away.

The first session with this highly disturbed client, therefore, is typical of that with most clients who are afraid that they will fail in some important way and that they therefore will be worthless. Even though the session is only a half hour in length (as almost all sessions are these days), and even though I know very little about the client's past or present life, I believe that if I can get across to him the notion that *he* is creating his anxiety and that *he* can effectively start undoing it in short order, he can be significantly helped during this first session. In case he subsequently shows that he has not understood my message or has not worked with the tools I have started to give him, then I merely go over the same ground several times, until he begins to see more clearly the scientific method of understanding and tackling his emotional problems that I am trying to teach him. But it is surprising how many seriously upset individuals are able to get at least part of my Socratic-like instruction immediately and to begin to make some use of it.

Although this particular client seems to have some difficulty in comprehending that it is his own perfectionistic demands on himself that are disturbing him (as shown by his frequent pauses and silences), I keep persisting at going over the same message until he seems to be getting it. With a more alert and faster-learning client, I would try to get over the same idea more quickly and then spend more time applying it to other parts of his life, or getting on to other aspects of his anxiety about homosexuality.

T143: Now what?

C144: I'll always be anxious (*inaudible*)—

T145: As long as you have necessities, demands, got-to's—

C146: (*Inaudible*)

T147: Because as soon as you say, "I've *got* to have *x*"—such as be straight—and there's the slightest possibility that you won't, then you'll say, "Wouldn't it be *awful* if I were not what I've *got* to be?" While if you're sticking to "It's *desirable* to be straight, but I'm not or might not be," you'll say, "Well, tough shit! So I'd be gay! I wouldn't *like* it. And I'd work against it if I *were* gay. But what's so goddamned *horrible* about having an undesirable trait?" You see?

C148: But that undesirable trait scares me.

T149: No! "*I* scare me, with my got-to's! It isn't the undesirable trait that scares me. Since I *must* be straight, then the mere thought of being gay scares me. But if I *want* to be straight, and right now I'm not, I'd be *concerned* but not *scared*." Do you see the difference?

C¹⁵⁰: I'd be very concerned about it—

T¹⁵¹: You'd be concerned, just like "I would *like* to have a good job. Today I am unemployed. I am *concerned* about getting a good job. I'd better get off my ass and get one. But if I've *got* to have a good job, and today I am unemployed, I'm distraught, I'm despairing, I'm anxious!" Isn't that so?

C¹⁵²: (*Nods in agreement*)

T¹⁵³: Now, you're always escalating your desires, your wishes, your preferences into needs, necessities, got-to's.

T¹⁵⁴: I'm sure I am.

C¹⁵⁵: Then what could you *do*?

C¹⁵⁶: (*Pause; silence*)

T¹⁵⁷: It's very obvious!

C¹⁵⁸: Stop demanding?

T¹⁵⁹: That's exactly right! Interrupt every demand—because as soon as you feel anxious at point C, the consequence, it's not because of A, the possibility that you might become gay, it's because of B, your belief: "Wouldn't it be *awful* if I became gay! I *must* be absolutely straight!" And you'd better change B!— your demand. Not your wishes. You want to remain straight; you don't want to be gay; it's a pain in the ass to be gay; it's abnormal to be gay in this culture. What a nuisance! "But I absolutely, for the rest of my life, must have a guarantee that I'll *never* have a gay thought and *always* remain straight!" *That's* your nutty demand.

C¹⁶⁰: That *is* my demand.

T¹⁶¹: So—suffer! I'll write you a guarantee—as long as you have that demand, you will suffer! Do you see why you'll suffer?

C¹⁶²: 'Cause I'll want that guarantee.

T¹⁶³: 'Cause you're *demanding* a guarantee.

C¹⁶⁴: So I keep on doubting.

T¹⁶⁵: You *have* to; 'cause there are no guarantees in the world! If you were that one out of a hundred who was straight, and the other ninety-nine were gay—how do we know that that won't be reversed five years from now?

C[166]: (*Pause; silence*)

T[167]: There *are* no guarantees in life! And you're saying, "There *must* be! I must be guaranteed *normal*, guaranteed to do the *right* thing, guaranteed to *succeed*, guaranteed to win people's *approval*." Well, lots of luck! All you're going to have with that nonsense is practically guaranteed misery!

As the therapist, I am possibly a bit too dogmatic here. I often put in qualifiers, at this point, and say things such as: "There are, *as far as we scientifically know*, no guarantees in life"; or, "*The chances are exceptionally high that*, with that hypothesis that you devoutly believe, you will be utterly miserable." With this client, for dramatic effect and because of time limitations, I did not put in these italicized qualifiers. Probably, they are unnecessary; since the client seems to be getting the main points I am making. But rational-emotive therapists would better take care that they are not dogmatic or authoritarian, since then they are doing the same thing that the client is doing, and cannot be scientifically upheld.

C[168]: (*Pause; silence*)

T[169]: Now, there are two words which people tell themselves which create just about all emotional disturbance. What do you think they might be?

C[170]: "I'm a shithead!"

T[171]: Yes, that's almost right. But those words would only create anxiety and depression, not anger. The two words usually are: "*It's awful* that I do this; and if *I* do it badly I'm a shithead; and if *they* do it badly to me, *they're* shitheads! And if the world is too hard, I can't stand it—*it's awful!*" Right?

C[172]: (*Nods in agreement*)

T[173]: Now, what two words could people use to get rid of their emotional disturbance? Just about every emotional disturbance could be eliminated if they really *believed* two words. What do you think *they* would be?

C[174]: "So what?"

T[175]: Or "Tough shit!" "So *I* do badly at times—so I'm 'abnormal' at times. So the world treats me unfairly at times. So life is rough. *Tough shit!* That's the way it is! I am fallible; they are fallible; so the world is the way it is! *Tough!*" If you would really accept that, about your limitations, about other people's limitations, and about the world's limitations, you'd wish things were better: you, they, and the world. But you wouldn't be mad. And you'd say: "If I ever became a homosexual, tough shit! I'd face it and do something about it. It wouldn't be good; it would be bad. Tough! But it wouldn't be *horrible* or *awful* or catastrophic." You see?

T^{176}: (*Pause; silence*)

I, as therapist, give the client every opportunity to respond and to agree with, rebut, or cavil with the points I make. Most clients have quite a few rejoinders, and a lively discussion ensues. This particular one is so depressed and confused that he thinks slowly and is probably afraid to make some rejoinders he thinks of making. Hence there is not too much of a dialogue. But the method of teaching by questioning, rather than of merely stating points or facts, is frequently used; and the client is often asked to fill in point B (his belief system), for example, after I have shown him what A (the activating event) and C (the emotional consequence) are. This method would probably take too long with the present client, and therefore when he does not answer, I frequently proceed and add to the point already made. Preferably, however, he would respond to my question or fill in the blank I had left for him; then I would correct his response if necessary and we would go on. Even this client responds, from time to time, when prodded. But he gives short answers and does not argue back very much—which probably would be better.

T^{177}: You very rarely say "Tough shit!" And you're always saying "It would be awful!" or "It's now awful!"

C^{178}: I always say demands.

T^{179}: Right! Now, if you want to change those demands, change them. But if you keep them, you'll get the same crummy results. Well, we haven't got any more time now. You go give it some thought. And there's no question, you could change. The question is, when are you going to give up those *demands*? Fortunately, they're *your* demands. You don't have to maintain them. You can get rid of them. Okay, you give them some thought. You can make another appointment.

C^{180}: I will.

I, as therapist, saw that the end of the session was approaching and somewhat briefly, from T[169] onward, got in the idea that all emotional disturbance seems to be created by two irrational words that people tell themselves, "It's awful!" and that it can be diminished or eliminated by their believing strongly in the essence of two other words, "Tough shit!" I usually present this point in more detail—particularly showing the individual that what he calls his "emotional" problem is really his having a problem *about* a problem. Some unfortunate event is occurring or may occur at point A (the activating event or activator), and he feels upset at C (the consequence). He usually wrongly thinks that A causes C; but, of course, B, his belief system, causes his emotional consequences. When these consequences are self-defeating or disordered, he is almost invariably telling himself a rational belief (rB) and an irrational belief (iB) at point B. I show him specifically what these are, using an example from his own life. Then I show him that his irrational belief is just about always a form of the sentence, "It's awful!" I also show him how this particular client's answer, "So what?" is not a very good one—since it implies that it is not important at *all* what happens to him at point A. Actually it usually is important; but it is not *all*-important or sacred that the point A occurrence be changed or improved. So the right answer is, when A is unfortunate or inefficient, "Tough shit!"—meaning, "That's the way this event is (or may be). I don't like it, and I want to get rid of it. But I can stand it; and there's no reason why it shouldn't exist (although it would be much better if it didn't). Now, let me see how I can temporarily gracefully lump it, then learn to deal with it, and finally, if possible, get back to it and change it."

I find that I am often able to get this point over during the first therapy session. Consequently, some alert and hard-working individuals immediately begin to use it in their lives and come back to the second session considerably improved, especially in regard to something or some person about which they are terribly angry. These clients are the minority, but they do exist. Most clients, after several somewhat repetitive sessions, are able to see and combat their "awfulizing" and much more consistently change it into acceptance of reality, even when it's grim. I did not assume that the client in this case would quickly get around to using the "Tough shit!" idea. But I thought that it would be good to present it to him for the first time, so that later repetitions might fall on more fertile ears.

Usually, when one of my clients is a fixed, compulsive homosexual or has fears of becoming one, I tell him something about homosexuality and particularly try to get him to distinguish between homosexual behavior or episodes and obsessiveness with being an exclusive homosexual. In the former instance, the individual is basically heterosexual (or bisexual) and from time to time has homosexual desires and sometimes overt activity; but he does so out of choice or preference, and not because he thinks that he *has* to do so. In the latter instance, he does not really have any choice but views himself as almost completely homosexual and believes that he can only desire and have sex-love satisfaction with members of his own sex. In this case, as I show in various of my writings, especially in the book *Homosexuality: Its Causes and Cure* (Ellis, 1965), the individual is disturbed, overly rigid, or fixated on homosexuality; and it would be preferable, though hardly necessary, that he acknowledge his having a hang-up and do something about overcoming it, so that he could thereafter, at the very least, have successful sex-love relations with members of the other sex as well as his own.

I often explain this to my clients and help them distinguish between their sporadic or noncompulsive homosexual behavior and their fixed homosexuality. I did not do this in this particular case mainly because of lack of time. I knew that I would get around it in subsequent sessions, and I did. I also knew that this client assumed that fixed homosexuality constituted something of a disturbance, but I also knew that he considered any homosexual leaning a flaw and an indication of his worthlessness. I was much more interested in this second matter, since it was a real hang-up. And I worked with him, during the next several sessions, to show him that he didn't have to be 100 percent *anything*; that probably no one was 100 percent heterosexual, and that being in that kind of rigid category of 100 percent heterosexuality (if one could ever make it) was probably to be almost as disturbed as being completely homosexual. He slowly and reluctantly seemed to accept this view, and as he did so, he became better and better. From the sixth session onward, he began to make real progress and to accept himself with his failings, including his obsession with the possibility of his being homosexual.

EIGHTH SESSION

T¹: Hi! What's doing?

C²: I keep—I pretty much got it all sorted out.

T³: Yeah? How have you got it sorted out?

C⁴: Well, there just are no shits. There are just *human beings* who make mistakes.

T⁵: All right. How, specifically, does that apply to you? Are you just a human being who can make mistakes?

C⁶: I can make mistakes, just as anyone else can. That's it.

T⁷: Right!

C⁸: It's just whether I'm a better human being or not, if I correct them. That's all.

T⁹: Right.

C¹⁰: If I *want* to correct them—

T¹¹: And sometimes even if you want to correct them, some of them can't be corrected—it's too late. What about that?

C¹²: Correct them too late?

T¹³: Yeah. Let's suppose you make a mistake, and it can't be corrected any more; it's too late.

C¹⁴: Fuck it, then! I gotta live with it that way then.

T¹⁵: That's right. You're still a fallible *human.*

C¹⁶: Um-hm. But there's nothing you can't correct.

T¹⁷: Well, no; that's not quite true. If you buy a stock and it goes down, it goes down! And that's it! So don't say that.

C¹⁸: Yeah.

T¹⁹: Most things, however, you can correct.

C²⁰: Well, anything that has to do with feeling like a shit, or anything else like that.

T²¹: That you can always correct—right?

C²²: Yes, that can always be corrected.

T²³: You never have to feel like a shit, no matter what you've done poorly.

C²⁴: Yeah. You know, and I'm saying—anything physical, anything that you have control over like your own self, you can always correct.

T²⁵: You can *not do it again.* If you went out and screwed a boy, you wouldn't have to keep screwing a boy.

C²⁶: No.

T²⁷: It would just be an error—

C²⁸: Yeah.

T²⁹: You could correct that error—

C³⁰: You could always correct it. As long as you have control over it yourself.

T³¹: Which you do—if you don't *blame* yourself. Then you have the control.

C³²: Yeah. But otherwise, anything outside of you, you can always *try* to correct. Sometimes it's beyond correcting, so—but you're *still* not a shit!

T³³: You're *never* a shit!

C³⁴: No, you can never—you're just a human being who has made a mistake, and you've got the right to try again.

T³⁵: Right!

C³⁶: Because that's what a human being is. And I've been thinking about it more and more. Sometimes I pretty much hold onto it, the idea of the whole thing. And I've thought it all out. And sometimes, you know, a shit comes back to me—with me.

T³⁷: "I did badly, or I thought badly, and therefore I'm no good!"

C³⁸: Yes, "and therefore I'm a shit!"

T³⁹: Yeah.

C⁴⁰: Yeah, that really hits me. Sometimes.

T⁴¹: But *then* what do you do?

C⁴²: Well, then I remember that, you know—well, I try to think of the classic case of—stereotyping. And, you know, they're just *human beings*, who make mistakes. That's what hits me harder than anything else—the stereotyping—which I'm slowly getting rid of, though.

T⁴³: Yeah: that human beings *shouldn't* make mistakes; and that they're lice when they do.

C⁴⁴: Yeah. But the stereotyping's there of the homosexual, the one who goes prancing down the street—which is quite comical now!

T⁴⁵: Yeah.

C⁴⁶: The stereotyping hits me harder than anything else does.

T⁴⁷: Because what do you think of when you think of that stereotyped "fairy"?

C⁴⁸: Oh, I think: "What a shit!"

T⁴⁹: *He* is?

C⁵⁰: He is. Or what a shit I could *become*.

T⁵¹: But how is *he* a shit? Let's suppose that he's one of the few homosexuals who is in that stereotyped "fairy"-like way. Suppose that he's prancing down the street, showing off, etc.

Now, why is *he* a shit?

C⁵²: Well, I think he's a—the reason why I think he might be a shit, even though there are no shits, there are no stereotypes, really—is because he's made a *fool* of himself, number one—

T⁵³: That's why he's *acting* badly. And he's really not making a fool of *himself*. He's acting foolishly. You can't *make* a complete fool of yourself; you can just act foolishly. Because that same guy, in business or something else, might act very sanely.

C⁵⁴: Yeah.

T⁵⁵: So in *that* respect he's acting foolishly.

C⁵⁶: Yes, he's acting foolishly.

T⁵⁷: Now, let's suppose he is. Why is he a shit?

C⁵⁸: Well, because—suppose he's the type of guy who doesn't like to make mistakes. And therefore, you're not supposed to act foolish.

T⁵⁹: Well, you see, that's your nonsense: that you're not *supposed* to act foolishly; the human is at all times supposed to act *well*, sanely, properly. But where *are* these humans who always act well?

C⁶⁰: There *are* none, really. There's always—one aspect in each of us where we act foolishly, and some little quirk we have.

T⁶¹: All right. But that's your *worst* stereotype: that a human is *supposed* to act non-foolishly.

C⁶²: Yeah.

Even though the client seems to be doing very well, and to be seeing for the first time that he *can* make mistakes without considering himself a louse for making them, I, as his therapist, suspect that he may only be giving lip service to this notion and not really be believing in it. I therefore persist in taking him up on his statements, to see if he really sticks by them. He admits that he sometimes does not; but it appears fairly obvious that he often does adhere to his new, less bigoted way of thinking. At the very least, he now seems to know what the right way to think is, and he is working toward thinking this way. He just hasn't reached it consistently or permanently, and I keep after him to make sure that he understands it even better during what seem to be his closing sessions, so that by the time he quits therapy, he will have the new philosophy more solidly under his belt.

At this point during the session, I go off into a discussion of extreme homosexuality and transsexualism with the client, to show him that even people in this "abnormal" category are not to be despised and are entitled to their peculiar ways. He seems to accept this illustration and to learn by it. I also try to show him that it is illegitimate to label an individual as a "Negro" or a "black" when he is really a *person* who, among many other traits, happens to have black skin. The client seems to accept this, too. He continues:

C^{63}: So as long as I keep thinking of a human being not being a shit, and yet one who makes mistakes, as long as I keep proving it to myself that that's all there is, and if I work at that, within time the problem will just leave. And I don't even think I'll have to work at it.

T^{64}: Right.

C^{65}: I think it will just come now. So I see it more and more, yet I still have these lags of going back to a shit. It's so much—so much more secure. But it makes for fucking misery! And a lot of it. Something I don't need! But now that I've gotten over the problem, I really get along with my girl friend a lot better, and everything else. I've noticed that.

T^{66}: Right.

C^{67}: And—I enjoy it more!

T^{68}: Yes, because you're not spending the time doubting, giving yourself a pain in the ass—

C^{69}: Yeah. I always used to give myself—I didn't complain to her—but I always used to give myself that pain in the ass because, you see, I've had homosexual experiences. And I always think of a little Kinsey scale, one to seven, or one to six, I forget. And I say, "Jesus, God! Where am I on that fucking scale?" Yeah. And—

T^{70}: "How do I *rate* myself?"

C^{71}: Yeah. And that's when it first started. It started out just rating myself. And then it went deeper and deeper and deeper and deeper. But I think I can go out now and go further up the scale. And, say—you know, like—"It doesn't matter. Really! It just matters whether I really want my girl friend or do I want a boy. Do I want to go out and—hunt down another man, and have him do the job?"

T⁷²: And that doesn't make it—

C⁷³: But that would be saying—I know it is a lot of bull. So why should I do *that* now? And you *can't* make out 100 percent all the time with broads. So I just keep thinking about human beings making mistakes and being allowed to change them and correct them. And being able to come back and say, "I might have done that. I might have had those experiences and everything else. But they're something I'll take for growing up, or take for what they *are*. I'll take for what they are, and they're worth. But I made a mistake; and I'm entitled to do that. But I'm also entitled to change that. I'm also entitled to come back and try." And I just keep thinking of that.

Now that he has got the idea that he doesn't have to condemn himself if he isn't completely heterosexual, the client begins to see clearly that he has followed this sequence: (1) He had some minor homosexual experiences. (2) He read the Kinsey reports and noted how they scaled homosexual behavior from one to six. (3) He began wondering what his rating on this scale might be. (4) He thought that if he had a high rating or was a "real" homosexual, he would be pretty worthless. (5) He therefore became obsessed with this kind of rating and kept asking himself if he were really a homosexual. (6) His relations with his girl friend suffered somewhat. Now that he agrees, at least at times, that he isn't a rotter even *if* he were largely homosexual, and now that he sees that he doesn't have to be 100 percent heterosexual, he is stopping his obsession with his sexuality and is getting along better with his girl friend.

At the end of this eighth session, the client feels that he is doing so well that he decides on a two-week instead of a one-week gap between sessions. He continued therapy for five subsequent sessions, then felt that he wanted to try it on his own. A follow-up report, six months after therapy ended, showed that he was no longer obsessed with sexual ideas, was continuing to get along better than ever with his girl friend, and rarely blamed himself for any act, even when he made a fairly serious mistake. His feelings of self-acceptance kept becoming stronger, and he felt that he had few problems any longer in that regard.

CHAPTER 5

A Young Woman with Feelings of Depression

PAUL A. HAUCK, Ph.D.

The client is a twenty-eight-year-old woman who was seen a few times one year prior to the present session because she was somewhat insecure about her impending divorce. At that time, she was able to weather her problems in this connection, and the therapy sessions were therefore terminated. She now returns to therapy in a state of moderate depression, accompanied by episodes of uncontrollable sobbing and anxiety over her depressed state.

FIRST SESSION

T¹: You were saying on the phone that you had a divorce in October and that you have not been depressed until about a week ago.

C²: Well, I'd say about three weeks ago. It's really hard to explain. When we got our divorce, we were still friends and everything. We got along fine. And then when I would see him, like a weekend or something, I was out with another guy and he happened to show up at the same place we were and he sat with us at the table, and we all just had fun together; and when I went home I was depressed. I don't know—my old feelings came back or something. And then the next weekend about the same thing happened; he takes the kids on weekends, and when he brought them home, he stayed for about an hour. We had coffee and talked at the kitchen table, and after he left, I cried and silly things like that; and then by the next Wednesday at the very most, I'd be fine again. And then this last week, the thing did not happen on the weekend. I wasn't with him at all. And when he brought the kids home, he did not stay or anything; and I was out with this date for a half hour or so, but I didn't have any of these feelings or anything; but then I was depressed the whole week, and I didn't know why. I didn't feel like I was depressed because of him or anything, but I think I still love him in a way; but I don't want to live with him, and I don't have any desire for him physically or anything. But I feel a certain feeling for him. I care about him. I suppose it is natural after all the years we were married.

T[3]:   Right. How long were you married?

C[4]:   Eight and a half years.

T[5]:   Eight and a half years. And you have how many children?

C[6]:   Three.

T[7]:   It sounds like your first two depressions were the result of kind of feeling a little sorry for yourself because you were lonely.

C[8]:   Right.

T[9]:   You had met him again, and wasn't it too bad that you couldn't make something out of the marriage; and "Gee, we had lovely memories together," and that kind of thing. Is that right?

C[10]: Right.

T[11]: But now you are suggesting that the last depression that you had, which has not let up, was due to something else.

C[12]: I think probably it is. I don't know. I found myself having very little patience with the kids, screaming at them, and then wishing I hadn't. And then at work all day long I sat there and just started crying for no reason. I mean no apparent reason. I just all of a sudden started crying and felt silly about it, but it wasn't something I felt I could control at the time. And I don't know why. I tried to think about it and wonder why I was feeling that way, if I was feeling sorry for myself, if I was lonely, or what it was. There is another situation. I don't like to admit it, but I was seeing a married man, and I think I am in love with him. And he says he loves me and all this stuff; and he says he is going to get a divorce. But he hasn't done it yet, and I think that might have something to do with the depression, too, because I've been seeing him since I got the divorce.

T¹³: How steadily?

C¹⁴: Well, at first it was about twice a week. Well, I see him every day at work, for one thing, but as far as seeing him alone, it was twice or maybe once a week.

T¹⁵: For how long?

C¹⁶: For six months.

T¹⁷: Well, I presume you have a fairly intense relationship going here.

C¹⁸: Right.

T¹⁹: And you have had intercourse with this man?

C²⁰: Yes.

T²¹: Okay. Now what happened? Why are you bringing that up now?

C²²: Because I think that maybe that had something to do with the depression, because it has been so long that we have been seeing each other, and he hasn't gotten a divorce yet.

T²³: Oh, I see.

C²⁴: And I was upset about that, for one thing, because he keeps saying he is going to, and he didn't.

T²⁵: And you were thinking about this about a week ago?

C²⁶: Well, I have been thinking about it for a long time. But I have been just sort of saying to myself—well, he will. And then I think last week I sort of got the idea in my head maybe he's not going to.

T²⁷: I see.

C²⁸: Because it has been—you know.

T²⁹: You began to really, really doubt last week whether he was really sincere.

C³⁰: Yes.

T³¹: I see. All right. Then what did you tell yourself about that situation when you began to realize that maybe this man is pulling a fast one on you? Or that he is not really in love with you and has no intentions of divorcing his wife?

C³²: What did I think about?

T³³: What did you think? What did you say to yourself?

C³⁴: Well, for the past couple months I've been—I keep telling him I'm not going to see him any more until he gets divorced because it's not right, for one thing, and it's not good for me, and it's not good for him and his wife and the kids, and the whole bit. Right? But then I change my mind, and then I ask him to come over or something after I've already said, "I'm not going to see you any more." And so, I don't know what I thought when I start thinking. I really think that he wants to get a divorce, but he doesn't have guts. That's what I think. Maybe I'm kidding myself, I don't know.

T^{35}: You have begun to wonder this past week whether you were in fact kidding yourself. For the first time you really began to seriously think that "maybe I'm being taken for a ride." Before that you were always more positively oriented or persuaded, shall we say? All right. Now you are asking me, I suppose, "Why do I get depressed? Why did I get depressed last week? What can I do about overcoming this depression?" Is that what you want to see me about?

C^{36}: Yes, and I think if I had certain goals— You told me once before that I shouldn't wrap myself up so much in one person, which is what I did with my husband. And this I am having a tendency to do again; and I think unless I develop other interests or widen my personality or something, the whole thing is going to happen again. And everybody says, "What do you want? What do you want to do with your life? Do you want a home and family, or do you want to be free?" And I don't know. I'm just kind of—I really don't know what I want. I guess sometimes I feel guilty because sometimes I feel like I'd rather not have the kids. I'd rather be free where I could do just anything I wanted to do. And then I feel guilty because I shouldn't feel this way. And, I don't know—I don't think it's any one thing. It's a combination of things that upsets me.

T^{37}: All right. I think we have to break down what you're doing. In order to control this feeling, we must understand all of the elements that are creating it. You see, actually, from what I hear now, there are probably two ways in which you are depressing yourself. Depression can be caused by one or more of three methods. The first one is to blame yourself for something that you are doing. The second is to pity yourself for something, and the third one is to pity somebody else. For example, if you were to see a child hobbling along with a cane, your heart might want to break over his misery, and you can get pretty depressed over thinking of other people's problems. But you can get obviously just as depressed over thinking of your own problems and how unfair it is, and where you are going, and so on; and I have the feeling that some of the time you are getting depressed because you are looking at your life and you are saying, "What's this all about? Poor me! Here I am not getting anyplace. I waited very faithfully for this man for half a year. I showed him my trust, and the son of a gun isn't coming through the way I hoped he would, and isn't that awful. I feel so sorry for myself because here I am being taken advantage of, and I've been a decent person about this whole thing." Right? Can you sense that that is part of your depression?

C^{38}: Yes, I suppose so.

T^{39}: I don't want you to agree just because I offered it as a suggestion. Do you sense or feel that self-pity is part of your problem?

C^{40}: Yes.

T^{41}: For example, those first two weeks when you were out with your husband, you got depressed after he went home.

C^{42}: Right.

T^{43}: That was self-pity, wasn't it?

C^{44}: Sure.

T^{45}: "Why can't we live together? Wouldn't it have been nice if he had been able to overlook some of my faults?" And this sort of thing. "And he didn't. That's terrible! I ought to feel so sorry for myself because I don't have what I want." Correct?

C^{46}: Yeah.

T^{47}: All right. So probably some of your depression is self-pity. Now I am wondering also whether or not being guilty is part of it—guilty because you are having an affair. Guilty because sometimes you want to reject your children, because they are in the way. I don't know. You fill that in for me. Can you? What do you think you are guilty about?

C^{48}: Well, I think you are right.

T^{49}: About what?

C^{50}: I feel guilty about not wanting the children. Most of the time I don't feel guilty about the affair because I never thought of it in that way. If it was somebody else, I would. I guess

I'm like most people. I don't apply the rules to myself. It's wrong for everybody else but it's okay for me.

T⁵¹: All right. So then you suspect that you are feeling guilty because of your feelings of not wanting the kids.

C⁵²: Yes.

T⁵³: What do you mean when you say you don't want them? You mean they should be given away? You wish you never had them? You wish they were dead? Or what are you talking about?

C⁵⁴: I don't know. I don't like the responsibility of the children. If they could just all play together. But you have to discipline them, and you have to teach them; you have to this, and you have to that, and I—

T⁵⁵: It gets to be a heavy burden. Is that what you mean?

C⁵⁶: Yes, but then—I mean—nobody made me have them. If I am mature enough to have them, then I should be mature enough to take care of them.

T⁵⁷: When you notice that sometimes you are not fully the mother that you want to be, then you blame yourself. Is that it? All right, now the question is, are you right for blaming yourself for being an inadequate and disinterested mother?

C⁵⁸: Well, it can't be anybody else's fault. Nobody else makes me do whatever I do or think whatever I think.

T⁵⁹: I didn't say fault. I grant you that what is happening there with the children is between you and the children, and therefore most of the things that go wrong might very well be your fault. Correct? I'm saying, "Should you blame yourself because it is your fault?" Do you know what I mean by *blame*? I mean something very precise when I say blame. I mean that you are not only dissatisfied with yourself as a mother, which might be very accurate and correct to say; but you are also dissatisfied with you as a person. In other words, you don't like yourself period. Not only don't you like your mothering, you don't like yourself as a *woman*, who happens to be a mother. You are not just saying that your mothering characteristics are wanting. That would be correct, because right now you don't feel very much like a mother. You've got responsibilities you don't want. It would be very nice to give the kids to someone else until they are ten years old, and then you can come back and take care of them. Right? Okay. So you are right when you say, "I don't think I'm being the greatest mother in the world to these kids." Then you say, "—and that makes me an awful, worthless, good-for-nothing human being." And that—that is when you get depressed. Not when you admit that you are not a good mother. It is when you convince yourself that you are not a good person because you happen not to be a good mother. Follow me?

C⁶⁰: Yes.

T⁶¹: Explain it to me then.

C⁶²: Well, I think what you mean is that—well, like, not everybody could be a good carpenter. You could try and try forever, and you could not be a good carpenter. But it's not your fault that you can't be a good carpenter because you have tried; and the same way, just because I am not a good mother does not mean that I am not a good person. But then there are other things that you are not good at too, so—

T⁶³: Well, now you are saying, of course, that it's okay that you are not a good mother as long as you are good in something else.

C⁶⁴: Yes.

T⁶⁵: You've got to be good in a bunch of other stuff. Now, *why* do you have to be? Why can't you be lousy at a lot of things? In other words, I could point out right here that you are probably a lousy bicycle driver, aren't you?

C⁶⁶: No.

T⁶⁷: No? Oh, I'm sorry. Okay. Are you a lousy—

C⁶⁸: Housekeeper.

T⁶⁹: Okay. You're a lousy housekeeper. You're a lousy housekeeper. You're a lousy mother. You're a lousy—what else?

C⁷⁰: The things that women are supposed to be.

T⁷¹: Most women *are* good at, you mean?

C⁷²: Okay.

T⁷³: Let's not say *supposed to* because that is simply not the way to define it. A lot of women say, "Why? There is no particular reason why I should be good at housekeeping."

C⁷⁴: Well, this is the way I feel. But then when—well, the majority of people, which you know, which is your society, right?

T⁷⁵: Right.

C[76]:   When the society you live in demands that you be a good
          mother and a good housekeeper, it's—hard to keep this atti-
          tude. You can't.

T[77]:   I agree it's hard to keep it. But it's harder if you don't. What
          you have to do is ask yourself whether society and all your
          friends are really correct. Are you a worthless person because
          you're not a good mother and a good housekeeper and have
          a few other failings along with those? Does that mean you
          are not a good person? Does that mean you have no value
          any more, at least to you? Now maybe in order to be valuable
          to these other people and friends of yours, maybe you have
          to be a good mother because that is the only kind of people
          they will respect. See? Okay. But does that mean just because
          you don't have their respect that you can't have your own
          respect? That is what has happened. You see when you get
          depressed the way you do, you are saying, "I can't respect
          myself any more and like myself. I am not important to *me*
          any more because I am not important to *them*, because I don't
          fulfill the expectations *they* want out of me." Now that is
          when you get depressed, when you think you are not impor-
          tant to yourself any more. If you said to yourself, "Well, I
          am still very important to me. I am a wonderful person. Now,
          that's not enough to make friends with those people. I am
          afraid they are going to reject me because in order for me
          to be friends with them I have to be a good mother, too.
          However, all right, so I'll have to put up with that. So I'm
          not going to have their friendship. See? That's just too bad."
          Would you be depressed then? If you had your own self-
          respect and still weren't a good mother and did not have their
          friendship, would you be depressed? Would you feel guilty?

   Dr. Hauck zeros in on the essence of the client's problem of depression: not the activating events (point A), her boyfriend's failure to
divorce his wife and marry her, and her disinterest in her children,
but her irrational belief system (point B). She is clearly telling herself
that she *should* be married after a six-month affair, and that she
is *supposed to* be a good mother; and that consequently it is *awful*
when she is not yet remarried and when she does not want to take
the responsibility for her children. He points out that she might

possibly accept herself as a person, despite her poor mothering, if she were only good at other things. But why, he asks (at least by implication), does she have to be good at *anything* in order to accept herself?

He finishes up this part of the session, however, with an inelegant solution: that she could convince herself, "Well, I am still very important to me. I am a wonderful person. I happen to be a rotten mother—that's true—but I am a wonderful human being." For practical purposes, this solution is all right since she can hold that she is a wonderful person merely because she exists, in spite of her failings. But philosophically, she has no more reason for calling herself a "wonderful person" than she has for calling herself a "bad person." Both designations are definitional or tautological and cannot really be empirically proven.

More elegantly, the therapist could try to get her to accept the fact that she is a person who does both good and bad *deeds* but that she does not have to rate her *self* at all. Instead of trying to help her gain *self-respect*—which is still a rating of herself—he could try to help her gain *self-acceptance*, which is a more objective term denoting that she exists, that she has both fortunate and unfortunate traits, and that she can still choose to focus on enjoying herself even if she always has poor traits and even if (in an extreme case) these traits far outweigh her good ones. *Self-acceptance* (or *self-choosing*) implies that she chooses to stay alive and seek joy (and avoid pain) but *not* to rate herself.

C⁷⁸: I don't know if I would feel guilty or not, but I'd be awfully lonely without any friends.

T⁷⁹: Well, of course. If you didn't have any friends, you would be very lonely. That's true. But probably you could find some other people. In all likelihood you would. People usually don't go around rejecting others willy-nilly. You must have some redeeming features, some other things that they like about you. Just as you can probably criticize some of your girl friends for some failings that they have, can't you?

C⁸⁰: I don't have any girl friends.

T⁸¹: You don't have any girl friends?

C⁸²: I don't like women.

T⁸³: Oh.

C⁸⁴: Because they talk about silly things that don't make any sense, like how many pains they had when they had their babies, and how much this operation hurt and that operation, and just dumb things, and about a new recipe or something. Really, I couldn't care less.

T85: Well, then, whose opinion are you worried about?

C86: I don't know.

T87: Just society's, you mean?

C88: I don't know.

T89: Your mother?

C90: My mother, my sister, my ex-husband.

T91: Oh, I see. Okay. So then they are the ones. All right. Then they are the ones you are talking about. "If they don't think I'm a worthwhile mother, then therefore I am not a worthwhile person; because in order for me to be a worthwhile person, I have to have their approval. In order to do that, I have to be a worthwhile mother." Right?

C92: Yes.

T93: Then the question is, *why*? Just suppose your mother doesn't accept you, and your sister doesn't accept you, and your husband doesn't accept you. Does that mean you are worthless and good for nothing?

C94: I guess that's the problem. I'm not independent enough to say I can—as long as I think I'm okay, I can make it. I haven't been that independent. I'm too dependent on other people. That's a big problem in itself. I mean—you know—I know I should not be so dependent on other people. When I got the divorce, the divorce was my idea in the first place. And how I had the guts to do it, I don't know, because I thought, "Well, I can do it. I'll show them. I can do it." And well, for a while I had a little trouble financially because I never had to handle money before. Then my brother-in-law sat down with me and figured out a budget and everything, and we got that all straightened out, and I've been doing okay with that.

T95: Well, why didn't you blame yourself for being a poor budgeter?

C96: I didn't have to. He blamed me. I didn't have to blame myself. Everybody else is doing it for me.

T97: Well, that's the point. You could have blamed yourself and gotten very depressed over that. You could have said, "Here

I am. I'm an adult. I *should* know how to handle money, and I don't. Aren't I awful?" and gone on into a deep depression over that, couldn't you?

C⁹⁸: Yes.

T⁹⁹: But you didn't. Instead of blaming yourself, you did something very interesting. What did you do?

C¹⁰⁰: Corrected myself.

T¹⁰¹: Yes, you corrected the problem as much as you could, didn't you? You did not focus on what a worthless person you are. You focused on the problem instead. By focusing on the problem—

C¹⁰²: I really didn't care. I can't understand why I even did anything about it, because I didn't care one way or another.

T¹⁰³: Care about what?

C¹⁰⁴: If the bills were paid or whether I was spending the money the way I was supposed to. I just had the attitude—well, what the heck, you know. I'll get some money some day.

T¹⁰⁵: When was this now?

C¹⁰⁶: When I was having trouble with the budget and—like bills being two weeks past due. I never—I didn't worry about it. Maybe I should have, but I didn't. I thought, "Okay, I'll get the money." You know, no big thing. And everybody kept saying, "You've got to pay your bills on time. You've got to pay them when they are due." Okay. So I had my brother-in-law set up a budget for me, and I had nothing to do with it. I told him all my bills and what the payments were, and he wrote it all down and looked at the calendar, and Friday I write out the checks for whatever he says I am supposed to pay. But that's not being independent. I'm dependent upon him to work out my budget, for if he hadn't done it, I couldn't have.

T¹⁰⁷: I see what you mean. But my other point is that you did not blame yourself because you were an inadequate budgeter. You could have blamed yourself because there is a big failure. See? Really, if you don't know how to budget your money, you might very well run into problems with it. All right. But you didn't say, "I'm a terrible budgeter; therefore, I'm a terrible person." You didn't say that, although that's a big failure, too. Isn't it? But in this case you are saying, "Look, I'm not only a bad mother, I am a bad person." My point is that no *behavior* makes you a bad *person*. The moment you decide that you are a bad person because you have a fault or a weakness, then you are going to get depressed. But you could still like yourself despite the fact that occasionally you don't want children and occasionally you don't think you are being the greatest mother in the world. But you can still like and respect yourself and not blame yourself. You'd be surprised to find you wouldn't be depressed. You still wouldn't be a good mother, would you? But you would not be depressed. That is what you are seeing me about, how to get over your depression. And I am sure you know how to do that—by never blaming yourself. Don't blame yourself, and you will feel much, much better. And then if you sense you have a problem and you want to overcome that problem, by not feeling depressed you will have the energy that you can apply to the problem and say, "Okay, now look. I guess I am not doing a great deal with my children. I'm not raising them the way I really want to. I wish I didn't have them at all—anyway, sometimes at least. However, I do; and therefore, I am going to have to learn how to handle this problem, so now what can I do? What can I learn by my past experiences that will enable me to be a better mother? What did I do last time that was wrong? How can I profit by my mistakes so they teach me how to be a better mother next time and so I don't repeat any mistakes?" Now, if you spent your time looking at it, rather than crucifying yourself for it, look at how much better that would be. Are you following me now?

The essence of the rational-emotive approach, during this session, is in Dr. Hauck's T[107] response. He sums up here the RET position that the client cannot possibly be a bad *person*, no matter what bad *act* she performs. He focuses particularly on her depression, since that is her worst presenting symptom; but in the process he may underemphasize some other points. Thus, in C[47] the client indicates that she is too dependent on other people, and he does not really tackle this problem of hers here, though he does point it out in other sessions. He could have shown her that her feelings of worthlessness and depression are intimately involved with, and in some ways are the same thing as, her feelings of dependency. For her basic philosophy seems to be: "Unless people accept me, I am worthless." And with this idea, she could hardly be anything *but* dependent. Moreover, he could point out, once she recognizes her dependency, she condemns herself for *that*—and she thereby ends up by being depressed, (1) because she cannot guarantee that she will do well and be acceptable to others, and (2) because she has a weakness that we call dependency.

In T¹⁰⁷, the therapist tells the client that she could still like herself despite the fact that occasionally she doesn't want children and is not the greatest mother in the world. She may wrongly interpret him, however, to mean that if she is continually, rather than occasionally, irresponsible in her motherhood functions, she is pretty worthless. So it would be better if he would make clear to her that she could accept herself (rather than *like* herself, which is again an inelegant term) even if she were *always* inept as a mother.

C¹⁰⁸: Yes, but I don't—

T¹⁰⁹: You don't what?

C¹¹⁰: I don't know exactly what I mean—I don't feel the responsibility of it. I don't—I don't feel the importance of disciplining the children and teaching them this and that. If I did, I probably would be doing it.

T¹¹¹: Yes.

C¹¹²: But I don't. Even if I wasn't depressed about it and blaming myself and so forth, I still don't think I would do anything constructive about it because I don't care that much whether I discipline them or not.

T¹¹³: All right. From now on, then, you won't be depressed. You are only depressed because you are blaming yourself *because* you don't care. If you really don't think there is any problem, and you don't even mind not yelling at the kids and disciplining them so much, then relax. Maybe you are right. Maybe you will raise better children than your sister, for example.

C¹¹⁴: I want them to mind, but I don't want to do the work of making them mind. Laziness?

T¹¹⁵: If you are right, and they turn out okay, then fine.

C¹¹⁶: Okay. But if they turn out bad, then it's all my fault again.

T¹¹⁷: That's right. Well, mostly it will be your fault.

C^{118}: Okay.

T^{119}: But how do you know? You have to take the chance. How are the children now? Are you happy with them?

C^{120}: Yes.

T^{121}: Okay. What don't you like about it? What is happening to them?

C^{122}: Well, they don't mind, and they talk back. I have to tell them more than two or three times to do something and end up screaming at them, which doesn't do a bit of good anyway.

T^{123}: Doesn't that motivate you towards wanting to know different methods of handling them? It is obvious that what you are doing now is not bringing you a great deal of pleasure. You are not going to enjoy your children if that goes on, are you? Well, maybe if you studied child rearing methods and we talked about that, for example, maybe we could teach you how to be a more efficient mother and show you what you are doing that brings this behavior on—this unpleasant behavior that you are getting tired of. You may be encouraging it without your knowing it.

C^{124}: I think I said something about I wanted my children to love me, or something like that. I'm afraid of making my children mad at me or something—which is wrong, but I still feel that way anyway. And this one guy told me, he said, "I don't care if my children love me or not as long as they respect me." I can't see this attitude at all. How can they respect you if they don't love you? What he calls respect is fear, and I don't want my children to be afraid of me, or I don't want them to mind because they are afraid they are going to get a beating or a spanking or—I don't know—maybe I expect too much out of humanity. I think people should be good because it's what to do, not because they are afraid of being punished. And I think that's what I think children should be, too, but I don't know how to make them be that way. I don't want to tell them, "You have got to do this, or you will get a spanking," or even if you don't say it, you give them that impression. You are still teaching them that they have to behave in a certain way, or they will be punished. I don't know whether it is right or whether it is wrong, but I feel that they should mind because—

T¹²⁵: Would you behave because of that reason when you were a child?

C¹²⁶: I don't remember when I was little, but when I was a teen-ager I was never—I can remember from probably age ten on up. And I did things that I was told to do or supposed to do because I was supposed to and because it was the right thing to do, not because of fear of punishment because I was never—I can never remember being spanked. My father slapped me across the face a couple of times and for, in my opinion, no reason, which infuriated me, rather than disciplining me. It didn't do a bit of good; it made me very rebellious at that. But I can never remember getting a spanking. But then I feel it didn't help me because I was spoiled, and I never did anything wrong. I mean I never—

T¹²⁷: Well, if you don't show people that there are unfortunate consequences from certain behaviors, then what is going to get them to change? Why should they change?

C¹²⁸: Well, can't people just want to be good?

T¹²⁹: I think a lot of people want to be good. They would all like to be—most of them at least would like to be good. However, how do you get them to do that? For example, you want to be good to yourself. You don't want to be depressed. Right? All right, but what has brought you here is finally the painful consequences of your not knowing how to do things any differently. Right? You have been suffering because you have been making certain mistakes. There has been, in a sense, a punishment to you because of your incorrect behavior. Right? That's why you are here. You get depressed, which is something that happened because you don't know how to do it any differently. You behave wrongly in some sense, you get depressed and that is painful, and now you are coming to me for help as to how to remove that pain. Well, if your children don't experience any kind of pain for certain behavior, how are they going to know that that behavior is wrong? What is to tell them that? How should a child know automatically whether or not a behavior is good or bad? He thinks that screaming back at you is pretty good because he can get his way by that, can't he? From his point of view it makes good sense to him to scream back at you because he can get his way, or he can stay up later. He reduces pain by arguing. He reduces pain. It has turned out to be a pretty smart method for him, hasn't it? And the only way you are going to get him to change that is by making that behavior somewhat painful. I don't mean you have to spank him. It may be sometimes that you might have to, but that isn't always what is called for. But somehow his behavior has got to bring some displeasure to him so that he will say to himself, "Hey, wait a minute. This isn't working for me anymore. I get more of a headache now than I used to. It's not getting me the pleasure that I once got; therefore, I'm going to have to change." You are asking the child to figure this all out by himself. But if he is not being really hurt by his behavior, why would he want to change it? You have to supply the hurt, mainly in the form of frustration or in the form of penalty. If they don't do what you say, then we will have to go over this in more detail at another time. But one of the things you are going to have to learn, if they don't behave, is to penalize them for misbehaving. You set the rule; you tell them what the penalty will be. If they break the rule, they get the penalty, and that's all. Then just let them suffer with their mistakes. Next time, they will think before they do the same thing. That way, incidentally, you may soon get to the point where you will be controlling your children, and after you control them and get them to behave more like what you want, what will happen to your feelings about them?

C¹³⁰: I'd like them better.

T¹³¹: You'd like them better. Right. And once you like them better, then what would happen—with the depression?

C¹³²: I guess I would feel I am doing a better job, and I would not feel so guilty.

T¹³³: Right. Mainly in the next sessions what we have to talk about again are the dynamics of depression, on the one hand, and also some sound mothering techniques on how to handle children better than you have been. Right?

C¹³⁴: Really? it's just an excuse, but I don't get home until 5:30 at night and then fix supper and do the dishes and give them their baths and go to bed. It doesn't leave too much time for play or anything.

T[135]: Yes, right. You have a tough job.

C[136]: And then, well, I've been working weekends, too, at the hospital.

T[137]: Well, okay, you've got a bad situation. We'll have to talk about what we can come up with—some kind of suggestions that will help you to become as efficient as possible. Because I think that will help your feelings after you get them changed to more what you like. Let's talk about this again. Okay?

Dr. Hauck spends a good deal of time showing the client that it would be far better if she paid more attention to becoming a more effective mother than to condemning herself for being an ineffective one. The techniques of handling her children that he discusses with her are correctly included in RET, because the rational-emotive therapist does not hesitate to instruct his clients in some of the more efficient methods of childrearing, sex techniques, business methods, and so on. The danger here, however, is that the therapist may get sidetracked from more important considerations.

Thus, in C[114] the client wonders whether she is lazy, because she wants to get good results from her children without doing the work to get these results. Dr. Hauck lets this point drop for the present (though he picked it up mentally and worked on it later). Frequently, however, he would show her right here that she is indeed "lazy" with her children—because she is irrationally believing that she *should* get good results with them without putting in any amount of work. He would also show her that she is following a short-range rather than a longer-range hedonistic view in this respect: striving mainly for the pleasure of the moment (tending to her own desires and neglecting to discipline her children) and not for the greater pleasure of the future (enjoying their good behavior).

In T[129], where Dr. Hauck attempts to show the client some of the principles of behavior modification in rearing her children, he says: "One of the things you are going to have to learn, if they don't behave, is to penalize them for misbehaving." To some degree, he is correct; but his use of the term "have to" may be overstated. She obviously doesn't *have to* penalize her children to get better behavioral results (though it might well *be better* if she does so). And if the therapist stresses *have to's, got to's, you must's,* and so on, then he is often unwittingly encouraging the client to use these misleading kinds of overgeneralizations and absolutes. Thus, if the client believes that she has to penalize her children in order to get them to behave, and she actually does not adhere to this imperative, she will almost certainly make herself inordinately guilty for not doing what she supposedly *has to* do. But if the therapist shows her, instead, that it would be better if she disciplines her children with some form of penalization, and she then fails to do so, she may more easily conclude, "Isn't it too bad that I didn't do what would be better," thereby making herself concerned but not guilty.

In the closing statement of the session, T[137], Dr. Hauck rightly indicates to the client that they can work on suggestions to help her become more efficient with her children; but he implies that these suggestions, and the good they do, will help her get her feelings straightened out. Actually, in RET we would not want the client to feel better about herself because she was handling her children more efficiently. Rather, we would want her to accept herself fully whether or not she becomes more responsible and effective in mothering her children. Greater efficacy in this respect is highly to be desired for several reasons, but not because she then would be a more worthwhile person, who could consequently like herself.

FOURTH SESSION

T[1]:   How have you been?

C[2]:   Fine. No depression.

T[3]:   Tell me about that.

C[4]:   I don't know what to tell you. I guess that I just kept busy enough that I haven't thought about anything, or something. I had no reason to be depressed. The past week the kids were in Nebraska with my mother, and I just kept busy.

T[5]:   They stayed in Nebraska?

C[6]:   For a week. They are supposed to come home today.

T[7]:   Well, I'm curious. Why aren't you depressed now? What has happened? Is it just the fact that they are not around, or were you depressed when they were around?

C[8]:   I don't know for sure, but I think—well, I've been dating a new guy, and I've just been so busy with him I haven't had time to think about myself, I guess.

T[9]:   You are implying that before when you were dating this other fellow, you got depressed over him?

C[10]:   Yes. I did once in a while, but since I started dating this new one, I haven't even wanted to see the other one or even thought about him or anything. And I'm glad.

T¹¹: I recall you saying that this was somewhat disturbing to you—this relationship. Again, what was it?

C¹²: He was married.

T¹³: And what was depressing about all that?

C¹⁴: Well, he said he was going to get a divorce and all this, and he didn't; and we've been seeing each other for about six months or so.

T¹⁵: Right. You were being strung along and getting nowhere. And I suggested you were getting depressed because you were feeling sorry for yourself because life was kind of dull, and you weren't doing anything about it. Correct?

C¹⁶: Right.

T¹⁷: All right. So what prompted you to drop him and go see someone else?

C¹⁸: Well, I was dating other guys anyway. But, you know—like, I would just have a couple drinks—well, I don't drink. I drink 7-Up, but I go to places where they drink. And I have 7-Up or something and dance a while, and I'd go home. No big date or anything like that. And it just so happened one night that the guy that I'm dating happened to be my ex-husband's best friend. And—well, he used to be. They're still friends, but they're not best friends. And he was there one night at one place where I usually go, and he asked me to dance, and we danced, and we danced the rest of the evening. And then he asked me to go out the next night, and we went out; and ever since then we've been together almost every day.

T¹⁹: So you're trying to tell me that you replaced this other fellow, and life is lovely again. Would you have been able to do that if you hadn't come to see me?

C²⁰: I don't know.

T²¹: Chances are that might have happened anyway, hm?

C²²: It's possible.

T²³: Yes. So have I been of any value to you?

C²⁴: Oh, I think so. Because now whenever I start feeling a little depressed, I try to talk to myself like—you know, "Well, are you feeling sorry for yourself? Are you feeling guilty or whatever? What's going on here? And quit it and get busy"—which

I never would have done before. I would have just gone on and stayed in a depressed state until somebody else brought me out of it. I can do it by myself now.

T²⁵: I see.

C²⁶: I did get a little upset one day, but I talked myself out of it. My ex-husband said he wanted to talk to me about something. And whenever he says anything like that, it is usually something I have done wrong or something he thinks he should correct me about.

T²⁷: Yes.

C²⁸: And he did not have time to talk right then because he had called me from work. And so I didn't know what it was, and I started worrying and tended to make things worse than what they are in my mind. And then I got to thinking, "Well, he said it wasn't—it's not serious, and there's no hurry. We can talk later. So it must not be anything too bad, or he would have said, 'I want to see you tonight and talk about it.'" So then I just decided—well, I couldn't think of anything I had done so terribly wrong, so I just talked myself out of worrying about it.

T²⁹: And ordinarily what might you have done?

C³⁰: I would have just gotten nervous and started crying and worrying and thinking, "What did I do now?" and "Gee, he's going to yell at me." And, you know, just more or less worry about it and try to think about what things were, and think up worse things than possibly it even could be.

T³¹: And you could have been pretty nervous and depressed—both—

C³²: Right.

T³³: —by the time you really got to talk to him. Right? Well, now. Why did you do that? You are suggesting that our talks helped you handle these things better?

C³⁴: Because I—as I say, before I would have just gone to pieces and worried and fretted until I found out what it was. And this time I didn't. I said to myself, "Well, okay, I did something wrong, you know?"

T³⁵: Yes. Well, that sounds like real improvement, doesn't it?

C³⁶: It sure does.

T³⁷: Because I wasn't there to handle it, and it is something quite different for you, as you know. Who made that difference? Santa Claus? Who? Who made the difference in how it was handled?

C[38]: I did.

T[39]: Yes, you did. So—okay. Maybe we are learning something, then, aren't we?

C[40]: It looks like it.

It is not clear, from the first part of this session, whether the client has been undepressed because she almost accidentally happens to have met a new and more attractive lover, with whom she has been busily diverted, or whether she has really benefited from the previous three sessions with therapist. But her response in C[34] indicates that she is now more willing to accept herself with possible wrongdoings and that therefore she may well be becoming less anxious and depressed when unpleasant events occur. The goal of RET, of course, is not to merely help her find pleasant diversions, such as a new lover, but to help her refuse to depress herself even when things go wrong in her life.

T[41]: Okay. Now with respect to the other thing—the handling of this new relationship that you have—you are normally being dated by a new fellow and falling into a new romance. That's usually pretty uplifting, and I don't see that I would contribute a great deal to that. You had a new relationship going here, which would have ordinarily pulled you out of your depression. I am asking myself, "Have I been of any value to you there?" And I wonder whether or not you would have been in the mood to go out and strike up a new relationship and take advantage of it if you had not been working on your prior depression.

C[42]: Right. No, because I probably would have been staying home as I was doing before. I wouldn't have gone anywhere. I wouldn't have had the opportunity to meet anyone. Before, I was just staying home and feeling sorry for myself.

T[43]: Oh, I see.

C[44]: And not going anywhere. Just maybe once a week or something like that I'd go for a couple hours, and then I'd go back home.

T⁴⁵: This way, I take it, you were in a good enough mood to really
        go out and swing around a little bit, and in this way you
        were able to meet somebody and change the course of your
        life again.

C⁴⁶: Right.

T⁴⁷: Okay. Good.

C⁴⁸: I've also been thinking about talking to my ex-husband and
        telling him that I want to have the kids back because I feel
        confident and in the mood to have them back. However, I
        hesitate because I think it might be too soon, and I'm not
        going to rush into a decision like that right away. But I have
        had a feeling which I think is good that I thought about want-
        ing the kids back.

T⁴⁹: That you are capable again. You are a strong person. You
        are in control of yourself. And, "I can handle the kids again"
        is what you are saying, right?

C⁵⁰: I think so.

T⁵¹: Yes. Wonderful. What does he think about that? Have you
        asked him?

C⁵²: Oh, no.

T⁵³: You haven't said it yet.

C⁵⁴: I'm not going to.

T⁵⁵: Oh. Until you feel stronger?

C⁵⁶: Right. Until I am absolutely sure. Right now I just think I
        want them back.

T⁵⁷: Yes.

C⁵⁸: But when I am absolutely sure, then—because if I say it now
        and then I get the kids back and something happens and I
        go back, then it's not good for the kids.

T⁵⁹: That's right. We want to be cautious about this. Then we
        can talk about other things that you do with the kids, mainly
        your self-discipline, your following through. How have you
        been doing on that?

C⁶⁰: Pretty good.

T⁶¹: Tell me about that.

C⁶²: I don't know if it—I don't know if it—I don't know—well,
        the fellow that I am dating is divorced and has three children
        and has custody of the kids, and so most of the time we have
        been spending with the kids. We have had the kids with us

all the time and—most of the time. And we go out after we put the kids to bed—then we go out together. And I don't know if I can handle my own—this is the whole thing—but his kids—. Now, like, if they are doing something they are not supposed to, I tell them "Don't," or "Stop doing that," or "Straighten up," or whatever. And I don't just say it off the top of my head and forget it, like I was doing with my own, you know I kind of absentmindedly tell them to stop it and then ignore them. I really don't know, because I haven't seen my kids for a week, and I don't know if I would be the same with them or not.

T⁶³: What about your self-discipline at home? Have you managed your own affairs better?

C⁶⁴: That's really hard to say. Well, the last time I was here I went home and said to myself as we discussed, "I'm not going to bed until I do so-and-so and such-and-such." And I did it. However, I really haven't been home enough to do anything since then. I've just been gone. I haven't been home. Of course, there isn't that much to do because I am not home. I'm at work all day and then I'm gone.

T⁶⁵: You are there by yourself so there isn't—you haven't had that much of an opportunity, although you seem to be beginning. You began to use a little bit more with his children. And then you just started using a little bit more self-discipline in your home, but you haven't had a real opportunity yet.

C⁶⁶: And I haven't been put under any pressure to do it. This is one thing that bothers me. If somebody says it has got to be done by a certain time or something like that—if I'm under pressure—lots of times I get—well, I get too nervous. I can't handle it or something.

T⁶⁷: Well, yes, I understand that. That wasn't really what I was referring to. I was referring to simply boring daily chores that had to be done and when you had to discipline yourself. Sometimes if you are very nervous you want to do it and can't. It is not a matter of discipline, but you get so nervous and so rattled that you can't do it. So we have to distinguish between sometimes not doing a job because you are nervous and sometimes not doing a job because you are undisciplined.

C[68]:   I think, and other people mentioned it too, that I am not quite so scatterbrained. I am using my head now.

T[69]:   Oh, really.

C[70]:   That shows something anyway.

T[71]:   Of course. Shows maybe you are settling down a little bit. Becoming a little bit more mature, a little more self-assured, right? Delightful. You look happier.

The client is by no means cured at the end of this part of the fourth session. As she notes in C[66], she still reacts badly to pressure and gets nervous when something has got to be done by a certain time. But she has stopped mooning around the house and consequently has been able to go out and meet a satisfactory partner. She also has been able to handle her new boyfriend's children. She feels strong enough to ask her husband if she can take back her own children. And others have noted that she is much less scatterbrained. Considering how anxious, sobbing, and depressed she was only a few weeks ago, it is highly probable that the rational-emotive approach taken by the therapist has been of considerable help to her. In the course of several subsequent sessions, she maintained her gains, was able to handle her own children much more satisfactorily, and remained undepressed. So Dr. Hauck's direct intervention not only seemed to work, but appeared to get highly satisfactory results in a brief period of time.

CHAPTER 6

A Husband and Wife Who Have Not Had Intercourse During Thirteen Years of Marriage

JOHN M. GULLO, M.A.

The husband, in the following case, is a 37-year-old teacher and his wife is a 39-year-old dietician. Although they have been married for thirteen years and have had a considerable amount of counseling, they have not yet been able to have successful intercourse.

FIRST SESSION

T¹: Well, what seems to be the difficulty?

H²: Well, what led us here was that—we have made some attempts off and on in our marital life to have intercourse and have children; and we seem to have a mental block there.

T³: Um-hm.

H⁴: And what—one last desperate thing—we thought maybe we might adopt a child. This might help us to break down this feeling if we got involved with an adopted baby. Now I realize this is a negative reason for doing this; but we felt this might be an answer. And, of course, that led us to the child welfare place over here. The director felt that we ought to make an appointment with somebody that we can talk about this problem to. And he mentioned you and we made the appointment. So that's where we are.

T⁵: Okay. Now, have you been able to have intercourse at all in your married life?

H⁶: Uh, I don't think so—

W⁷: No.

H⁸: Except that—I guess that first attempt we made we didn't succeed.

T⁹: Yeah. Okay. How long have you been married now?

W¹⁰: Thirteen years.

T¹¹: Thirteen years?

W¹²: Um-hm.

T¹³: And how old are you?

W¹⁴: I'm—thirty-nine. I had to stop and think. (*Chuckles*)

H¹⁵: Thirty-seven.

T¹⁶: Thirty-seven. Okay. Now, what happens when you start to have intercourse? Do you get an erection, or are you unable to maintain it or what?

H¹⁷: Yeah, yeah, I don't think I'm able to achieve this. There's some sort of a mental block there at this time. So, therefore, we just put this thing in our background.

T¹⁸: Um-hm.

H¹⁹: We feel that we've given this a lot of thought over the years, you know, and at times we've tried to think this thing out rationally. And we've sought help, and it seems like the help hasn't been help, and so we've just sort—oh, just thought we'd wait till maybe a more convenient time to work this out. And then of course, as I say, the years go by.

T²⁰: What kind of help have you had previously?

H²¹: The first help was—did you ever hear of—did you ever know Dr. S—— at Temple University?

T²²: Yeah.

H²³: Well (*bitterly*), I had five minutes of help from him.

T²⁴: Yeah?

W²⁵: That was the first year of our marriage.

H²⁶: Yeah, that was the first year of our marriage, when we knew that something was wrong here. And he put a student that was working under him with me, and with the fee that I had to pay going to school at that time, and—we had a bad rapport between him, and we—it just didn't work out. That's all. So there was the first attempt. And—then—after that, probably a year or two after that—I did seek another psychiatrist. Didn't charge me anything. Which I felt bad about (*laughs*), 'cause I felt he wasn't giving me his attention. It just seemed like he wasn't interested. And he gave me—prescribed some pills to relax me. And—but it didn't seem like anything came out of that either. He was a fellow that taught psychology at the college, and I don't think he was—

W²⁷: He was one of my professors.

H²⁸: Yeah.

W²⁹: While I was going to school.

H³⁰: And I don't think he really understood the problem.

W³¹: No.

H³²: Then—then we tried—

W³³: I think, at the time, that he thought I just shouldn't be going to school, holding down a job, being married, more or less. And I think he thought that was my problem. He encouraged me to quit school, which I finally did—which I finally did.

H³⁴: Yeah.

W³⁵: But I don't think he really understood our problem. Because there were so many other students that were going to school that were overcoming the obstacles. So I don't feel—that wasn't it.

H³⁶: Um-hm.

H³⁷: Then the next thing we went to the University of Wisconsin Hospital, and we sought a doctor there about either this particular problem, or didn't we mention artificial insemination at that particular time?

W³⁸: Um-hm.

H³⁹: And we really didn't get any help from him. He was a medical doctor.

W⁴⁰: How far were we living from there—I mean from the University of Wisconsin?

H⁴¹: About ninety miles.

W⁴²: Well, they said they were going to set up appointments for me. So, that again was kind of a problem getting back and forth.

H⁴³: And following that, was that the last one till we moved here?

W⁴⁴: Yeah, that—

H⁴⁵: I think so.

W⁴⁶: —that we together have tried to get help from. There are times that both of us separately were going to medical doctors and would ask for advice. But we could never get any help from them either. Any doctor that ever examined me told me that there wasn't any reason that I couldn't have a child. But they didn't seem to give us any hope for the situation.

T[47]: Um-hm.

H[48]: We have—I mean, we've looked into our own backgrounds and feel we've sort of rationalized out these reasons. And we know that it's wrong and everything. But it's like—you know, you're taught not to touch a hot stove, and when you get up to it, you withdraw. And it just seems to be that reaction here.

T[49]: Yes, that's right. And so the point is that you have to overcome this false way of looking at things.

H[50]: Yes, and, of course, one time it really bothered me whether I had a false concept on all of life, you know. But I don't think that's the case. I feel I'm all right, and I dislike people who have false views on things when they can have right views. And so here I am in this particular instance, which we *know* that somehow we've been in a bad or wrong groove in this particular thing. It seems so easy to get out, and yet for us it hasn't been—for one reason or another.

T[51]: Okay, I think I can show you what things are going on in your head that are perpetuating this problem. There are usually two major reasons. What we want to find out from you are just exactly what some of the details are of one or both of these reasons. Reason A is fear of failure, and reason B is sexual puritanism, which usually is involved here also.

H[52]: I think it's probably a combination between both of those; and I think we both recognize that.

T[53]: Okay. So then the problem is, as in any superstition—since this is probably one of the best ways of describing any emotional problem—it's just superstitious thinking. Now, how do you get over the black cat superstition? How do you get over any superstition, such as the one that breaking a mirror is going to give you seven years' bad luck?

H[54]: Well, the thing to do is to break the mirror and see—

T[55]: Yeah!

H[56]: —that God doesn't strike you dead or something.

T[57]: Right.

Even though the therapist, John Gullo, as yet knows very little about the specific circumstances leading up to this couple's sexual problem, he takes a chance and guesses that it is largely caused by fear of failure and sexual puritanism. He does this largely on theoretical grounds and on the basis of his prior experience with sexually failing couples. Although it may seem presumptuous of him to proclaim his interpretation so early in the therapeutic process, he assumes that there is a high chance that his guess has some validity and that it may well save this couple considerable time, trouble, and expense. If his guess happened to be wrong, or if the clients resisted it, he might well backtrack on it. But, as is so frequently the case in RET, it seems to ring a bell with the clients and thereby furthers therapeutic progress.

RET practitioners are frequently accused of having an authoritarian or dogmatic manner when they hazard these kinds of interpretations so early in the course of therapy. In one way, however, they are simply being more honest and direct than psychoanalytic, client-centered, experiential, or existentialist therapists—all of whom have their own distinct hypotheses about the client's disturbances as soon as they obtain a little data on his problem, but most of whom subtly and long-windedly try to get him to see "for himself" what their hypotheses are and actually (and more dishonestly) indoctrinate him with their views. In RET, the client is fairly and squarely told, usually quickly in the game, what the therapist's hypotheses about him are. Then he has many chances to challenge, resist, and bring up evidence against these hypotheses if he does not wish to accept them. If he does accept them (as seems to be most frequently the case in virtually all kinds of therapy), he and the therapist save a great deal of time. In this particular case, both clients seem to be quite ready to accept the therapist's initial interpretations; therefore, he proceeds in a fairly rapid-fire manner.

H[58]: Well, we realize that, except when it comes to something like intercourse. All right, we say that; but when it comes time, then nothing happens. (*Laughs*)

W[59]: We're—

H[60]: It's not like, breaking—

W[61]: We're really dandy at talking to each other; and boy, we're really going to do it! And then—

H[62]: I think I got drunk one time. I thought maybe that might help, you know.

W[63]: (*Laughs*)

T[64]: Listen, that's a darn good technique to use, sometimes.

H[65]: But it just put me to sleep, see. (*Laughs*)

T[66]: Well, you had too much.

H[67]: So—

T[68]: Well, there are a number of helpful things which you can do to get you a little relaxed in this process. But what we want to do is to get some details now, 'cause I may even have to teach you some aspects of sex play to help you out in this connection also. Now one technique which you can do to help you relax is just what you said a minute ago: Have a few beers or have a glass of wine or something.

H[69]: That does help a little!

T[70]: That will help you sometimes.

W[71]: And what happened. You did that once and got so stuffed you said you were uncomfortable or something, and—

H[72]: Well—

W[73]: You know!

H[74]: Yeah, I—well—it doesn't matter—

W[75]: (*Laughs*)

T[76]: Okay. Now, how often do you attempt to have any kind of sex?

H[77]: Well, before we were married—in fact one of the—I think one of the reasons we decided to get married was because we thought we just couldn't contain ourselves any longer, and we didn't want to break any moral codes that we had accepted as being valid and so forth. So we got married. And I think at the beginning there we did try when we first got married. And then we felt that because we were so busy, and with school, and there's a lot of pressure—that we thought we'd wait a little bit on this till we got settled down. But then—oh, occasionally after that it would come up, you know, but then we'd quickly put it aside again. And down through the years it's just been occasional.

W[78]: Until, for awhile, it went for years without us even discussing it.

H[79]: For awhile we thought maybe it was the best thing that we just—just put it completely out. And we realized this wasn't the solution either. And the last year, I'd say, we're becoming more and more interested in doing something about this.

T⁸⁰: Yeah. Now, are you able to achieve any possible satisfaction masturbating?

H⁸¹: Yeah.

T⁸²: And how often do you engage in that?

H⁸³: Oh, just occasionally. Maybe it's probably accidental.

T⁸⁴: And how about you?

W⁸⁵: Not too often.

T⁸⁶: Well, are you able to obtain satisfaction in that way?

W⁸⁷: A very little.

T⁸⁸: Now have either of you attempted to masturbate in each other's presence?

H⁸⁹: No.

W⁹⁰: No.

T⁹¹: Well, this is another technique that you could use to get both of you interested in each other. The both of you, or one of you, it doesn't really make much difference, could masturbate in each other's presence. Then you will maintain some degree of excitement, and then you can try to have intercourse. And as soon as you penetrate her, what you can do to help him maintain his erection is close your legs over his penis. Because this will put pressure on the penis and keep the blood in there.

W⁹²: Um-hm.

T⁹³: It will help you. So there are three or four things that you can do now, technique-wise, to help you with this problem. But now we have to get down, more specifically, to just exactly what you are saying to yourself when you get ready to engage in sex with your wife. What happens?

H⁹⁴: Well, I've thought a great deal about this, and I feel it goes back to a lot of things that I was told or taught to be true when I was very, very young and inexperienced. See, when I was born—my mother had a cesarean operation, which about killed her. And I think I had another sister that was born and that died very shortly after some childbirth trouble. And—she—my mother was sort of a neurotic woman, you know. Of course, as a child you don't really understand these things, all these things. But you could feel the emotion. And—, it was always a feeling that anything that has to do with sex or childbirth or anything is something that is terrible and—brings you to the point of death, and—is evil, I mean all of this is tied up in there. I think this is the opinion that I came away with when I left my home, which I know is not right. And—when I think—when I—when we suggest this to each other and when we maybe decide to try this, I think of these—this comes up very hard in my mind: that I might be hurting her, I might cause her death or disfigure her, or—bring her misery. I mean, to put her in the same state that my mother was in, which I don't wish—I didn't want—wish for anyone. 'Cause I think that my mother didn't have a very happy life. I think that's the feeling that I get.

T[95]: So your irrational idea here is that you're saying to yourself when you get ready to have sex with her, "Wouldn't it be *awful* if I—if she got pregnant and died?"

H[96]: Yes, yes.

T[97]: "That would mean I couldn't take it."

H[98]: Yeah.

T[99]: Well, *why* would that be awful?

H[100]: Well, because I think—this might be a paradox, but because I love her so much.

T[101]: Yeah, but why would it be *awful* if she died?

H[102]: Because this is a party that I have chosen to be my helper. And she has chosen to be my helper. And she has chosen me. And she respects me, and I respect her.

T[103]: Okay. But you see, you're saying two things here now. A is "I want her to be with me the rest of my life. I don't want her to die before her time and before my time." And B is "If she does, it's awful, terrible. It's dreadful." Now why would it be so awful, so terrible? Not, why would it be bad?—'cause it would be bad. It would be unfortunate if this were to occur.

Mr. Gullo is doing here what a rational-emotive practitioner usually does in cases of sexual inadequacy: first, he is finding out the kind of inadequacy involved and is suggesting practical ways of countering it (as Masters and Johnson [1970] would tend to do with their clients and as many other marriage counselors and sexologists would do); and second, he is zeroing in on their self-deprecating and unrealistic philosophies about themselves and their sex experiences. In regard to these philosophies, he is trying to show the clients exactly what these are, why they are self-defeating, and what they can do about challenging and questioning them and ultimately replacing them with more realistic values.

H[104]: Well, I'm not saying that death in itself is a terrible tragedy. I don't believe that.

T[105]: No, I know that.

H[106]: But I feel that if I—if I am the instrument of a tragedy, this would be—maybe this is reflecting back on me; there's a selfish feeling here—that this would be a tragedy that I have had a part in.

T[107]: And if this were to happen, this would mean that something—that "I'm a real louse."

H[108]: Yeah, because my mother often threw up her particular problems to my father. I mean he was blamed, and therefore I have a great affection for my father, and I never did have too much affection for my mother.

T[109]: So you overpersonalized them. You assumed that you would be responsible for her death.

H[110]: Yes, I have probably had those feelings. Maybe not that strong. I've had the feeling, maybe, of just an abnormal life or something, you know.

T[111]: Yeah.

H[112]: But I think death enters into it.

T[113]: Yeah.

H[114]: Not the death in itself—but—to be a cause of it. An unnecessary type of death or something. I think probably that my wife's background, too, has contributed a little bit to this. She had a very stern, self-righteous father that—

W[115]: Who had three children, though.

H[116]: Hm?

W[117]: Four children. I mean—

H[118]: Yeah, I know that. But I think this affected you and your sister, a great deal.

W[119]: Probably.

H[120]: Your sister—how old is your sister, forty-two, forty-three?

W[121]: Yeah.

H¹²²: And she just had a child about a year ago.

W¹²³: 'Course we—

H¹²⁴: About a year and a half ago.

W¹²⁵: We never discussed it with each other, so I don't know what is the cause of her delayed pregnancy.

T¹²⁶: Um-hm.

W¹²⁷: Well, I don't believe that her problem is the same as ours.

H¹²⁸: Well, I think it was tied in.

W¹²⁹: Uh, well, I do, too, because I think the first few years of their marriage was very difficult. Because her husband would accuse her of being childish or immature in accepting responsibility. And she probably was. I don't know. I—

H¹³⁰: But I think in this family, though, there is a resentment built up against the father.

W¹³¹: Well, I think—

H¹³²: I mean—

W¹³³: Yeah, it's not only the resentment.

H¹³⁴: I mean respect, an old-world respect, as a figure of authority. But also a resentment—

W¹³⁵: I think I resented him more than my sister did.

H¹³⁶: That you couldn't express your own feeling. Well, she—I think she was more—

W¹³⁷: And I think I—

H¹³⁸: We don't want to get in a family fight here. (*Laughs*)

W¹³⁹: (*Laughs*)

H¹⁴⁰: But she was more capable of just accepting whatever he said, whereas you just sort of rebelled against some things he said.

T¹⁴¹: Yeah. Okay, then. Getting back to your particular reason for inadequacy, then, is the idea that you will be the cause of her death as a result of pregnancy. And that (*a*) her death would be terrible, and (*b*) you would be a louse for having caused it. Is that right?

H¹⁴²: Well, it might take me a day to think about that—that logic. (*Laughs*) But it seems that would be tied in.

The clients, who are somewhat sophisticated and who have had some amount of psychoanalytic psychotherapy, would prefer to connect their present attitudes to intercourse, and the male's fear of hurting the female through engaging in it, with the indoctrinations of their family members. This may certainly to some extent be true, since they may have picked up negative ideas toward sex from their parents. But this may also not be true, since the husband's failure to keep persisting at having intercourse with his wife may be much more a result of his fear of failure than of his fear of getting her pregnant and thereby "hurting" her; and it is very easy for him (and his wife) to use childhood-imbibed superstitions as a cop-out in this respect. Rather than get embroiled in speculative assumptions about what happened during both the clients' childhoods and how that affects them now, Mr. Gullo sticks to the main points, which easily can be validated: namely, that if the husband believes that intercourse with his wife might lead to pregnancy and that such pregnancy might also result in her death, he also (and more importantly) believes that he would be a louse, under those circumstances, for causing her demise. His view of his own "lousehood," and not the high probability of his causing his wife's death (which he may have falsely picked up from his parents), is the real issue; and this is what the therapist wants to emphasize.

T[143]: Well, why would you be a louse if this were true? Let's assume now that she got pregnant, and she died giving birth. Why would that make you out a louse?

H[144]: Well—I think it would be a tie-in to what I've been told—what I would be.

T[145]: Yeah, but does that make you a louse? Here, all of these years you've been told that you'd be a louse—

H[146]: No.

T[147]: —if you did this.

H[148]: No, definitely not. I don't think it would.

T[149]: But you—but you really *do* believe it would!

H[150]: But I—I—it must be a very strong subconscious feeling.

T[151]: Yes. It's very strong, so strong that this is what's maintaining your problem. If you keep telling yourself over and over again, "Yes, I would be a louse if this would occur"—in other words, you make yourself guilty. This is what guilt is.

H[152]: Yeah, I think I would make myself guilty in this aspect.

T[153]: Right.

H[154]: Right.

T[155]: Well, now, let's say, if I call you a camel, does that make you one?

H[156]: A camel?

T[157]: Um-hm. If I called you one, would that make you one?

H[158]: No, no, hm-m.

T[159]: Now—now, you see this is—

H[160]: But if I—if I had the experience of having to sleep and live
with camels all my life, which I hated, and you call me that,
that would have a very personal meaning to me then. Now
I lived in an environment where this was—these thoughts
and feelings expressed— And, therefore, when I tell myself
this, it has a more emotional personal meaning.

T[161]: Mm, that's where you—that's where we agree: that you have
this strong influence to think this way. But then the cause,
the reason you *still* have the problem, is because *you* are maintaining it in your own head. You still carry on this self-brain-
washing in your own—

H[162]: Yeah.

T[163]: —head by telling—

H[164]: Yeah.

T[165]: —yourself over and over again: "Yes—

H[166]: Well, I think—

T[167]: —yes, I would be a louse."

H[168]: I think I sort of realize that. But then I have to ask the
question, "Why do I keep maintaining it?" 'Cause I know it's
not a right, healthy attitude in this particular aspect.

T[169]: Because (a) it's—you're not challenging this idea. You won't,
you're not continuing to do—

H[170]: Yeah, but *why* don't I challenge it?

T[171]: Because—

H[172]: Why do I easily let this dominate me?

T[173]: Because, as human beings, this is the way we all are. We
have difficulty giving up our ideas. It's a natural kind of resistance that we all face. And then because you're inured to doing
this all of the time. You haven't got any practice questioning
or challenging this superstition. You've had considerable practice doing just the opposite. And now it requires work. So
you try it a time or two, and you say, "Oh, *hell*! I work so
hard to try and get over it, and it just doesn't seem to work!
I guess there's no hope at all!"

W[174]: Um-hm.

T[175]: You see what I mean?

H[176]: Um-hm.

T[177]: And you still, in the back of your mind, it seems to me, also have this fear of failure that comes as a secondary aspect. "Here I've tried to have sex with my wife and I've failed. And so if I try again, what am I going to do? Am I going to fail again? Since I've always failed in the past, it looks like I'll *always* fail! So why even try at all?" So then you give up, and you kind of run away from having the sex activity.

H[178]: Yeah, I think this—it's a pretty good analysis.

T[179]: Okay, so now the question is, how do you get over it? You have to do two things now. (*a*) You have to question and challenge vigorously this false notion that you have.

H[180]: Um-hm.

T[181]: And then (*b*) you have to do the work. You have to act. As John Dewey said many years ago—the famous educator—"Nothing is ever really learned until it's acted upon." So the same would apply to the black cat superstition. You not only have to ask yourself, "How could the color black possibly affect my life? Where's the magic?" Then you have to go and pat the black cat on the head. So you then not only have to challenge these ideas: "Why would I be a louse, if she were to die and why is it so awful to fail?" You also have to force yourself to have relations with her.

H[182]: It seems, though, that over the years I have sort of asked myself—maybe not exactly this way—but I've said to myself, "This is irrational. This is not right." But—I mean, I've thought it out like this. But that hasn't been enough to overcome the resistance, you see.

T[183]: Because, probably, you're *blaming yourself* for being irrational.

H[184]: Well, yes, because it's quite a paradox. Uh, as I said, at one time in my life I thought maybe—all through my life I have had a warped view on everything. If it's warped here, then it must carry through—that was one thing Dr. S——, in his five minutes—he didn't think I was crazy, you know. That's all. So—

T[185]: I don't think you're crazy either. You just happen to have an exaggerated view of sex and self-blaming that many other people have in a lesser degree.

H[186]: Yeah.

T[187]: Your problem is a common one, incidentally. I see lots of people with this particular problem, although for some of them it hasn't gone on to this great a length.

H[188]: Um. Probably if we could have—you know, maybe have got this earlier, as I say, it wouldn't have worn such a groove in our thinking. I think of this.

T[189]: That's right.

H[190]: But we do truly want to do something about this. And—as I say, we've sort of gotten, it seemed to me, the runaround in many areas, though maybe we didn't follow through on some of the ideas that they did present hard enough. I don't know; I'm not blaming these other people entirely.

T[191]: Yeah.

H[192]: I'm sure they—I'm sure you can get a good idea, and the minute you walk out that door you can completely ignore that idea.

T[193]: Yeah. Well, I'm going to try to make sure that doesn't happen. I'm going to make it as concrete as possible and give you a homework assignment to do. 'Cause in the kind of counseling that I do, we give concrete homework assignments so people can get over their disturbances. And you can get a couple of books if you want to go into more detail about this— specifically things that I'll say to you. But now I think it's important for you to realize that this apparently is one of the major reasons why you haven't been able to do much about it. You got the secondary disturbance of blaming yourself because of your irrational "Well, that's irrational for me to think this way." And, "Man that's really awful. How nutty can a guy get?" And so you blame yourself. You're overgeneralizing. You're condemning the sinner instead of the sin. You're condemning yourself instead of the act. You say, "Because my act is bad, I as a whole person am a louse." This is what guilt is.

H[194]: Yeah.

Mr. Gullo drives home a most important point here. Many clients come to therapy already knowing that they are thinking and acting irrationally, and they then wonder why this knowledge does not help them behave more rationally. One of the main reasons for this, the therapist points out, is because they are really telling themselves two things: (a) "I am acting irrationally," and (b) "I should not be behaving in this manner, and am therefore pretty worthless for being irrational!" This second idea not only adds to their original irrationality (which almost always consists of their condemning themselves for something they have done or not done), but it also prevents them from looking at it and doing anything effective about it. For while the client is condemning himself for being irrational, he will rarely have the time and energy to discover why he behaves (or what he is telling himself to make himself behave) irrationally, and he will therefore not really get back to trying to solve his original problem. RET, because of its consistent anti-blaming aspect, is one of the few forms of psychotherapy that tackles the individual's secondary set of symptoms—that is, his blaming himself for blaming himself. This secondary irrationality is frequently worse than his original one, and infinitely complicates his disturbance.

T[195]: And this is why all guilt is irrational.

H[196]: Theologically now, with my strong religious upbringing, I (*laughing*) might have some things to say on that.

T[197]: Well, there's one other way that we use guilt, and that's in the legal sense of the word. Which means that you're responsible for having done the act, the wrong act. Now what I'm talking—the kind of guilt I'm talking about is that (a) you're responsible for having done the act; and then (b) you're a total louse, a worm for having done it. Now, by this definition, all guilt is irrational because you condemn yourself for your act.

H[198]: Yeah, I agree. This is a faulty concept.

T[199]: Right.

H[200]: Guilt. This type of guilt that, for one thing, condemns a whole man.

T[201]: And this is irresponsibility. This is immorality.

H[202]: Though—though I do feel that—man is a whole person, though. I mean, what his mind may do does affect his whole body. I mean he is—he is a unit. And what—and—and to separate one thing and say this is bad where the rest of him is good may be—I don't make that much of a difference. Maybe this is why I feel a complete guilt. That I feel that I'm a whole person: body, soul, spirit, and mind.

T²⁰³: Yes, well, you're going to have to make this difference. Because there is this difference in reality. Now an individual is an ongoing process. And he consists of a set of likes and a set of dislikes. And when you do a wrong act, this doesn't mean that you, a whole person, are a louse for having done that act.

H²⁰⁴: But that act, though, affects your whole person. This is what I'm getting at.

T²⁰⁵: It may affect you, but it doesn't mean that you are totally worthless.

H²⁰⁶: No, I agree with you there.

T²⁰⁷: And that's what you're—that's the trap I think you're falling into, which you always fall into. You equate your *worth as a person* with your *act*. You don't hold the opposite existentialistic view that you're a good person just because you're alive. Incidentally, you go against your own religious precepts, inasmuch as God reportedly said that to err is human and would better be forgiven.

H²⁰⁸: Yeah.

T²⁰⁹: And you're not forgiving yourself.

H²¹⁰: Yeah, I think it's one thing to say—like, to forgive myself and feel that I'm not a louse and so forth. It's one thing to say that. But when something has been programmed into you, then it's not easy. I mean, you can say that, but the reality is not there.

T²¹¹: Now I agree with you there. What I'm trying to get you to do is not *easy*. But it is harder not to do it than to do it. It's going to be difficult at first for you to stop and think when you begin to create this anxiety and guilt in you. You have to stop and say, "Now, wait a minute. *Why* would I be such a louse if this happened? Let's assume my wife really did get pregnant and died in childbirth. So, how does that make me a louse? It's just too bad. It's not *awful*."

H²¹²: Well, I have a better, a deeper feeling than it's just too bad. I think—I think I have a deeper feeling than that.

T²¹³: Yeah, that's your problem—you have *too* deep a feeling. And you have to come up to the level of reality, which is simply that it's only *too bad*. Beyond that it becomes technically what we call tautological. You are now defining it as lousy *beyond* reality, and therefore you make yourself *feel* bad. You see what I mean?

H²¹⁴: (*Nods affirmatively*)

T²¹⁵: And you're going to have to face the fact that it *would* be just too bad. It's not awful. Nothing in life that I know of could you really call awful, terrible, or equal to "I can't stand it—what a louse I'd be."

H²¹⁶: Yeah.

The therapist is trying to make clear—though it is difficult to get over this point to almost any human being—that nothing is truly awful in the universe since the term *awful* is meaningless or has surplus, magical meaning. To say that an event, such as one's killing one's wife by getting her pregnant and having her die in childbirth, is bad, unfortunate, disadvantageous, deplorable, or undesirable, is often true because this is an empirically-founded statement, which can be observably validated. Thus, the real misfortunes or disadvantages of killing one's wife—e.g., injury to her, loss of her companionship, the trouble of finding a new wife, difficulty of breaking the emotional bonds to her, and so on—can easily be found and delineated; and it would be quite odd if one held that it was good or advantageous to bring about her demise in this manner. But the awfulness, horror, or catastrophe of killing her could hardly ever be substantiated empirically. For the belief, "It is awful that I killed her!" not only includes the real disadvantages listed above but it also denotes the assumptions (*a*) "I can't stand the disadvantages of killing her"; (*b*) "I should not or must not have killed her"; (*c*) "I am thoroughly worthless as a human being for killing her"; (*d*) "I don't deserve to continue to live or to enjoy myself in any way whatever now that I have killed her"; and (*e*) "God or the universe will cruelly punish me, on this earth or in the hereafter, for having killed her." All these assumptions are magical, unprovable, or disprovable hypotheses; and although it is empirically observable that anyone who believes in these theological propositions will almost certainly create most miserable results—he will feel guilty and ashamed, will tend to feel worthless, will be severely depressed (perhaps for his entire lifetime), and may even deliberately punish or kill himself—the existence of these results is no proof whatever of the hypotheses. It is merely proof that when one believes in "awfulness," one feels awful and experiences unpleasant consequences additional to those indigenous to one's "awful" acts.

T²¹⁷: Incidentally, for you as a whole person to be worthless, you would have to say that all of your acts are worthless. Now you know that you have good acts and bad acts.

H²¹⁸: Yes, I—in fact—I mean—like, within each person I think there's this love and hate, belief and unbelief, and we're a composite type of individual—well, I can see that.

T²¹⁹: But incidentally, it's ironical because here you are; you keep focusing so much on the disadvantages of what might occur that you don't even realize that the probability, I would say, is statistically quite low that your wife would end up dying in childbirth.

H²²⁰: I realize that. I've read the statistics. I'm familiar with them.

T²²¹: And, then, the other reason why you need not get overconcerned about childbirth is that you know there are ways—most enjoyable, normal ways—of having sex relations without intercourse that you could engage in. Right?

H²²²: I guess so.

T²²³: So you see where focusing on this one aspect, intercourse, is really hanging you up now.

H²²⁴: Um-hm.

T²²⁵: It prevents you from looking at these other areas which you could try to enjoy. And this may also be another thing you want to try doing if you continue to have this sex difficulty. You might try caressing each other and giving each other satisfaction without intercourse. This might be an additional technique that you could use.

H²²⁶: Wouldn't that be—in the background, wouldn't there be—too, a negative, a repulsive factor here, too, against any woman? I mean—wouldn't this be a part of it? That, because of this—I mean no matter who it'd be, her or somebody else, there'd be a seething hatred or repulsive factor, too?

T²²⁷: Well, there very well could be if you—if you believe that (a) sex is dirty, and you make yourself repulsed in that respect. And then (b) you overgeneralize, thinking your mother is such a witch that in life you assume that every other woman is a witch also. You could develop resentment there. Now is that what you're suggesting that you're probably also doing?

H²²⁸: Yeah, maybe it's not only just the sex part, but maybe her as a woman. I mean, there might be this feeling here.

T²²⁹: Well, what would be repulsive?

H²³⁰: Just the mere fact of—that she's a woman, I guess. I mean, would there be an illegitimacy in this type of feeling?

T²³¹: But what would you say to yourself? "See, here's a woman," and why, what would you say to yourself to get this feeling of repulsion?

H²³²: Well, I thought maybe this might bring back some—just by her very presence near me, that this might bring back unpleasant memories and emotions and feelings.

T²³³: Yeah. And what are some of these unpleasant emotions or feelings?

H²³⁴: Well, I don't think—I mean April means any specific thing; but I think maybe just her very presence would—

T²³⁵: Yeah, but you would have to tell yourself something about her presence. You'd have to bring the past up now, in your own head.

H²³⁶: Yeah.

T²³⁷: And what kind of specific things do you say to yourself about bringing the past up here? How do you compare her to your mother?

H²³⁸: I don't know if I can answer that right now.

T²³⁹: Well, what was it about your mother that you disliked?

H²⁴⁰: —domineering—unforgiving. And, of course, being ill contributed toward this.

T²⁴¹: All right. Now, do you feel that way about having a relationship with your wife *now*? "Well, my own mother was domineering, so if I start to show my feeling, show any form of affection with my wife, maybe she'll lord it over me, maybe she'll become domineering to me. Maybe she won't forgive me, especially if I fail to maintain an erection. Maybe she'll really condemn me for that. And wouldn't that be *awful!*"

H²⁴²: I mean—as I say—some of these feelings here. I mean April has—we've always assured each other that we would be forgiving. She's no comparison to my mother.

W²⁴³: Although I do think I might have contributed to some of this, because when we were first married, I had a natural fear of this. I mean I had never had any experience either, so I didn't know what to expect. Maybe—maybe in a way I pulled away from him or something. And then, with these feelings that he already had, I might have repulsed him myself. I don't know. But I couldn't say that he's all to blame. I probably contributed to it, too.

T²⁴⁴: Well, yeah, there's probably some contribution that you've made here, but his problem is largely in his *head*. It's not *you*!

W²⁴⁵: I don't know.

T²⁴⁶: Well, he's—what I'm suggesting here is that he's the cause of his own problem. He has had past serious influences that have helped him to think and feel and lead his life this way. But he's still the cause, for now when he gets repulsed by you, it's what's going on up here (*pointing to his head*) that's repulsing him, not you intrinsically. No human being could emotionally hurt or harm or cause another individual to be upset. This we do ourselves by what we tell ourselves about another person's acts. A famous philosopher, Epictetus, said this over two thousand years ago. "It's not things or events that upset people but their *view* of these things." And in our A-B-C formulation A is something that happens to you, a fact, something in reality. Let's take it on his level—his sexual inadequacy. "I'm not able to maintain an erection." And then at point C he's feeling anxious, guilty, upset. And it's not A that's the cause of C but B: what he *tells himself* about A, his failure. At point B he tells himself, as we all do, two things: one sane and one insane. The sane sentence is: "I don't like it because I failed at A. Or, "I don't like it because my wife isn't sexy to me right now." And the second sentence at point B is: "And because I don't like it, it's *awful*. It's terrible. It shouldn't be this way. What a louse I am for having failed." That is what creates your emotion at C. Are you with me?

H²⁴⁷: Um-hm.

T²⁴⁸: In other words, you feel the way you think. Now, you could *influence* him to be repulsed by—

W²⁴⁹: That's what I mean. I might do this.

T²⁵⁰: Now, that's what you're talking about. But I didn't want you to feel that you were the *cause* of his emotion.

W²⁵¹: I used to think so.

T²⁵²: Well, most everybody thinks so unfortunately.

Mr. Gullo rightly points out that the wife might have some influence over her husband and could help him to believe that he was a blackguard for getting her pregnant or for failing her sexually, but that this would not truly be the cause of the husband's sex problem, since he could only really create his own catastrophizing philosophy in his own head. Technically, even the influence of others is quite unimportant unless the individual actively agrees with this influence and makes it his own view. This is what the rational-emotive therapist frequently demonstrates: that no matter how "influencing" a child's parents were, he had to be suggestible to their words, gestures, and attitudes. Perhaps more importantly, he later had to keep reindoctrinating himself with the nonsense that they tried to get him to believe. Consequently, psychoanalytic and behavior conditioning theories, which emphasize the "influence" of the individual's past on his present life, fail to stress his active agreement with these prior "influences," neglect to show him how he is still actively going along with these "pulls," and hence provide him with a foolish rationalization for his contemporary disturbances. The true "causes" of the individual's irrationalities are (a) his original gullibility when he was younger and (b) his retained gullibility and self-instruction today. Outside "influences" certainly exist and are relevant; but they can easily be, and by the disturbed individual (and the inefficient therapist!) usually are, enormously overstressed.

W²⁵³: And that made me more miserable than the fact that we weren't having intercourse. Feeling that I—that there was a lack in me or something—that he had no desire for me.

T²⁵⁴: Yeah. Now he's doing just the reverse. He thinks that he would be the cause of your death, which in a way he would be, though not to the degree to which he thinks he would be. But the most important thing is that you're really condemning yourself, as far as I can tell. For (a) your failure to satisfy her, and (b) because you feel that—how to state this?—well, because you would feel that you would be responsible for some awful, awful, dire catastrophe that would happen; that if something is fearsome or dangerous, you should completely refrain from it. You see? (*Pause*) Now it is hard to get over this; you do have to stop and think. There's just no other way of getting over it. And then you have to put into action this kind of insight. Insight is not enough. 'Cause you know all these years that it just doesn't do that much good.

H[255]: It's very easy to have other things, I mean involve yourself or busy yourself in other things; you forget about the particular problem.

T[256]: Right.

H[257]: And we have done that. We have talked it over between ourselves and discussed it and said, "Well, maybe the time will come when we're not so busy." But the thing is, you continually involve yourself.

T[258]: Yeah. You rationalize.

W[259]: Well, there are times we've even asked each other, "Do we really want to have a family or do we enjoy our freedom?" Maybe this is why we don't try to do anything. Maybe we're just having such a good time that we don't want to have anything to spoil it.

T[260]: Yeah. Well, I think that that is a cop-out, too. I think basically the problem is one of a lot of guilt involved and sexual puritanism and fear of failure. And that's the real cause. And then, in order to not see that, you keep thinking all these other specious reasons for why you might not be making it with each other. Because incidentally you could start taking birth control pills and not have a family and have a ball sexually. This may be the other hang-up that you have also. That sex is only for procreation. Now is that—were you taught that also?

H[261]: No—I don't know if I was exactly taught that or not, but I disagree on that viewpoint. I think—sex should be for fun.

T[262]: Okay, good, we have no problem there; and—I agree right down the line on that. I don't agree with the Roman Catholic position at all on that. You might be a Roman Catholic; I don't know. I was a Roman Catholic.

H[263]: That's the position that I—that we came out of religiously— we came out of a very fundamental, straight background.

'Course we're not that now. And it has a very sick view of sex.

T[264]: Yeah, you're not that way now in theory, but you're still carrying around with you, in the back of your head, *old-time religion*. That's really what's—

H[265]: Yeah, that's right.

W[266]: Yeah, um-hm.

T[267]: —still with you. And we have to get you over that.

The therapist suspects that the clients' fundamentalist religious views may have had something to do with their sexual inhibitions and evasions; and although they are presumably not as rigid in that area as they previously were, he thinks that they well may have remnants of the old-time religion. In RET, the therapist often explores whether the client's present irrational ideas spring from his early-imbibed religious orthodoxies; if so, these orthodoxies are questioned. Usually, as in the present instance, the client is able to retain moderate religious views but is induced to challenge his extreme dogmas that interfere with his sexual and his nonsexual functioning.

Mr. Gullo, in the conclusion of this session (which, because of space limitations, is not included in this chapter), tries to show the clients, and especially the husband, that they are trying to be too perfectionistically good, and that it would be better if each of them were a little more self-interested rather than overly altruistic. He also emphasizes the husband's looking at his self-defeating beliefs about sexual failure and his disputing these beliefs: "It is pure drivel that it's terrible if sex failure occurs. So it does. You can tell yourself, 'What enormous difference does it make if I fail? If I fail, I fail. Let me see what I can do to be less failing next time.' Or, 'Isn't it interesting? Here I'm failing again. Now, let me see what I can do to succeed a little better in this sex relationship with my wife the next time.' So if you focus on trying to enjoy yourself with her, instead of focusing on how horrible it is if you fail, then your chances of success become pretty good."

The therapist ends this first session by giving the couple the homework assignment of trying to have sex relations with each other every day that week, and of challenging their catastrophizing when they have these relations. He also assigns them three books to read: *Sex Without Guilt* (Ellis, 1970), *A Guide to Rational Living* (Ellis and Harper, 1970), and *The Art and Science of Love* (Ellis, 1969b). Usually, the second of these books is regularly assigned after the first session of RET; but in cases involving puritanical sex blocks or sexual inadequacy, the other two books are also frequently assigned.

During the next three sessions, which occurred at intervals of about two weeks, the clients made slow but steady progress. They kept trying to have sex relations, at first with minimal results since the husband was rarely able to keep or maintain an erection; and on those few occasions when he was able to do so, the wife complained about being uncomfortable in the sexual positions that they were mainly using. During the fifth session, the husband reported that they both tired easily during sex relations, and he was unable to have an orgasm. Mr. Gullo probed for the details of the positions they were using, and discovered that the wife mainly rested on her back with her legs straight up in the air, and that they both found that inconvenient, and she found it particularly tiring. He recommended that she try holding her legs back to her chest, or that her husband hold them up with his arms or shoulders. This advice seemed to help them considerably.

When the couple were lax about working on their sex problem together, the therapist induced them to make a list of the advantages of their doing so and the disadvantages, especially to their relationship, of their not doing so. They made these lists and kept reading them to each other. In fact, using one of the behavior therapy methods that are employed in RET, they were instructed not to allow themselves to have any meals until they first read these lists to each other. This forced them to remind themselves of their purposes and their therapeutic goals at least three times a day. The therapist also induced them to make a chart of their attempts at intercourse, so they could have, day by day, a visible record of how seriously they were trying to overcome their problem.

During these sessions, Mr. Gullo kept alternating between discussing practical techniques of sex relations and showing the husband and wife what irrational ideas they were telling themselves to stop themselves from making a sufficient number of attempts, and then checking to see whether they were actively and persistently disputing these irrational ideas.

The sixth session occurred about three months after the first one.

SIXTH SESSION

T[1]: Well, how have things been going?

H[2]: Well, we think we've got our problem solved now! (*Laughs*)

T³: Well, good! Good!

W⁴: We're doing real good.

H⁵: Yeah. We really are. And—we think we're on our way. (*Laughs*)

T⁶: You've had intercourse how many times successfully, then? Approximately?

H⁷: Well, we don't know how many times, but as much as we can.

T⁸: Yeah.

H⁹: And—there's been a few days we haven't because of just long hours and things like that.

T¹⁰: Just couldn't get to it?

H¹¹: Conflicts in schedule and stuff. But—it's as regular as we can make it.

W¹²: Um-hm. We don't have the same feelings about it we did—

H¹³: Yeah.

W¹⁴: —you know. We look forward to it now, whereas it was a real problem before.

T¹⁵: Um-hm.

H¹⁶: And so it's—it seems to be all right.

T¹⁷: You have an orgasm when you're having intercourse?

H¹⁸: (*Nods head yes*)

T¹⁹: You do?

H²⁰: Right.

T²¹: Good, good! And you're satisfied also?

W²²: Um-hm.

T²³: Better, better!! (*Laughs*)

H²⁴: (*Laughs*)

W²⁵: (*Laughs*) Most of the time. Now last time—we both realized that we were kind of rushing things, I think, last time. I didn't enjoy it too much, but it was all right.

T²⁶: Um—

W²⁷: We know that we should spend a little more time, you know. But we just didn't that time.

T²⁸: Um-hm. Are you getting tired?

W²⁹: No. (*Laughs*)

H³⁰: (*Laughs*)

W³¹: I guess I'm—

H³²: She's holding up pretty well now.

W[33]:   —doing all right. I thought maybe it was just—

T[34]:   Practice?

W[35]:   —tensions or—yeah, lot of practice—

T[36]:   And tenseness?

W[37]:   Um-hm. Now it doesn't bother me at all.

T[38]:   Have you tried some different positions to—

W[39]:   Yeah.

T[40]:   —see how that affects you?

W[41]:   Um-hm. They probably have been as successful as the original one we still stick to.

T[42]:   Um-hm.

W[43]:   But—

T[44]:   Well, probably—

W[45]:   —people develop better ways after a while.

T[46]:   Right. That's just what I was going to say.

W[47]:   Yeah. I think we're doing real good.

T[48]:   That's good! I'm very glad to hear that.

In various responses, such as T[3], T[21], T[23], and T[48], Mr. Gullo not only acknowledges the clients' progress, but shows his pleasure and approval at their new behavior. This, of course, is a technique of reinforcement and constitutes one of the ways in which rational-emotive therapy is a form of behavior therapy. Even nondirective treatment, as has been shown in several experimental studies, is reinforcing when the therapist says "um-hm" to the client's improved behavior and ignores or questions his disturbed behavior. In RET, there is an honest, full-fledged attempt to reinforce changes that are helpful to the client.

H[49]:   We're waiting for a family now. (*Laughs*)

W[50]:   (*Laughs*)

T[51]:   (*Laughs*) Do you have any problems with fertility or anything like that?

H[52]:   Yeah, I've been—see, when we started out on this thing, we went to the family planning thing over here.

T[53]:   Um-hm.

H[54]:   Well, see, one of the things we wanted was to adopt a child. And one of the things was to get a fertility test. And I went

to the doctor, and he gave me this test and said that I was—
that I had about one chance out of seven of impregnating
my wife if we had intercourse regularly. And so he gave me
this prescription for pills, which I've been taking ever since.
Two pills twice a day. In fact, I should make another appointment with him. Supposed to go in about three months, and
then he's going to take another test.

T⁵⁵: And the medication is to increase your fertility?

H⁵⁶: Yeah.

T⁵⁷: And how about you?

W⁵⁸: Well—we decided there wasn't any reason to test me further
until he got up to what he should be—

H⁵⁹: Any time I make an appointment now we'll recheck on this.
If I can take it—take his [the doctor's] attitude.

W⁶⁰: Well, you can stand that!

H⁶¹: (*Laughs*)

As shown in the wife's response, W⁶⁰, and in her husband's good-
natured laugh after this response, there is an indication that they
have not merely learned some new sexual techniques but have also
been working at changing their basic attitudes toward frustrations
and disappointments. Previously, they had received what they considered to be real attention and poor treatment from the physicians
and therapists they had seen, and they were clearly resentful of
this kind of treatment. Now they seem to realize that they can stand
being treated cavalierly or ineffectively and that other people's attitudes do not have to affect them too seriously. It may well be this
very change in their thinking, with a consequent rise in their level
of tolerance for frustration, that has enabled them during the period
of therapy to persist at overcoming their sex difficulties. Previously,
they have always given up on attempts at intercourse, soon after
disappointing results were obtained; but this time, in spite of initial
problems, they persisted until they succeeded. As I have noted in
a paper on the nature of disturbed marital interaction (Ellis, 1966),
whatever the original causes of a husband's or a wife's emotional
upsets are, the main thing that keeps perpetuating these upsets
is his or her unwillingness to work at changing the disturbed feelings
and behavior. This time, both partners seem to have combated their
ideas that persistence at troublesome adjustments to each other is
too hard and that they shouldn't have to work at sex relations that

are "supposed to" occur spontaneously; and they have consequently (at long last!) reached a point where they semi-automatically are enjoying intercourse.

T⁶²: Well, what's his attitude like?

H⁶³: Oh, I don't know. He's just typical—just rush in, rush out, you know. Take a pill. We've had this runaround before, and so I think it sort of disgusted me a little bit.

T⁶⁴: Well—

W⁶⁵: I think you'll feel differently when you go back this time.

H⁶⁶: But he sure wasn't interested in my problem. You know.

T⁶⁷: Maybe because he knows he doesn't know what to do about it. (*Laughs*) Except, you know, medically speaking.

H⁶⁸: Well, yeah, medically. I mean—you—well, that's fine. But—

T⁶⁹: You mean, he didn't even seem to be interested in it medically?

H⁷⁰: Yeah, he did medically, and I say he wrote out a prescription for the pills and told me to come back in three months.

T⁷¹: Um-hm.

W⁷²: But he didn't give you any solutions for what to do in the meantime.

H⁷³: No.

W⁷⁴: Well, my doctor didn't either! They don't know what to tell you!

T⁷⁵: That's right, they don't. (*Laughs*) That's why we're in the business.

W⁷⁶: And if it hadn't been for the agency who recommended us to you, we'd still be getting the same runaround. No matter how many pills it took, it wouldn't help us any!

T⁷⁷: Yeah.

W⁷⁸: So we'll just have to be patient now and find out what happens.

T⁷⁹: Well, I guess you've solved your problem then. Is there anything—?

W⁸⁰: You've come real close to it! (*Laughs*)

H⁸¹: Um-hm, yeah. Just—

W⁸²: Yeah, we really have.

H⁸³: —wanted to say we're very happy about it! (*Laughs*)

W⁸⁴: Yeah.

T⁸⁵: So am I!

H[86]: (*Laughs*)

W[87]: Yes. It really—really, it's a small miracle. It really is.

H[88]: You thought you had a loser on your hands, didn't you? (*Laughs*)

T[89]: No, I didn't. No, not really. But I'm just happy that it got solved this quickly.

H[90]: Well—well, we wanted to and—we felt we had some real obstacles. And—we worked it out. Whether it's too late, I don't know.

W[91]: (*Laughs*)

T[92]: No, it's not at all too late. At any rate even if you weren't able to get her pregnant, at least you'd have the happiness and satisfaction and pleasure of having sex together.

W[93]: Um-hm.

T[94]: Plus the closeness that usually goes with it.

W[95]: Well, that was a good thing.

H[96]: Yeah.

W[97]: But that—that doesn't completely satisfy us, because that wasn't our original intent.

T[98]: No, 'cause you wanted to have the children, along with it.

W[99]: Yeah.

T[100]: Yeah.

H[101]: 'Course if we find that we're still unable to have children, I think we can still go through an adoption agency. We could.

T[102]: Um-hm.

H[103]: 'Course we want to try ourselves.

T[104]: Oh, yeah; I would, too.

W[105]: Yeah.

H[106]: Yeah.

T[107]: You might also investigate the possibility of going on birth control pills for one month because they make it easy to get pregnant once you stop taking them.

W[108]: Probably should try that.

H[109]: (*Laughs*)

W[110]: (*Laughs*) I'll try anything. Well, we have really—this last period, you know, of trying—we have really been elated at our success, you know. And—it's been a wonderful experience for us.

T[111]: It's like courtship all over again.

W[112]: (*Laughs*) Yeah!

H[113]: (*Laughs*)

W[114]: Well, it's like being married! (*Laughs*)

H[115]: (*Laughs*)

W[116]: We spent all this time all these years with not really knowing what it's all about. It's real good experience.

H[117]: Which seems silly, you know, but it happened.

W[118]: When you look back on it. But, you know, we never really found anyone that would help us.

T[119]: Um-hm.

W[120]: And we, maybe that's why we have progressed. I don't know if we've made good progress, but at least I think we have. And I think the reason we have is because this is the first time we've ever found an answer that we could work on. And we both have really tried. And I think we will continue to, now that we have the answer.

T[121]: I'm sure you will. Because you've reached a point where there's no—no returning to that old pattern of abstinence.

W[122]: Um-hm.

T[123]: From now on it's going to be an enjoyable thing and will increase as time permits.

H[124]: Well, we don't have those fears—which has been a radical change, you know. And—I think this was—this was the initial thing that kept us back at the beginning—certain fears. Now we just don't think about them.

W[125]: No.

According to the testimony of the clients, especially as shown in W[120], they were most helped because for the first time, after years of trying various forms of treatment, they "found an answer that we could work on." This is precisely the goal of RET: to give the individual something very specific and concrete that he can work on. First, he is shown exactly what he is convincing himself to make himself upset. Second, he learns how to verbally and theoretically dispute or challenge his own false beliefs. Third, he is given clear-cut activity homework assignments to help break up his old patterns of crooked thinking and self-defeating activities. Fourth, he is some-times provided with alternative ways of behaving and tested tech-niques of improving his performances (sexual or nonsexual). All these new teachings—and they are exactly that—can be fairly easily understood by almost any reasonable, intelligent individual and can be tested in practice. As White, Fichtenbaum, and Dollard (1969) have shown, there is "some measured evidence that what a patient learns to think and say during therapy is related to changes in his behavior. An association was found between verbal learning of messages and behavior relevant to these messages. Learning of therapeutic messages was found to be related to improvement in overall mental health. Thus the findings seem to support the value of explicit goals and message teaching in short-term treatment [p. 293]." Although their study of learning in therapy was done in a Freudian psychoanalytic setting, it beautifully epitomizes the constant clinical findings that are made during the practice of rational-emotive therapy.

T[126]: Well, I don't know what else I can do for you, or get you to do for yourself.

W[127]: Well, you know, we were talking it over whether we should come back anymore. And we thought maybe we probably should—maybe one more check, maybe at a month or two, you know.

T[128]: Okay.

H[129]: 'Cause I want to check with the doctor again to see if my fertility has improved any. Don't you think it'd be wise, maybe one more?

T[130]: Yeah, I think so. A month—would you like to come back in a month, then, or would you like it a little longer?

H[131]: Well, maybe. Let's see, check my date calendar. (*Laughs*) What about the twenty-ninth of next month? That's a little more than a month.

T[132]: Yeah, that's fine.

H[133]: Do you think it should be that soon? Or should it be in the following month?

T[134]: Oh, I think probably that would be a good time.

W[135]: The end of next month then?

T[136]: Um-hm.

H[137]: Okay. Thanks for the real tremendous help you've given us.

W[138]: Yes. If it weren't for you, we would never have gotten it solved.

T[139]: You have only yourselves to thank, since you had to do the
         work. Good luck to you.
H[140]: Thank you very much!
W[141]: Yes, thank you very much!

Following their last session, the husband and wife continued to
have even more frequent and increasingly satisfying sex relations.
Several months later, the wife became pregnant, and they were both
elated. They talked to John Gullo on the phone and profusely thanked
him again for his help. After the birth of their first child, they
kept having successful and highly pleasurable sex activities, including intercourse, about two to three times a week. They still have
other difficulties in their relationship but consider them minor and
do not feel in need of any further psychological aid at the present
time (over two years after the completion of therapy).

CHAPTER 7

A Relapsed Client with Severe Phobic Reactions

MAXIE C. MAULTSBY, JR., M.D.

The client is a twenty-four-year-old married undergraduate student who was hospitalized for a psychotic episode and who later had thirty sessions of traditional psychotherapy, which, he claimed, were not very helpful. Before hospitalization he had the delusion that he had a guardian angel who protected him from all harm and would prevent him from getting hurt even if he jumped in front of speeding trucks—which he thought was an exciting and (because of his magical "protection") harmless habit. However, he was finally struck by a truck, received a severe concussion, and developed an extreme fear of noises, which he thought would result in his having another concussion. He also had, when first seen for rational-emotive therapy, severe feelings of anxiety and inferiority, suicidal thoughts, difficulty sleeping, poor study habits, and pronounced feelings of guilt and depression.

After fifty sessions of group RET, the client reported significant improvement in most of his problems, especially his phobic reactions and his sleeping difficulties. But a year later he reported that his gains were being whittled away, that he was becoming terribly afraid of another concussion and a consequent major loss of his intelligence; that he was afraid of cops, rock throwers, rioters, and fires that might lead to an accident that would result in his having a concussion; that he again felt very stupid in his school work; and that he tended to blame many of his personal failings on his original accident. He therefore wanted to return to therapy.

FIRST SESSION

T[1]: Give me an idea of how you are experiencing life now. What's going on in relation to the things that originally caused you to come to therapy two years ago.

C²: Well, speaking sort of from an overview of my life, I feel that I am a lot more rational than I was when I first began seeing you. I am much happier than when I first began seeing you.

T³: Let's see, when was the last time I saw you?

C⁴: When you ended the group, a year and a half ago.

T⁵: Okay. So it's been over a year, hm? What's it been like? I mean what have you been doing, etc.?

C⁶: Well, when therapy ended, my wife and I took a long, very pleasant summer vacation. It was really wonderful. But when I got back into school, I felt I began to slip.

T⁷: Slip? Slip how?

C⁸: Slip back into some of the old patterns, but not to the same depth. I mean I was still able to handle my problems, because most of them were essentially the same old shit.

T⁹: Yes, you mean the problems were the same as those that originally caused you to come to RET.

C¹⁰: Yes, I felt I was slipping more and more; it was like I didn't have enough RET inside me to make the transaction without you.

T¹¹: Why do you say that? What do you use as evidence?

C¹²: Well, I am assuming that if I had had enough RET, I would not have slipped back.

T¹³: Well, let me see; how many sessions did you have?

C¹⁴: About a year, over a year.

T¹⁵: But they weren't all individual, were they?

C¹⁶: No, only two of them were individual, and they were in the first month. I really enjoyed the group. The way I felt at that time, I felt that the group was more beneficial for me than individual therapy.

T¹⁷: Let's see, you had eleven months of once-a-week group RET making a total of about forty-five group sessions in the course of a year. Okay, now what have you been doing on your own since then?

C¹⁸: You mean therapy? I did homework for four or five months after therapy.

T¹⁹: Why did you stop doing it?

C²⁰: I didn't just stop, you know. Slowly and slowly you do less and less.

T²¹: Why?

C²²: I don't know.

T²³: During the time you were doing less and less, were you having fewer and fewer problems?

C²⁴: Well, yes, that has something to do with it; and also it was during the summer, you know, the first escape. We traveled all summer, and we camped a lot of the time. I wasn't in the position to do homeworks; I didn't have paper, I didn't have pencils, I didn't have light. When school started, I tried to pick it up again.

T²⁵: For how long did you try?

C²⁶: I don't know. It was almost like I would forget about it; I would concentrate on the problem, you know, and just not recall that the way to deal with it was to do homework.

T²⁷: In other words, you would be confronted with an emotional conflict, and you would get so caught up in it, you wouldn't think about rational thinking and rationally handling the situation. Right?

C²⁸: Well, I would think of rationally handling it—I mean I would say some of the phrases, but it didn't occur to me to sit down and do a written homework. Sometimes I would think, "Do homework on this." And then I would say, "First see if you are advanced far enough in RET to handle it inside"; but then for some reason I just wouldn't get around to doing the written homework. I remember just before therapy ended, I was beginning to be able to internalize the whole process.

T²⁹: What you mean by that is, when you were confronted with a stressful situation, you would immediately start thinking about the situation using rational concepts as opposed to your pre-therapy way of thinking. The concept of *internalization* is foreign to, and therefore meaningless in, RET theory. We usually say that your rational thinking had become so well learned that it is situationally or cue-controlled, like a reflex response; or rational thinking was becoming your preferred way of thinking about your whole life.

C³⁰: Yes, it was becoming—what you call "thought shorthand."

T³¹: Yes, the rational view of life was then eliciting reflex-like rational responses in you to the same environmental cues to which you formerly had reflex-like irrational responses. That's what thought shorthand means. It's the end product of having thoroughly learned something, be it a habit of thought or a habit of physical action. And written homework, being a reasoned analysis of emotional conflicts, makes the process of replacing irrational thinking with rational thinking more efficient.

C³²: It also makes it necessary.

T³³: What?

C³⁴: Doing homework. The great advantage of homework is that you have to do it.

T³⁵: You mean homework forces you to think rationally?

C³⁶: Yeah, that's right.

The sessions with this client particularly illustrate the great extent to which homework assignments and homework reports are used in RET. Desensitization is an important part of behavior therapy (Wolpe, 1958; Wolpe and Lazarus, 1966) and consists largely of presenting an individual who has a phobia with a repetitious image of or actual contact with the thing or event of which he is afraid, so that he becomes gradually acclimated to it and therefore presumably unafraid of it. In its classic form, contact or in vivo desensitization was employed by Mary Cover Jones (1924), who conditioned a young child who was afraid of a rabbit to be unafraid by gradually putting a live rabbit closer and closer to him while he was engaged in a pleasant occupation, eating. Alexander Herzberg (1945), originally a Freudian analyst, adapted this method for use with psychotherapy clients by giving them activity homework assignments to do in between therapy sessions, so that they would desensitize themselves to stimuli that they considered extremely fear-provoking.

When I first was experimenting with changing clients' basic attitudes by rational-emotive methods, I realized that such change was much more likely to be effective if I gave them outside homework assignments, which consisted of (1) the doing of presumably "dangerous" tasks, such as dating members of the other sex, taking automobile or airplane rides, or going on job interviews; and (2) active self-depropagandization, often with the use of paper and pencil, in regard to the irrational ideas they had about doing "dangerous" things (or about their obsessions, compulsions, withdrawal, inertia, and other disturbed symptoms). Sparked by the work of some of my associates in this respect, especially Dr. H. Jon Geis and Dr. Maxie C. Maultsby, Jr., I developed a regular Homework Report which has been experimentally used at the Institute for Advanced Study in Rational Psychotherapy in New York City for the past few years. The latest revision of this form is reprinted in Figures 1 and 2. It has several important sections:

HOMEWORK REPORT

Consultation Center

Institute for Advanced Study in Rational Psychotherapy

45 East 65th Street, New York, N.Y. 10021 / (212) LEhigh 5-0822

Name .... Date .... Therapist ....

Instructions: Please draw a circle around the number in front of those feelings listed in the first column that troubled you *most* during the period since your last therapy session. Then, in the *second* column, indicate the amount of work you did on each circled item; and, in the *third* column, the results of the work you did.

		Amount of Work Done				Results of Work		
		Much	Some	Little or none		Good	Fair	Poor
Undesirable Emotional Feelings								
1a	Anger or great irritability	1b	....	....	1c	....	....	
2a	Anxiety, severe worry, or fear	2b	....	....	2c	....	....	
3a	Boredom or dullness	3b	....	....	3c	....	....	
4a	Failure to achieve	4b	....	....	4c	....	....	
5a	Frustration	5b	....	....	5c	....	....	
6a	Guilt or self-condemnation	6b	....	....	6c	....	....	
7a	Hopelessness or depression	7b	....	....	7c	....	....	
8a	Great loneliness	8b	....	....	8c	....	....	
9a	Helplessness	9b	....	....	9c	....	....	
10a	Self-pity	10b	....	....	10c	....	....	
11a	Uncontrollability	11b	....	....	11c	....	....	
12a	Worthlessness or inferiority	12b	....	....	12c	....	....	
13a	Other (specify)	13b	....	....	13c	....	....	
	....	....	....	....	....	....	....	
Undesirable Actions or Habits								
14a	Avoiding responsibility	14b	....	....	14c	....	....	
15a	Acting unfairly to others	15b	....	....	15c	....	....	
16a	Being late to appointments	16b	....	....	16c	....	....	
17a	Being undisciplined	17b	....	....	17c	....	....	
18a	Demanding attention	18b	....	....	18c	....	....	
19a	Physically attacking others	19b	....	....	19c	....	....	
20a	Putting off important things	20b	....	....	20c	....	....	
21a	Telling people off harshly	21b	....	....	21c	....	....	
22a	Whining or crying	22b	....	....	22c	....	....	
23a	Withdrawing from activity	23b	....	....	23c	....	....	
24a	Overdrinking of alcohol	24b	....	....	24c	....	....	
25a	Overeating	25b	....	....	25c	....	....	
26a	Oversleeping	26b	....	....	26c	....	....	
27a	Undersleeping	27b	....	....	27c	....	....	
28a	Oversmoking	28b	....	....	28c	....	....	
29a	Taking too many drugs or pills	29b	....	....	29c	....	....	
30a	Other (specify)	30b	....	....	30c	....	....	
	....	....	....	....	....	....	....	
Irrational Ideas or Philosophies								
31a	People must love or approve of me	31b	....	....	31c	....	....	
32a	Making mistakes is terrible	32b	....	....	32c	....	....	
33a	People should be condemned for their wrongdoings	33b	....	....	33c	....	....	
34a	It's terrible when things go wrong	34b	....	....	34c	....	....	
35a	My emotions can't be controlled	35b	....	....	35c	....	....	
36a	Threatening situations have to keep me terribly worried	36b	....	....	36c	....	....	
37a	Self-discipline is too hard to achieve	37b	....	....	37c	....	....	
38a	Bad effects of my childhood still have to control my life	38b	....	....	38c	....	....	
39a	I can't stand the way certain people act	39b	....	....	39c	....	....	
40a	Other (specify)	40b	....	....	40c	....	....	
	....	....	....	....	....	....	....	

(please complete other side)

Figure 1. Page one of Homework Report

1. On page one, the client indicates how he has been feeling, acting, and thinking since the last therapy session, as well as how much work he has done to change his undesirable emotional feelings, his undesirable actions or habits, and his irrational ideas or philosophies. He thereby indicates, to himself and to his therapist (to whom he

---

PLEASE PRINT! BE BRIEF AND LEGIBLE! ANSWER QUESTION C FIRST; THEN ANSWER THE OTHER QUESTIONS

A. ACTIVATING EVENT you recently experienced about which you became upset or disturbed. (Examples: *"I went for job interview." "My mate screamed at me."*) ....

rB. Rational BELIEF or idea you had about this Activating Event. (Examples: *"It would be unfortunate if I were rejected for the job." "How annoying to have my mate scream at me!"*) ....

iB. Irrational BELIEF or idea you had about this Activating Event. (Examples: *"It would be catastrophic if I were rejected for the job; I would be pretty worthless as a person." "I can't stand my mate's screaming; she is horrible for screaming at me!"*) ....

C. CONSEQUENCES of your irrational BELIEF (iB) about the Activating Event listed in Question A. State here the one most disturbing emotion, behavior, or CONSEQUENCE you experienced recently. (Examples: *"I was anxious." "I was hostile." "I had stomach pains."*) ....

D. DISPUTING, questioning, or challenging you can use to change your irrational BELIEF (iB). (Examples: *"Why would it be catastrophic and how would I become a worthless person if I were rejected for the job?" "Why can't I stand my mate screaming and why is she horrible for screaming at me?"*) ....

cE. Cognitive EFFECT or answer you obtained from DISPUTING your irrational BELIEF (iB). Examples: *"It would not be catastrophic, but merely unfortunate, if I were rejected for the job; my giving a poor interview would not make me a worthless person." "Although I'll never like my mate's screaming, I can stand it; he or she is not horrible but merely a fallible person for screaming."*) ....

bE. Behavioral EFFECT or result of your DISPUTING your irrational BELIEF (iB). (Examples: *"I felt less anxious." "I felt less hostile to my mate." "My stomach pains vanished."*) ....

F. If you did not challenge your irrational BELIEF (iB), why did you not? ....

G. Activities you would most like to *stop* that you are now doing ....

H. Activities you would most like to *start* that you are not doing ....

I. Emotions and ideas you would most like to change ....

J. Specific homework assignment(s) given you by your therapist, your group, or yourself ....

K. What did you actually do to carry out the assignment(s)? ....

L. Check the item which describes how much you have worked at your last homework assignment(s): ....(a) almost every day .... (b) several times a week .... (c) occasionally .... (d) hardly ever.

M. How many times in the past week have you specifically worked at changing and DISPUTING your irrational BELIEFS (iBs)? ....

N. What other things have you specifically done to change your irrational BELIEFS and your disturbed emotional CONSEQUENCES? ....

O. Check the item which describes how much reading you have recently done of the material on rational-emotive therapy .... (a) a considerable amount .... (b) a moderate amount .... (c) little or none.

P. Things you would now like to discuss most with your therapist or group ....

Figure 2. Page two of Homework Report

gives this report just before each session), exactly where he is now and how much work he is doing to help himself improve. The material on page one also gives, if collected and reviewed after a series of these reports have been handed in, a consistent set of progress (or lack of progress!) notes on the client.

2. On page two, questions A to E give a brief outline of the theory and practice of RET and force the client, if he regularly fills out the answers, to see his disturbances in the light of RET constructs and to learn how to apply these constructs to himself. When he comes in, at the beginning of an individual or group session of RET, the therapist frequently reads aloud his answers to questions A to E and "marks" them, as homework assignments are often marked in an educational setting, in the sense of showing the client whether or not he has filled out the blanks correctly. The therapist particularly examines the section of the form where the client has filled in the rational and the irrational beliefs to make sure that the client has filled them in properly and is able clearly to distinguish between these two kinds of ideas. It is almost incredible how many exceptionally bright and well-educated individuals are not able, at first, to make a clear-cut distinction between their rational and irrational beliefs, and are able to do so only after the therapist has corrected their homework assignments several times.

3. Questions F to P on the Homework Report indicate how much the client has worked at disputing his main irrational belief in the interim from the previous therapy session to the present one; what specific homework assignment he was given and how he worked at completing it; the activities and emotions he would most like to change; and various other revelant information. All or some of these questions are reviewed by the therapist, and the client is shown how to continue to do or to improve his homework in the future and is impressed with the value of homework thinking and activity.

Dr. Maultsby, in working with the client in the present case, uses his own homework report, which is fairly similar to the one printed in these pages; and he goes over these "homeworks" during the session, usually by having the client read what he has written on them in between the sessions and then discussing his homework statements with him. As will be noted in these sessions, he makes the "homeworks" a very important part of the therapeutic process. Other rational-emotive therapists may not stress this part of RET as much as he does, but they usually give it a prominent place in their sessions with clients.

T^{37}: Well, tell me, when you stopped therapy, what did you think about stopping? Did you feel fairly confident that you would be able to go on by yourself, or did you have reservations, or what?

C^{38}: By the time the therapy stopped, I was beginning to feel very, very elated with the therapy; I was beginning to finally see some basic, substantial changes in my way of thinking; and I felt very rationally that "Wow! I can handle anything now! Like this is great!" I became quite obnoxious about it, according to my wife and some of my better friends; you know, whenever anyone would have a problem, I would give them what I conceived was the rational response, and a lot of people got sick of me opening my mouth up on their problems with RET all of the time. But, I didn't care. I didn't care what they thought about me. And I really felt good. But then the therapy ended, and I wasn't fully prepared for it, and I felt like—you know—well, "I don't want this to be over, but maybe I can do it myself anyway." I now feel like if I could have had another couple of months, it might have been sufficient—I don't know. Maybe it was just a question of time—I don't know.

T^{39}: What you are describing happens with about a fourth of my patients—they get to the point that you described: they are really feeling great; for the first time they are really in control of themselves; and when they find that they are able to recognize someone else's irrational behavior and comment calmly and objectively on it, the experience becomes almost intoxicating, and they end up behaving irrationally "rational."

C^{40}: Oh, yes, this is what I am saying. Friends would do something, and I would say, "Look, you dummy!"—which of course was an irrational thing to do.

T^{41}: That's right, it was irrational because it resulted in significant environmental conflict for you. But, what's worse, often when clients reach that point in successful RET they usually convince themselves, "Now I am rational. Everything I say or do is rational. Therefore, I don't have to do any more homework. I don't have to objectively examine my perceptions and thoughts. I am rational; everything I think is by definition rational."

C⁴²: Yes, they have overconfidence.

T⁴³: Yes, and that is the most common reason they stop doing written homework. And by stopping, they deny themselves the opportunity to objectively examine and reflect on their thoughts. They try to do it in their head; but because they can entertain only one thought at any one moment, they can never really carefully examine their thoughts. Also, because they are then convinced that their thinking is always rational anyway, they have little motivation for carefully checking their thoughts against objective reality. That works fine, as long as they are not trying to handle emotional stress. But at that stage of therapy, in a stressful situation their initial *emotional responses* tend to still be their pre-therapy ones, even though their *thoughts* may be rational. If they don't do homeworks on those events, that fact tends to be ignored, and the clients conclude that, since their emotions were undesirable in spite of their having had rational thoughts, therapy is not working or they must be "slipping." The idea that therapy isn't working leads to less attention to their thoughts, and soon they are having as many, if not more, irrational than rational thoughts. Then trying to think a problem through in their heads becomes a waste of time; irrational and rational ideas are unwittingly mixed, and soon they return to therapy.

C⁴⁴: But, at the same time, isn't that the goal, I mean, to be able to do homework in your head?

T⁴⁵: Not really. The goal is to get clients to the point that even if they have an irrational emotional response, due to relative lack of practice in responding rationally, they remain in rational contact with reality. They will know that they are having an inappropriate, irrational emotional response. They will also know they still need to put forth more conscious effort to make their emotional response coincide with their rational thinking. They will realize that it is not that therapy isn't working, because they know therapy never works. They will remind themselves that they always must work at therapy. And they will try harder to teach themselves to respond appropriately to their rational thoughts rather than giving in to their irrational feelings. Take you, for example. One of the

reasons you came back to therapy is that you are again having
your phobic-like fear of being hit on the head. Now if you
see a stone building two blocks away being wrecked, you might
immediately start getting your old fear response to the idea
that a piece of stone might fall off and hit you on the head
and give you a concussion and cause you to be psychotic again.
Even though you get the old fear response, if you are still
practicing the rational thought process about it, you would
be constantly thinking things like, "It's silly to have this response to that situation. After all, from two blocks away it
is very unlikely that a rock could hit me. However, it would
be possible if I passed the building under the area of wreckage.
For that reason, I will now calmly cross the street. Because
the chances of a rock coming all the way across the street
and hitting me are so slight, to maintain my fear response
would then be most inappropriate." Now, even though you
were still having an irrational feeling of fear, if those rational
thought processes were firmly established as your reflex or
automatic way of thinking, you would remain in cognitive
control of yourself. By virtue of that control, you would decrease your irrational fear response. On the other hand, if
you had irrational thoughts—like "Oh my God, I am going
to get hit! I know I am going to get hit! Isn't it terrible if
I get hit! I better stop going here and take another street.
Oh, this is awful!"—plus the fear that was elicited by the sight
of the falling stones, even if you caught yourself sufficiently
to say to yourself, "Gee whiz, wait a minute, this is irrational;
maybe I should try to rationally handle this," the fact that
you had to "catch" yourself would mean, that you have not
learned the rational mental processes well enough to handle
the problem in your head effectively. For that reason, if written homework is indicated, mental analysis will probably be
doomed to failure. Also, were you in rational mental control
and merely crossed the street and passed on by the building,
even if your fear response had not lasted throughout the whole
experience, once you got home it would still be well to do
a written homework analysis of the whole event just to make
sure that your mental processes were really rational. If you
decided they were, then you know that all you need do is

more imagery to eliminate the external, cue-controlled fear response. Do you follow me?

C[46]: Yes.

T[47]: Now, after having done and checked a written homework, you realistically conclude, "Yes, I was thinking rationally in that situation; it is just that I haven't yet completely changed my emotional response," that will mean that you have learned rational behavior well at the neocortical or thinking centers of your brain. Your limbic system or the emotional centers of your brain are still responding the way they usually have, and you'd better put forth more time and effort in practice to change that. The first step would be therapeutic imagery, followed by voluntarily exposing yourself to the stimulus situation again and trying to more rationally control your fear response.

The therapist gives the client, in these last several exchanges, an explanation of why he'd better work very hard at his homework, in between sessions, in order to get deeper and more consistently held improvement. As a result of his previous sessions and his own work, he has partially learned to think rationally about accidents, so that the neocortical centers of his brain often respond in a sensible manner to the prospect of, say, a rock hitting him and giving him a concussion. But he *also* believes, perhaps in the limbic areas of his brain, that if he did get hit by a rock and had a concussion again, he would have to go through the same sort of psychotic episode that he previously had. Moreover, he still concludes (as humans are wont to conclude) that if this happened again, it would be awful or terrible (rather than merely inconvenient or disadvantageous). Consequently, he frequently responds with his old phobic reactions (to which, again in the limbic areas of his brain, he is still somewhat habituated).

The theory of RET, as Dr. Maultsby points out, is that since the deepest levels of the client's thinking and acting dysfunctionally have probably been arrived at by his continually, repetitively convincing himself that accidents can easily occur and that it would be awful if they did occur, and by his steadily acting (in his overt habits) on these unfounded assumptions, the main way for him to counterattack his deepest-seated convictions and behavior patterns is for him now to continually, repetitively, and steadily contradict these assumptions and behaviors. That is what the homework reports and assignments, given to him by the therapist or himself, largely do: serve as this kind of an ongoing, reiterated thinking-emoting-behaving counter-conditioning. If he does them incisively, forcefully, and repetitively enough, he will ultimately believe, feel, and act, on both his cortical and his subcortical levels of behaving, in a semiautomatically sensible fashion.

C^{48}:   Yes, tomorrow is May 9.
T^{49}:   Yes, so what?
C^{50}:   That is the anniversary of my accident.
T^{51}:   My response to that is the same as it was at the first May 9 anniversary.
C^{52}:   I know, I know, but I have been getting a little more apprehensive as the time gets closer. And then the riots [between students and police] broke out. I live in the middle of the riot area, and I don't know what is causing what. But since the riots started, I seem to be really getting more and more worried that something might happen to me. Tell me, do you think this is irrational? I went out, and I bought twenty dollars' worth of lumber, and I boarded up all of our windows.
T^{53}:   What do you think about it?
C^{54}:   I think that it is a way of insuring that nobody will throw rocks through the window and possibly hit me or my wife. It can also keep the police from throwing tear gas in the apartment.
T^{55}:   All right. Why do you ask me if I think it is rational? I mean, the whole point of teaching you how to do, and insisting that you do, written homework is to give you a definite, specific way of determining whether or not something is rational: namely analyzing it in the A-B-C-D homework format. Now, you obviously were feeling some apprehension or fear, which motivated you to put up the boarding, right? Now, to decide whether that was rational or irrational behavior you need to do a homework report on it and consider the facts and events as you gave them to me. If your self-talk were the same as you described it here, I would probably think that your behavior was rational. My reasons would be, (1) I understand that the police threw tear gas into the lobby of the hospital; that

indicates that police can get pretty wild and indiscriminate about where they throw tear gas. (2) At the height of police-student confrontations, according to the news reports, the police often break as many windows as the students do. (3) I understand the police have indiscriminately thrown tear gas into apartments in your area during riots. Consequently those are very realistic reasons for boarding up the windows of homes in potential riot areas. However, those facts don't necessarily mean that you were responding to rational thinking when you boarded your windows. You can behave "rationally" for irrational reasons. We need to consider your primary motivation in making your decision. I was talking about protecting your wife and yourself from tear gas and protecting your windows from already demonstrated probable damage. But if your primary concern was the possibility of a rock coming through the window, hitting you on the head, causing a concussion and psychosis, because that is very unlikely, I would be less likely to call your thinking rational. Then I'd have to say your behavior was irrationally motivated and advise a homework analysis. If you had done homework, you would have been better able to determine for yourself if your behavior were rational or not. Do you see what I mean?

C⁵⁶: The probable danger was my first motivation. I don't know if I invented other ones or not.

T⁵⁷: Well, look at it like this: From what you described, to want to protect yourself from tear gas seems perfectly realistic and sufficient reason to board up your windows. So it becomes a matter of your relative concern, of fear of the probable dangers already described, versus the most improbable event of a rock being thrown through the window, hitting you on the head, and causing another concussion. If the latter were your primary concern, then boarding up the windows would probably be an example of objectively rational behavior, done for very irrational reasons. Therefore you would need to do a written homework on the situation to redirect your thinking toward the objective reality. Do you see what I mean?

C⁵⁸: I think the riot occurring near the magic day had a lot to do with it. It seemed like there was greater justification than there would be had either one occurred separately.

T[59]:   No, no, no. That's merely a misperception and a more subtle
         form of self-deception. It is like saying, "If I have three or
         four unfortunate things happen to me, then it is logical to
         get upset; but if only one unfortunate thing happens, it would
         be illogical to get upset." The reality is, when more than one
         unfortunate thing happens to you, you may have a greater
         stimulus to get upset. But since getting upset is unnecessary
         in order to do whatever you can about the unfortunate events,
         and since being upset may interfere with your doing what
         you can do to change the unfortunate situation, you risk
         merely adding injury to insult by getting upset. The point
         is, it is irrational to get undesirably upset about *anything*,
         ever. Granted, because no human is perfect, everyone will get
         upset some time. But that fact does not make the act of get-
         ting emotionally upset a less irrational act. It's like, everyone
         will ultimately die; but that does not make death a healthy
         or desirable event.

   Dr. Maultsby emphasizes here two of the points that are quite
frequently made in RET: (1) Human upsetness does not stem from
activating events, no matter how unfortunate and unfair these may
be, but from the individual's belief system about these events—from
the conscious or unconscious *shoulds, oughts,* and *musts* he foolishly
connects with, or contends should be connected with, them. Consequently, he never really has to get upset. (2) When he does become
irrationally overconcerned or overemotional about anything, he
usually decreases his chances of correcting and truly protecting himself in regard to that thing. By making himself, for example, utterly
panicked about student-police riots, he reduces his chances of (*a*)
calmly avoiding such riots himself and (*b*) working vigorously, in
conjunction with other concerned citizens, to reduce the incidence
of rioting. As soon as he escalates the rational belief, "I very much
want to avoid getting hurt in riots and suffering a possible concussion thereby" into the irrational belief, "I absolutely must not be
hurt in a riot, for that would completely destroy me!" he not only
needlessly upsets himself (as opposed to cautiously alerting himself),
but he also tends significantly to reduce his ability to cope with
rioting in case it does occur as well as his ability to possibly do
something to prevent rioting.

C[60]: But if everybody does something, wouldn't it be irrational if one person didn't do it?

T[61]: No, no, no. We are not concerned here with everybody; we are concerned only with you and your life. What other people may or may not be doing has no necessary bearing on you. As long as your behavior meets these two criteria for rational behavior—(1) it keeps you alive, and (2) it gets you what you want out of life without significant personal or environmental conflict—your behavior will be rational and you can forget other people. Now, I say "forget other people," but what I mean is, refuse to inappropriately concern yourself with them. As long as you behave in a manner that keeps you out of significant environmental conflict, you will be doing all the usual courteous, civil things toward people, and you will refrain from doing uncivil, cruel things to people. That is all any sane person or society asks of anyone.

C[62]: Then, what you are saying is that rational thinking is independent of anything else, and no amount of misery or misfortune that piles up on one person should be able to snap him.

T[63]: No, I am not saying that. I am saying that however many unfortunate things happen to you, to respond to them irrationally is just adding another unfortunate event to the ones you already have.

C[64]: Doesn't it become more likely that a person will get upset if he has a lot of problems at once?

T[65]: Yes, it becomes more likely, but it does not become any more justifiable. It isn't any more logical; it isn't more reasonable. That is what I have been trying to explain to you. When you listen to the tape of this session, maybe you will see it. The main point for you to see here is that you are trying to make your increased probability of responding irrationally justify your behaving irrationally. That is the same type of reasoning the police and National Guard use for killing people. They say things like "Well, if they hadn't been calling us pigs and been saying XYZ things, we wouldn't have gotten mad enough to shoot them." I say "Bullshit!" If a person is not sane enough to distinguish a pig from a human being, then society is being irresponsible to the taxpayers to put a gun in that person's hands. Granted it is more difficult to control oneself when people are saying personally distasteful things, but if it were required that all people allowed to carry guns first undergo a course of RET, we would have fewer people killed because of inability to distinguish between pigs and human beings, or other such childish behavior. Rather than giving in to irrational impulses to kill people when it is more difficult than usual to control oneself, it is more sane, more logical and rational, to put forth more effort to control oneself. Do you see what I mean? So, even though there have been riots or there is the potential for riots in your neighborhood, there still is no logical justification for you to begin behaving irrationally. From a rational point of view, you now have all the more reason to try harder than ever to behave rationally. Do you understand what I mean?

In his T[65] response, Dr. Maultsby brings out two important aspects of RET. First, he refers to the client's listening to the tape recording of his session. It is frequently found, in rational-emotive therapy, that if a client makes a recording of his therapy session and takes it home with him to play over and over (usually on a cassette recorder), he gets much more out of the session. This is because during the session he is so absorbed in responding to the therapist that he often does not hear all that goes on in the course of it. Moreover, even when he does hear clearly, he easily forgets many of the therapist's salient points—not merely because he is resisting therapy or because he wants to forget, but also because, being human, he has a fallible memory and easily and naturally forgets even things he very much wants to retain. Again, if he listens to the session several times during the week, he thereby gets a repetitive message from the therapist and keeps reminding himself about what his problem actually is and what some of the ways are he can work effectively on it. For several reasons, then, recordings appear to be an important aid to RET sessions.

Secondly, Dr. Maultsby tries to show the client not only that RET is an effective form of treatment for disturbed individuals but that it can be generally applied to the problems of so-called normal or healthy persons and even to the social problems of the world. For if, as he notes, people really thought straightly about themselves and others, and refused to condemn those with whom they significantly differ (as the students condemn the "pig" cops, and the cops condemn the "communist" students), the world would probably be a better place in which to live. Although this generalized, social aspect of RET may not come into play in a series of therapy sessions, it often is useful to refer to it, as the therapist does in this response.

C66:   Yes, but what about the headaches? I don't see any way of rationally dealing with a headache. I mean, you know you just have it, and you handle your reaction to it as rationally as you can, but you still have it. I mean, rational thinking can't make your head stop hurting.

T67:   Well, it depends on what causes the headache. Now, if your headache is the result of nervous tension, then of course rational thinking would be the therapy of choice. If your headache is the result of somebody hitting you on the head with a billy club, then rational therapy won't help the pain, but RET *could* help you learn how to avoid being beaten over the head. Do you see what I mean? What RET can do about headaches is a function of the probable cause of the headache.

C68:   Is it unreasonable to assume that the probable cause of my headaches is my old concussion?

T69:   Yes, it is most unreasonable.

C70:   Well, my concern is with dealing with the headaches, and hopefully there will be something that can end them.

T71:   How do you deal with them now?

C72:   How do I deal with them? I find that the best way to deal with them is to go to sleep, to take a nap.

T73:   Okay. Does that usually control them?

C74:   Well, when I wake up they are usually gone.

T75:   Headaches due to concussion do not consistently respond to sleep. On the other hand, headaches due to irrationally handled mental and emotional stress very often respond well to sleep. Excessive sleep is a common neurotic way of avoiding or decreasing anxiety. Also, just because your life situation seems to be going well, that does not mean that you have to be free of all mental and emotional stress.

C76:   That almost sounds Freudian.

T77:   No, not at all. I'm not talking about any unconscious stress.

I am thinking of the stereotype of the poor little rich kid who says, "I have everything; I should be happy, but I am not." You see what I mean?

C[78]: In my case I seem to get them in all emotional situations, when I'm happy or unhappy.

T[79]: Yes, but regardless of how happy you are, if for any reason you become irrationally concerned about the possibility of having a headache or the possibility of getting hit on the head, you can create an anxiety response. For people who think irrationally, there is no necessary inverse relationship between happiness and worry. Many such people worry because they are happy; they worry about the possibility of their happiness ending. In effect, such people are afraid not to worry. As a matter of fact, wasn't that one of your old habits?

C[80]: Yes.

T[81]: Yes, I remember, when you would realize that for a short period of time you have not worried about something, you immediately began to worry about having overlooked something that you "should" be worried about, and you worried about that.

C[82]: Yes. But it seems that what you are really saying is that the way to deal with the headaches is not to deal with the headaches, but to deal with the things which are probably producing the headache.

T[83]: Yes and no. It is logical to take a pain-killer for the headache, provided you consult an internist for the investigation of possible physical causes for them. Also, if you have mental and emotional problems that are often associated with headache, it would be well to investigate and evaluate those possible causes of your headache, do you see what I mean?

C[84]: Yes.

T[85]: I think that your current situation is no different in kind from your original situation. You are not perceiving your world as realistically as you are capable of doing, and you are not thinking as rationally as you apparently were when you left RET. If that is true, you cannot get the same type of rational results you were getting then. In other words, what has happened to you was perfectly predictable on the basis of rational learning theory.

Benefiting from rational therapy is no different in its process from benefiting from learning a foreign language. When you learn a foreign language, you are in fact learning a new way to think. You are learning how to think about the same things but using different sounds, words, etc. In RET you are still learning a new way to think, but you are learning to think different things in response to the same stimulus. The point is, you are learning a new way to think. Since you have taken a foreign language, you know that after a year of diligently studying and practicing it, you can be at the point that would be analogous to where you were in RET when therapy was stopped. You could meet a person who spoke the foreign language, and you could start talking with him without having to do much mental translation. You could probably be thinking and talking for the most part in the foreign language, thereby making your conversation relatively fluent and natural.

When you stopped taking the course, you no longer went to the language lab; you no longer studied nor practiced. Most probably, if you tried to practice with your American friends who took the same course, they rebuffed you by saying, "Look, man, the course is over. I don't want to hear that anymore," just as your friends did when you attempted to practice rational thinking on them. Being out of therapy and no longer being reinforced for practicing rational thinking, your tendency was to go back to your old pre-therapy habits of perceiving and thinking. Because you knew that way best, once you started actively using it, you tended to immediately fall back into the old response patterns because they were still easier for you than the rational ones were. And, as with the foreign language, if even though you stopped actively trying to practice it with other people, you continued mentally practicing by yourself, listening to tapes, and reading and writing in the language, you would not have lost much of your ability to use it. The same would have been true of your skills at perceiving and thinking rationally. But once therapy stopped, and your friends refused to tolerate your practicing on them, you stopped using the principles you had learned in RET. Because your life then was going fairly well, you probably convinced yourself that you did not need to practice any more because you were "rational." But, the reality even then of what you knew best was your pre-therapy irrational thinking habits. So as situations arose—and, more specifically, as emotionally charged situations arose—because of your years of practice with irrational responses, you were much more likely to respond irrationally than to respond rationally. Because you were no longer doing homeworks, you had shut yourself completely off from RET, except for your memory. You tried to mentally solve your problems, and at first maybe you did have some success. But, gradually the strength of your irrational tendencies took over and pretty soon you gave up completely. That is my analysis of the situation.

The rational solution is to reverse that process. You are not the only one who has the same problem. I find that about 10 percent of my patients recontact me complaining that RET either "is not working" or "is not working like it used to." To efficiently handle such cases, I have worked out a relapse routine. It's all explained in this handout. You take the handout and read it at least five times before your next session.

As is also noted in some of the other cases in this book, Dr. Maultsby does not hesitate to use bibliotherapy in addition to the other RET methods that he employs. For it has been found that some of the main messages or teachings that are often conveyed during RET sessions can also be included in written articles or books; that clients, when given this pertinent material, frequently read it over and over, making their own significant underlinings; that they sometimes specifically refer to it when they are especially anxious, depressed, guilty, or angry; and that they may even get as much or more of the RET message via this type of reading than they do during their actual individual or group sessions.

Consequently, most RET clients are given handouts after the first session or during subsequent sessions of therapy; and they are also encouraged to read certain RET books—especially, *How to Live With a Neurotic* (Ellis, 1969a); *A Guide to Rational Living* (Ellis & Harper, 1970); *A Guide to Successful Marriage* (Ellis & Harper, 1968); *Reason and Emotion in Psychotherapy* (Ellis, 1962); and *How to Prevent Your Child from Becoming a Neurotic Adult* (Ellis, Wolfe, & Moseley,

1966). Clinical findings, so far, consistently show such reading may be enormously helpful to some clients.

The specific handout that Dr. Maultsby gave the client in this case was one he wrote himself, "Why Former RET Clients May Need and Desire Further Therapy." It explains, in much more detail than some of his comments in the first session, why RET sometimes doesn't continue to work with certain clients; what skills are usually required for optimal mental and emotional health; how individuals can lead "normal" lives even when they are born and reared with a strong tendency to lead "abnormal" ones; why both environment and heredity are important factors in emotional disturbance; and how and why some clients stop working at RET. It gives excerpts from sessions with a nineteen-year-old girl and a twenty-year-old college student, both of whom had relapsed. It ends with this section on the important characteristics of relapsed clients:

Both clients cited had all of the characteristics former RET clients have who are likely to desire and return for further therapy at some future date:

1. They did not give up the unrealistic belief that they as human beings are the same as their behavior. Instead of continuing, as they were taught in RET, merely to rate their *performances* and not their *selves*, they irrationally returned to rating these *selves*. Seeing that they at first successfully used rational thinking to solve some of the serious problems they brought to therapy, these clients concluded, "I am now rational." To them that meant that they couldn't possibly have seriously irrational thoughts or beliefs. Therefore, they saw little point in continuing to do homework or even bothering to think, using the rational rhetoric and/or the rational thought framework. They no longer viewed their emotional difficulties as evidence that they might not be thinking rationally, but mainly viewed them as evidence that "RET isn't working" or "I didn't have enough RET inside of me" at the end of their first series of therapy sessions. They viewed RET as a magical power operating independently of themselves and of their pre-RET attitudes.

2. Even though they had done well in therapy, they refused to discuss some of their irrational ideas while they were in treatment, probably because they believed that those ideas either were rational or were superior to any conflicting ideas that the therapist or their therapy group might have brought to their attention. So they carried their undiscussed irrational attitudes and beliefs away from RET unchanged. Because these residual beliefs were irrational, they were constant sources of inappropriate emotional behavior—which the clients then mistook as evidence that "RET is no longer working."

3. Even though these relapsed clients occasionally did effective written homework analysis of their current problems, thereby demonstrating that they could still work with RET methods, at some point they usually stopped doing homework altogether.

In summary, former RET clients can well use further therapy when they either never completely replace their pre-therapy irrational ideas with rational ones or they stop working with and acting on the more rational beliefs they learned in RET. When either or both of these things happen, they often return to their pre-RET thought patterns, and they get poor emotional and behavior results consonant with their irrational beliefs.

SECOND SESSION

The client returns for his second session a week later, reports that he has been too busy to do any homework reports, that he catastrophized about passing some of his courses at school, and that he has returned to his old habit of not being able to sleep very well at night. The therapist shows him, once again, that it is unlikely that he will get and remain better unless he makes sure that he finds the time to do steady homework analysis. He also spends a good deal of the session explaining to the client what the difference is between his *wanting* very much to do something, such as succeed at school, and his thinking that he *has to* succeed in this respect. The former goal, he indicates is functional, while the latter goal results in extreme anxiety and malfunctioning. But the former goal, or any set of rational goals, is not likely to be achieved until the client gets back to consistently doing homeworks.

The therapist keeps after the client, during the next few sessions, to do his homework assignments regularly and to keep listening to the tape recordings of the sessions themselves. As he does this, the client seems to get back into the routine, which he used during his original series of sessions, of taking RET much more seriously and applying it a good many times a week, in between his therapeutic sessions.

FIFTH SESSION

The client shows some progress but is not sure that it is not mainly because things are going better for him and that therefore he has had a good mood change. The therapist shows him that he can keep himself in a good mood through using RET, even when things go wrong in his life. The client then reports on another of the homework assignments that he has been doing in between sessions:

C^1:   Okay, here is another homework. Facts and events: I took the dog and went out to the farm where we have a garden to work. I felt extremely happy, almost ecstatic for an extended period of time. Self-talk during the time: This is so great. We have this huge garden; we are growing our own vegetables. We met Tom and Judy who are very warm and interesting people; we have free use of their farm any time we want to come out here and enjoy the countryside. We have a place to run the dog; we have a place to stay whenever we want to; we have companions for the dog; it is a beautiful day, and it really feels good to be doing work outside; and I am very, very happy. Emotions: Ecstatic happiness, a kind of joy. Rational self-talk: It is fortunate that I have met some interesting people who allow us the use of their land at will; however it is not great, and it does not merit this outpouring of positive emotion. And once again, making my emotions primarily dependent upon external reality that I have little control over. It would be well were I to make my emotions dependent upon internal cues which I create myself. By following the same reasoning, were Tom and Judy to suddenly grow cold and deny us the use of their land, or the day to grow cold and rainy, or were I unable to use my muscles, then I would be plunged into despair as profound as my joy is ecstatic. What has happened is all positive, advantageous, but it was accidental, not attained because I defined it as part of my goals for my most satisfactory life adjustment. Rational emotions: Happiness, definite positive emotions, deep contentment.

T²: Good. It sounds like you are progressing. Now, did I tell you about therapeutic imagery?

C³: No.

T⁴: Well, when you get to the point where you can write consistently rational homeworks like that, then it would be well to set aside a minimum of a half-hour per day in which you do therapeutic imagery. Therapeutic imagery is merely mentally rehearsing events that you have worked out rationally in the homeworks.

C⁵: Starting with the rational emotions.

T⁶: Yes. Now, you re-create the whole scene mentally, but you ignore all of your irrational self-talk and concentrate only on your rational self-talk, the rational emotions you will learn

to have as a result of consistently thinking and believing your
rational self-talk. You are mentally rehearsing or mentally
picturing yourself behaving rationally, having rationally desirable and logical emotional responses. That's how you efficiently build the cognitive maps that guide your therapeutic
self-change. Understand?

C[7]:   Yes.

T[8]:   That's therapeutic imagery. That's where you correct past
irrational behavior. It is also where you learn to efficiently
control irrational fears and phobias. You see, one of the main
reasons people maintain irrational behavior is they don't have
realistic mental frames of reference for behaving otherwise.
They can't picture themselves behaving any differently from
the way they always have. However, after you nave taught
yourself the realistic, rational attitude toward your problem
or behavior, therapeutic imagery allows you to mentally practice emoting that behavior, thereby increasing the probability
of success in the real-life situation. For example, for the client
who has always had bad relations with her parents: Before
she goes home for vacation, I get her to start therapeutic
imagery, seeing herself utilizing the basic concepts of rational
thinking, like "I don't have to get upset; it really isn't terrible;
I can stand it; it's merely inconvenient; getting upset serves
no useful purpose," and soon she sees herself actually achieving those goals. Understand?

C[9]:   Yes. It is taking a probable event and its appropriate emotions, working with them to get a realistic mental picture
of how you want to behave.

T[10]:   Right.

RET, once its philosophic premises are accepted, can make use
of a large variety of therapeutic methods, including the technique
of therapeutic imagery outlined by the therapist during this session.
At first blush, this might appear to be a form of "positive thinking,"
as originally espoused by Emile Coué (1923) and later revived on
a grand scale by Norman Vincent Peale (1962). For in Couéism, for
example, the individual tells himself something like, "Day by day
in every way I'm getting better and better," and suggestively influ-

ences himself in this manner so that sometimes he actually *does* get better; and in Peale's form of "positive thinking," a fairly similar methodology is employed.

In RET, however, therapeutic imagery is employed not merely for the individual to convince himself that somehow, through the help of God or his own magical powers, he will get better, but that he doesn't *have* to think negatively and that he *can* contradict his irrational ideas. Thus, in the illustration Dr. Maultsby uses in response T^8, the individual who is going home for a vacation and has always had bad relations with her parents does not, normally, realize that these poor relations do not stem from her parents' unfortunate behavior at point A, but from her irrational belief system at point B—from her vigorously convincing herself, "They shouldn't act the way they do. I can't stand it! It's awful that they're acting that way! I have to get upset when I see them and they behave in that crummy manner. Maybe if I get terribly upset at them, they'll actually change." In RET, she would learn to pointedly dispute, contradict, and challenge these unvalidatable hypotheses. By RET therapeutic imagery she can imagine herself doing this kind of challenging, and through this kind of imagery she can actually rehearse speaking to herself differently about her parents and then behave differently toward them when she actually sees them.

Therapeutic imagery, therefore, as Dr. Maultsby indicates to his client, reinforces and strengthens rational thinking by helping the individual become convinced that she can think much more rationally than she usually does. If she, pollyanna-like, tells herself, "Let me envision myself actually getting along well with my parents and that will make me get along with them," she is merely voicing a pious hope and quite probably will later fall into her old negative patterns toward them, even if she at first treats them somewhat better. But if she tells herself, "Let me envision working at changing my own philosophy about my parents and using my newer, more rational philosophy when I meet them again on my vacation," she will have a better chance of helping herself think straight (instead of merely acting as if she were thinking straight) and thereby of changing some of her fundamental irrational assumptions. It is not that positive thinking or various kinds of role-playing cannot work in therapy, for there is much clinical and some experimental evidence that they can. But they generally are inelegant solutions to the problem of human disturbance and are much enhanced and deepened when they are combined with a genuine irrational-philosophy-attacking method, for which RET is most noted.

C¹¹: Okay, I have another homework I want to read. What hap-
        pened was I was on the way to the gas station; a car pulled
        up alongside of me very quietly, and I did not notice it. Then
        it suddenly accelerated very loudly. The noise frightened me
        very much. I swerved in the opposite direction, almost striking
        a parked car. Self-talk: The whole thing happened so quickly
        that I was unaware of the actual self-talk. I assumed that
        it was an example of thought-shorthand-produced response,
        and the relationships must have gone something like this: The
        car is going to hit me, and I'll get into another accident and
        have another concussion and mess up my whole life. Emotions:
        Fear. Possible self-talk. Since it was thought shorthand, I
        wasn't sure how to handle it.

T¹²: Well, remember a basic RET assumption is that behavior
        always makes sense. So all you have to do is reference yourself
        and your past behavior potentials and behavior patterns, and
        then try to explain your behavior in a way that would make
        sense to you. Usually, you can make an accurate estimate of
        what most probably you are responding to, and therefore you
        can decide what would be more rational responses.

C¹³: What I wrote was: The noise of a car accelerating beside me
        means nothing. What else could I logically expect to hear on
        a busy street near rush hour? I have heard that noise hundreds
        of times, every time I drive a car, and usually I pay no atten-
        tion to it. Simply because I noticed it once means nothing
        except that the car next to me accelerated. Even if it had
        hit me, which would have been unfortunate, from that position
        the chances of sustaining another concussion would have been
        very, very small. And even if I did have another concussion,
        that too would not be catastrophic, only very unpleasant; I
        probably could handle it in the same way I have learned to
        handle the first concussion. Therefore, the rational emotion
        to that situation now is indifference.

T¹⁴: Right.

C¹⁵: Then later on in the day, thinking about this, I got depressed
        about failing to be more rational than I am.

T¹⁶: Now then you were being irrational about being irrational,
        which is also being irrational.

C¹⁷: So I did a homework on it.

T[18]: Great, and I hope that you pointed out to yourself that you are only a fallible human being, which means that you are going to make mistakes even in your pursuit of rational thinking, and even now responding irrationally doesn't mean that you have lost all of your gains. It just means that at that time you were not responding as rationally as you would like to have responded nor as rationally as you hope to become able to consistently do.

C[19]: Should I read that homework on the depression over not being rational?

T[20]: No, time is up; we can go over it next time if you want to check it out, but I am sure it was okay if you included points I just made. All the things I said are on the tape, so if there is anything you are still concerned about in the next session, we will go over it then.

In RET, it can hardly be emphasized enough that the client, as the therapist notes in T[18], is a fallible human being, and that his fallibility extends to RET itself. If he thinks that he has to be perfectly rational, he will of course fail to achieve that goal. And then he will either condemn himself and feel anxious and guilty; or else he will cover up and assume that he is being rational, when he is not; or else he will tend to conclude that there is no use in his even attempting to be rational and will give up entirely on his homework. If he accepts himself as a human who can be fairly sensible, but who often is not, and who can keep steadily working to improve but never completely achieve his own rationality, he will finally strike a medium and accept himself with his errors, while still trying ceaselessly to minimize these errors.

Glasser (1965), Mowrer (1964), and other therapists of the "reality" school tend to stress that the client is utterly capable of controlling his own destiny, that he is quite responsible for his actions, and that therefore he'd damned well better admit this and better do something about changing his behavior. This is, of course, correct; and showing the client this frequently does him a service, in that it shows him that there is no other way for him to improve than his working his head off to do so. RET therapists frequently do the same thing and have, in fact, been doing so for years before "reality" therapy was invented. They have also been confronting clients very directly with their wrongdoings, and insisting that these clients would better stop their nonsense and admit to themselves and others that they are really lousing themselves up, long before the Synanon-type group leaders (Yablonsky, 1965) and the encounter movement therapists (Burton, 1969) started to use direct confrontation methods.

The RET message, however, is significantly different from the reality therapy message, in that if clients do not get off their rumps, accept responsibility for their own disordered behavior, and act concertedly to help themselves—which is quite frequently the case—the therapist by no means insinuates that they are no-goodniks who deserve to suffer but very clearly tries to show them that they can still accept themselves in spite of their goofing. He thereby invariably helps them to accept themselves while he is trying to induce them to change their dysfunctional behavior. This method may occasionally boomerang, since the disturbed individual may use RET as a cop-out, and tell himself, "Well, I'm not really a louse for shirking my responsibilities to myself and others; therefore I might as well keep shirking." For the most part, however, he does not seem to cop out in this manner and instead does learn to change his behavior without condemning himself. In fact, the RET hypothesis is that he thereby has a better chance of ridding himself of his symptoms (since he does not divert himself into foolish, time- and energy-wasting self-condemnation), and that he also winds up with a more elegant, more deeply philosophic solution to his general and specific problems.

That is to say, where the client in reality therapy may do the right thing for the wrong reasons—correct his behavior because he would view himself (as his therapist, too, might view him) as a crumb if he did not correct it—the RET client tends to do the right thing for the right reasons—correct his behavior because he thereby is likely to become a happier and at the same time more tolerant person. The RET client winds up more truly independent of the need for others' approval than virtually any other kind of client; and this advantage presumably outweighs the advantages of techniques of exhortation used in certain other kinds of treatment.

SIXTH SESSION

The therapist continues to prod the client to do his homework assignments, and goes over them regularly with him during the sessions, to correct them and to suggest better and more specific ways for him to perceive and to counterattack his irrational ideas.

Here is a typical exchange where the client does his homework assignment reasonably well, but where the therapist shows him how to be still more precise about doing it.

C¹: Now for the homework. I did a homework on my failure to be rational. Do you remember that I told you that I depressed myself because of my irrational reaction to the thing about the car?

T²: Oh, yes, I remember.

C³: I depressed myself because of my fear reaction to the sudden and unexpected acceleration of the car next to me. Irrational Belief: "There I go again, acting like a fool because some noise scared me. I haven't learned anything in therapy; I just go right on having these ridiculous reactions to the simplest noises; it is like being afraid of the dark, for heaven's sake! This is not going to get any better; it is all because I am so stupid!" Emotions: Depression, resignation to an unhappy life. Rational self-talk: "Simply because I acted in an irrational manner in this particular case or in any other case, this is no realistic reason to depress myself. I can get rid of those kinds of emotions and reactions if I work hard enough and long enough at RET. The failure to utilize RET in this particular case has nothing to do with my intelligence. In any case, I am not stupid. I am above average in intelligence and performance. To depress myself over my failure to use RET in the car incident is a much more irrational reaction than the initial fear reaction.

T⁴: Now, that homework is indirectly, rather than directly, rationally done. To have gotten the most mileage out of your D [disputing] section, it would have been better to start with a sentence-for-sentence challenge of your B [belief] section, because those were the specific thoughts that resulted in your depression, you see?

C⁵: Yes.

T⁶: Also, if I wanted to label a theme in that homework, it would be "a typical example of your automatized catastrophizing habit," you see?

C⁷: Yes.

T[8]:   Read the first sentence.

C[9]:   Of the D?

T[10]:   Of the B.

C[11]:   The B. "There I go again acting like a fool just because some
         noise scared me."

T[12]:   Okay. Now, I would have responded to that sentence with,
         "If I defined the way I acted as being the way a fool would
         act, okay, I acted like a fool. But because I realize that *I* am
         not the same as my *behavior*, there is no reason to be upset
         because I behaved foolishly." Number two?

Dr. Maultsby refers again, in his response T[12], to the point that
"[because] *I* am not the same as my *behavior*, there is no reason
to be upset because I behaved foolishly." This is a point that many
RET clients have difficulty getting, and that has to be gone over
several times in most cases. For the individual, of course, *is* his
behavior in the sense that (1) he himself, and nobody else, performs
this behavior, and he is therefore responsible for it; and (2) his total-
ity, his being, his existence consists essentially of all the behavior
he engages in and will ever in the future perform.

But what the RET therapist means when he points out to the
client that he is not the same thing as his behavior is the following:

1. All the individual's behavior cannot possibly ever be known.
Therefore, there is no accurate way of seeing what he *is*, though
there are fairly accurate means of measuring various aspects of what
he *does*—for example, how well he does at studying, working, playing
sports, and so on.

2. To say that a human being *is* anything is invariably an overgeneralization, and a misleading one. As Bourland (1969), a general
semanticist, has shown, to employ any form of the verb *to be* about
a person is to overcategorize him and his actions. Thus, if we say
"John plays ball a good deal of the time," or "John has some excellent
ball-playing abilities," we may be saying something accurate about
John. But if we say "John *is* a ball-player," we strongly imply that
he does practically nothing but play ball. And if we say, "John *is*
an excellent ball-player," we imply that he does well at virtually
all aspects of ball-playing, when the chances are he actually does
poorly at some of them and well at several aspects. Similarly, if
Dr. Maultsby's client tells himself, "Some of my actions were foolish," he may be correct. But if he adds, "Therefore I am a fool,"
he is almost certainly overgeneralizing and is hence incorrect.

3. A human being is an ongoing *process* and is constantly changing. It is therefore inaccurate to measure him on the basis of any of his past or present behavior—which merely shows, at most, what he has done up to now but doesn't necessarily show what he may do from now on.

4. Although it may be theoretically possible (albeit very difficult) to rate or assess a person over and above assessing his behavior, it is usually unwise to make this assessment. For once we say something like "John is good because his acts are good" or "John is bad because his acts are bad," we tend to make a self-fulfilling prophecy about him—at least, if he accepts our judgment of him. For if John views himself as good, he will tend to continue to do good deeds, and if he views himself as bad, he will tend to continue to do bad deeds. Our (and his own) assessments of him, therefore, importantly tend to influence his future acts. Moreover, since John (being human) will invariably be error-prone and fallible, and since he sooner or later will inevitably do some pretty poor acts, we will tend ultimately to view him as bad rather than as good, he will tend to accept our view of him, and he will wind up influencing himself to act badly rather than well.

What Dr. Maultsby is trying to accomplish with this client, consequently, is to persuade him to keep rating or measuring his traits and performances but not to keep rating or measuring himself. He *has* various inadequacies or incompetencies (as all humans, even bright and educated ones, do); but he *is* not these failings.

C¹³: "I haven't learned anything in therapy."

T¹⁴: All right, I would have said, "That is typical of my unrealistic all-or-none thinking. To believe that because I haven't perfectly performed, I haven't learned anything, is nonsense." Do you see what I mean?

C¹⁵: Yes.

T¹⁶: And it would be well to point that out to yourself, and not only that, it would have also been well to point out to yourself the great advantage to you it would be, were you to eliminate your habit of doing all-or-none thinking. It is that ability to go from 0 to 180 degrees in an instant that results in your having widely fluctuating, instantaneous neurotic responses. You understand what I mean?

C¹⁷: Yes.

T¹⁸: You didn't speak directly to those things, and therefore your
       habit of using them remained relatively untouched. But that's
       the habit you need to deal with directly in your D section.
       What you did was describe the result that will probably come
       from having successfully eliminated that habit; but you left
       the habit untouched.

C¹⁹: You mean I just deal with the situation in general?

T²⁰: Right, the situation that resulted from those cues. But the
       most efficient thing would be to direct your homework to
       the cues themselves. Once you have eliminated the cues, your
       irrational responses will no longer be elicited. You will then
       respond only to cues for rational responses. Understand?

C²¹: Yes. Do you want the next one?

T²²: Yes.

C²³: "I just go right on having these ridiculous reactions to the
       simplest noises."

T²⁴: All right. I would have said, "That is not true. That situation
       certainly would not qualify for a situation of 'the simplest
       noise,' whatever that is. I probably don't respond to the sim-
       plest noises in that manner. I am just exaggerating and inap-
       propriately generalizing." What was the next one?

The therapist correctly points out here that the client is not merely
responding to the simplest noise, and is therefore unrealistically
exaggerating about his responses. More to the point, he is probably
doing this because he unrealistically and perfectionistically demands
that he not respond to any noise or that he respond perfectly well
to every noise. He is not really asking himself, therefore, whether
he is appropriately reacting to noises, but is looking for something
to condemn himself for and is finding it in his reaction to noise.
His general self-condemning philosophy, therefore, rather than his
specific reaction to noises, is the real issue here; and it is this that
is encouraging him to exaggerate about his responses to noise.

C²⁵: "It is like being afraid of the dark, for heaven's sake!"

T²⁶: And it isn't like being afraid of the dark, for heaven's sake.
       You see what I mean? After having directly responded in
       a rational manner to each of those sentences, then what you
       wrote would have made a logical closure to the homework;

and you would have handled both the cues as well as the responses to them. The whole process would have become potentially more effective. Then had you used your potentially very valuable talent to make yourself feel as appropriately in response to your thoughts as you feel in response to the reality, then you would have recreated the whole situation in your mind. That is, you would have done therapeutic imagery on the event, and you would have mentally pictured yourself behaving in the same situation with rational instead of your irrational responses, and you would have made yourself have the appropriate feelings for those rational responses. That way, you would have most efficiently handled the event and improved the probability of behaving in a more rational manner in the future under similar circumstances.

C²⁷: There's one more sentence. "This is never going to get any better, and it is all because I am so stupid!"

T²⁸: The rational response there is: "Right, it's this that never gets anywhere. But I already have gotten better, and I intend to continue. There is no such thing as a stupid human being, only a fallible human being. Far better for me to stick to the objective reality than engage in meaningless self-name-calling." Understand?

C²⁹: Yes.

What the therapist means by "There is no such thing as a stupid human being, only a fallible human being," is that a person is never stupid just because some of his acts are. He is always fallible, and therefore, no matter how basically intelligent he is, he can always be expected to act stupidly at times. It is consequently far better for the client to stick to the objective reality that his act was stupid rather than to call himself names—"a stupid person"—for acting in this manner.

T³⁰: Also if you believe (1) that it is never going to get any better, and (2) that it is your stupidity that is causing it, your depression becomes perfectly logical. It's that well-learned habit of thinking—using those irrational ideas—that needs to be eliminated. For example, "It's never going to get any better;

I am always doing it; I haven't learned anything; I am so stupid." Those attitudes and beliefs are the things that caused your feeling. Granted, you can bring the feeling under control after you create it, but that is only the practical RET solution, not the elegant one. The elegant solution would be to eliminate the cognitive ones for those irrational feelings.

Dr. Maultsby points out that when the client believes what he does believe—that things are not going to get any better and that it is his own innate stupidity that is causing them to be as bad as they are—he will naturally, logically make himself depressed. He can then, if he wishes, accept his depression and not give himself too much of a hassle about having it (thereby making himself depressed about being depressed). But he can more elegantly get rid of his two basic irrational ideas, and thus eliminate his depressed feelings entirely.

TWELFTH SESSION

The therapist feels that the client has been doing considerably better from the sixth to the twelfth sessions, because he keeps reporting that he is going through situations at school, at his teaching, and in his personal life that are similar to those that he had catastrophized about before but that he is taking most of them in stride and not upsetting himself about them. So the therapist decides to take stock of the way things are going at the beginning of the twelfth session, to see whether it is necessary for the client to keep coming on a once-a-week basis.

Usually, in RET, the number of sessions is cut down because (1) the client notes that he has relatively little to talk about any more, or (2) the therapist notes that and recommends that the client come in less often, and see how he can get along with fewer sessions. Where, originally, the client has a great deal to say, and especially to complain about, after a while he usually keeps reporting that he is not upsetting himself any longer, even though unfortunate events keep occurring in his life.

In the present case, the therapist and the client both agree, at the end of the twelfth session, that the client is doing quite well and that therefore it is advisable that he have only occasional subsequent sessions—unless he suddenly starts getting seriously upset again, in which case he is to immediately call for an appointment and to resume regular therapy again. The first part of the twelfth session follows.

T¹: This is your twelfth relapse session, so let's take stock of where you are now compared to when we started four months ago.

C²: I really feel very good. I feel very untroubled by the kinds of things that would have troubled me in the past. For example, I'm involved in two situations right now to which in the past I usually reacted very badly; but now, I don't think I'm being self-defeating. I haven't had any irrational responses as far as I can see. I am handling things very well. I know I am handling them to the extent that I am not having any anxiety or depressions.

T³: What are the situations?

C⁴: Well, the first situation is teaching. This is really something, I can't help being impressed with myself about. The kind of teaching I am doing is called intern teaching. The way it is supposed to work is the university department finds a cooperating teacher in the Five Towns School System, and then, I, as an intern, am assigned to that teacher; and I am in her classroom for a semester, every day, regular hours, and she leads me gradually from no teaching of the class at all in the beginning to 100 percent of teaching the class at the end. She leads me in very gradually, you know, day by day and week by week. She is always there with me showing me what to do, telling me what she thought I did right or did wrong, etc. It is a good idea. Well, unfortunately or perhaps fortunately, this school I am in, they don't have enough staff to go around. So they took me and another student teacher just like myself and put us in a classroom with thirty second-graders, all alone, no cooperating teacher at all, and they said, "Go ahead—do it." I know that in the past I would have reacted to that in complete panic, especially looking at my experience at the lab school, where there was just me and one other kid, and I was having a lot of problems.

T⁵: You mean this past summer?

C⁶: Yes.

T[7]:   Oh yes, I remember your coming in, and you were moaning
         about nothing was right, and you were doing everything
         wrong, etc. How did that turn out?

C[8]:   In the end it turned out to be a very split thing. Had some
         really positive aspects about it and some very negative aspects
         and not very much in the middle. I think it was because of
         the very atypical way in which they structured the school.
         I know I am never going to be faced in the public school system
         in a situation where I work on a one-to-one basis with a kid.
         I mean, I will always have at least thirty, probably more.

T[9]:   Right.

C[10]:   And the difference between then and now is really phenome-
         nal. I mean, I enjoy what I am doing when it is enjoyable;
         and when it is not enjoyable I only think these two things;
         it is a job, number one; and number two, it is something I
         have to do to get through school. In the past the problem
         was I always rated myself in relation to other people. You
         know, "I should be as good a teacher as Mrs. X"—you know—
         "just because I am here. And I just can't be doing any worse
         than she is because I have all these kids in my trust and care,
         and the public school system is paying me money, and I should
         be doing well, and I'm not." Whereas now I realize the reality
         of the situation is that I am a student teacher who is in a
         classroom situation. I don't know anything about the school,
         this particular school; and I don't know anything about their
         way of doing things, their books, etc. But I have to learn,
         that's all, and it takes time. While I am learning, I know I
         am going to be as good a teacher as at least half the people
         here; but that's unimportant.

T[11]:   How would you assess your management of your life situation
         now and your emotional control, etc.

C[12]:   I think I am becoming rational.

T[13]:   Suppose you could stay right where you are now psycho-emo-
         tionally, the rest of your life. Would that be satisfactory to
         you? Would you be able to pursue your life in a personally
         satisfactory manner?

C[14]:   I don't think I would stay here.

T[15]:   What do you mean?

C[16]:   Well, I perceive that I can go farther with being rational than merely handling what is happening now. There is a step beyond handling what happens to me now.

T¹⁷: You mean the step of causing what you want to happen?

C¹⁸: Yes, the difference between the practical and the elegant approach to life. If I continue to handle or react to situations as rationally as I am now, I see no reason why, in probably several months' time, I wouldn't be ready to go on to the next step, the elegant approach.

T¹⁹: I notice you didn't bring your homework book today.

C²⁰: I didn't have any problems.

T²¹: You mean you didn't write any homeworks?

C²²: No, I haven't had any problems to write about since I was here the last time I was here.

T²³: Look, you always have topics for homework. If your current day-to-day life is satisfactory, then do at least one homework per week on past problems and conflicts. What I am trying to say is, you spent your whole life developing the irrational thought patterns that you were using before you came to therapy, and it is unrealistic to expect that in the relatively short period of time that you have been in therapy you have eliminated all of them. Also, I don't expect you or anyone to accomplish that in the time you are in therapy. But by getting you to get in the habit of doing a homework or two once a week, whether you are having personal problems or not, you will be efficiently facilitating the generalizing process of rational thinking. You will be forcing yourself to be constantly checking your perceptions and thoughts. You will forever be alert to irrational, operational assumptions not touched on in therapy. Continued homework is a check on whether or not you are gradually resuming your old ways of conceptualizing and formulating ideas, etc. Do you see what I mean?

C²⁴: Yes.

T²⁵: It is like what every coach would love to have all his athletes doing, with reference to physical conditioning during the off season. Naturally he doesn't expect them to go out and do four hours of calisthenics every day. But he also knows that if they did thirty minutes a day, they would approach the season with better physical condition, thereby decreasing the probability for injury, etc. Understand?

C²⁶: Yes.

T²⁷: So, it is the same kind of thing here. Realistically perceiving and rationally thinking are skills. The more you practice them, the more mileage you will get out of them per unit time spent practicing, when you are trying to get on top of some pressing emotional problem.

C²⁸: Oh, yes, I see what you mean.

T²⁹: Most of my clients use homework more like an aspirin. Just as when they have a headache they rush to the medicine cabinet and get an aspirin, they only think of homework when they have a problem. Actually, you get the most mileage out of homework by doing it when you are between problems. That way, you decrease the probability of having problems.

C³⁰: Not only are you benefiting from doing the homework then, you are free of all the psycho-emotional tension that accompanies homework on present problems.

T³¹: Right, and you are able to more calmly and leisurely explore your thinking, examine and extend it. When you are dealing with a problem, your primary concern is to get the most rational views of it and try to make yourself respond rationally to them. But if you are not caught up in emotional conflict, you can just explore all of the various rational ways that you can function. Do you see?

C³²: Yes.

T³³: Also, it's a good idea to do homework on your friends' problems. That gives you an opportunity to apply rational thinking to someone else's irrational views.

C³⁴: If I did homework on someone else's problems, do I do it as a therapist for them—I mean, in the sense that I am telling them what I think they should do? Or do I do it in the sense of me putting myself in their place?

T³⁵: You do it only as a hypothetical situation, trying to decide what you or any rational person might rationally do. You do not do as you did when you first stopped therapy, namely go around therapizing your friends. You would write up your understanding of the problem in terms like this. "If I assume that what he said was true, then the rational point of view would be this. But if he said that and really meant it, what are the rational implications? What would be his operational assumptions." Do you see what I mean?

C36:   Yes.

In T23, the therapist points out that the client can keep working at doing homework even when things are going well with him, and that he'd better keep doing so in order to continue and to solidify his gains. This is a rather different therapeutic concept than the common insight-will-make-everything-better concept of the "psychodynamic" therapies or the now-that-you-can-trust-me-you-can-go-on-trusting-other-people-too of the "relationship" therapies. In RET, the goal is to give the client a new method of looking at himself and the world, and it is assumed that once he learns this method he can use it to stop upsetting himself in the future about virtually anything that may happen to him. But it is also assumed that his old biologically-based and learned habits of crooked thinking will tend to reassert themselves if he does not keep working quite hard at practicing the therapy-learned habits. Consequently, it is practically necessary, as Dr. Maultsby points out to this client, that he continue to work against his old habits and in favor of the new one, especially by continuing to do homework assignments, even when he is rarely bothered by the symptoms with which he was afflicted when he returned to therapy.

Again, in T27, the therapist notes that "realistically perceiving and rationally thinking are skills" and that the more the client practices these skills, the more mileage he is likely to get out of them. In this respect, as I have often pointed out to my own clients, RET somewhat resembles the client's learning to play golf or chess, or to use statistical methods. For although a good teacher (or even a book) can help him learn these kinds of skills, and although at a certain point in his life he may be very adept at using them, if he doesn't keep practicing, practicing, and practicing at continuing to employ them in the present and future, he soon becomes rusty and is no longer particularly good at exercising them. He may later, at almost any time, relearn these skills; but the relearning process, like the original learning process, requires a great deal of hard-headed, shoulder-to-the-wheel practice. Although RET is in many ways a more complex skill than golf, chess, or statistics, and although it is one that in many respects goes against the grain of the individual's hereditary predispositions and his prior environmental conditioning, it requires a similar amount of time and practice before the individual becomes truly proficient and semi-automatically sustained in using it. In fact, it might be said, just *because* RET involves considerable complexity, and just because it goes against important hereditary-environmental grains, the severely and chronically disturbed individual (whose name may be indeed legion!) probably would better practice it enormously and for quite a period of time during and after therapy before he can expect to make it his "second nature."

When Dr. Maultsby, in his T^{35} response, advises the client against going around "therapizing your friends," he does not mean that the client should never do this—because in RET, the client is frequently encouraged to use some of the rational-emotive principles with his friends, as well as on himself, in order to give himself additional practice with them, and in order to help him answer difficult questions that others (and he himself) might raise against some of the RET ideas. What Dr. Maultsby means here is that the client shirked his responsibilities to himself, after his first series of RET group sessions, when he only used RET principles with his friends and not with himself. If he uses these principles (*a*) directly with his friends when they bring up problems to him, (*b*) indirectly, in the manner that Dr. Maultsby outlines in T^{35}, and (*c*) directly with his own problems in his homework analyses, then he will be in several ways learning them quite thoroughly and helping himself automatically to believe in and act on them.

T^{37}:   Okay, since you are feeling so good today, I want to go over the original list of problems that you wrote up as reasons for coming back to therapy four months ago. The first thing you have is fear of being struck in the head and sustaining a concussion and losing your intelligence, etc.

C^{38}:   I am still afraid of being struck on the head in the sense that I don't want it to happen to me. I imagine I am more sensitized to looking for things, you know, that could possibly strike me on the head and result in another concussion.

T^{39}:   Okay, but is this fear interfering with your ability to function? Is it a problem for you now? Does it result in your not going out of the house as it formerly did?

C^{40}:   No, it hasn't been a problem. I am in a pretty safe situation right now that probably has something to do with it. I mean, I'm not climbing mountains.

T^{41}: But, when you were in group therapy before, you were working in a factory, and you seemed to be handling that pretty well. Still the job was dangerous enough for you to wear a hard hat.

C^{42}: There is no comparison to that situation at all.

T^{43}: What do you mean, no comparison?

C^{44}: Even that was a great fear in comparison to the way I feel now. Then, I used to walk down the street and worry about a car jumping up on the curb and hitting me or the roof of the house falling in on me. I don't do that anymore at all.

T^{45}: What about your preoccupation with loss of intelligence and thinking that you were stupid, etc? Putting the blame for your personal problems and negative feelings on the accident?

C^{46}: That is not a problem at all now. I noticed just the other day I can't even get excited any more even if I try.

T^{47}: You mean you test yourself?

C^{48}: Yes.

T^{49}: On the academic level, you said that it was difficult for you to realize that your mind will not do what you want. What do you mean by that?

C^{50}: Well, by that I mean prior to my accident I was functioning at one intellectual level, and since my accident I am functioning at a lower level.

T^{51}: Exactly at what level are you functioning at?

C^{52}: I feel that it is lower, but that is the way it is. You know, there is nothing you can do about it.

T^{53}: You say that you feel that way, but is there any objective reason for you to feel that way.

C^{54}: Yes, I think so. My grade point average in school before and after my accident.

T^{55}: What was your grade point average?

C^{56}: Well, before my accident it was a three-point, and after my accident it went down to about a two-point.

T^{57}: But what is it now?

C^{58}: Now? I couldn't tell you right now because my grades right now are either B's or incompletes. It has to be at least 3-point to stay in grad school.

T^{59}: Well, you talk about the difference between B's and A's and what—

C⁶⁰: Not all A's, a lot of A's and a lot of B's.

T⁶¹: Well, I think it would be hard to demonstrate any clear-cut significant difference on that basis between your current level of function and prior to the accident. You said you had trouble getting along with your family. Mother-in-law insists on controlling your life.

C⁶²: She hasn't changed.

T⁶³: What are you doing about that?

C⁶⁴: That has changed. I don't upset myself about her at all anymore. She can try all she wants to, but I don't allow her to manipulate my wife and myself.

T⁶⁵: What other evidence could you cite to indicate that you are any better now than you were when you started coming to therapy four months ago? In other words, why do you think that your twelve RET sessions have been a benefit to you?

C⁶⁶: The most tangible thing is that I feel a lot better in my approach to life.

T⁶⁷: I don't see anything tangible about that.

C⁶⁸: Well, the school situation I am in—comparing that now to doing essentially the same thing in lab school over the past summer, and seeing the two different ways in which I handled things.

T⁶⁹: All right, what are the two different ways?

C⁷⁰: Well, in lab school this summer I got myself all uptight over my inadequacies as a teacher—as a teacher interacting with other teachers, as a teacher interacting with a kid, as a teacher interacting with school materials, as a teacher thinking up activities for the kids to do, things to say to them, all of those kinds of things, I used to get very upset about—you know— losing sleep, deriding myself, things like that. Now, I accept the fact that I am not a stupid teacher, but that I am going to make mistakes for years, especially after just being dumped into a classroom, contrary to the way I had assumed it was going to be, with a cooperating teacher leading and guiding me, etc.

T⁷¹: Now, one of the things I think you could get from continuing to do homework is the realization that much of your vocabulary is meaningless nonsense. You say, "dumped into the classroom." Earlier you said, "thrown into the classroom." Nobody dumped you into the classroom, nobody threw you in. And for you it is important to correct those exaggerations, because you have the capacity to make yourself feel appropriate to those words and concepts; and you in fact do it, and that is where you get into trouble. You see, you need to develop a lot of skill in communicating with yourself in the most unemotional, accurate terms possible. By doing it consistently, then you will develop the habit of feeling appropriate to those realistic perceptions of reality. You understand?

C⁷²: Yes. The other thing, I am basing my feelings of greater rationality on, in relation to where they were before, is the fact that I am about to be drafted and I am handling that in the same rational way that I am handling my teaching situation. I realize that with reference to the army, no matter what they decide about taking me, I still have the choice to go or not and to not upset myself about the consequences either way.

In T⁷¹, Dr. Maultsby shows the client that he is habituated to forms of expression that in themselves help him to think crookedly. This is true of most clients, and it is often an important part of RET that the therapist indicates to them what their poor terminology is and how they can keep changing it. Thus, innumerable people keep using terms such as "They made me feel awful when they did that thing to me"; and the therapist corrects, "You mean, *you* made you feel awful when you perceived that thing they did to you." Or the client says: "I should have acted differently"; and the therapist corrects: "You mean, *it would have been better* if you acted differently; but there is really no reason why you *should* have done what would have been much better." Or the client reports: "I've got to stop eating so much!" and the therapist corrects: "You mean, it would be highly desirable, for several reasons, if you stopped eating so much; but as long as you insist that you've got to, you'll probably make yourself so guilty when you do overeat that you'll create sufficient hypertension to help you continue compulsively eating!"

This correction by the rational-emotive therapist of the client's meaningless or misleading vocabulary may seem like semantic hairsplitting, but often it is very important. For as long as people continue to employ erroneous, emotionalized terminology, they will tend to keep propagandizing themselves with irrational ideas; and when they speak more precisely and scientifically, they will tend to help themselves think in a saner, less magical manner. As one of the parting shots in this session, Dr. Maultsby reminds the client that he can, with some work on his part, change his habitual way of speaking and thereby help himself change some of his crooked thinking.

Dr. Maultsby's client had a few sporadic sessions of RET after his twelfth session, continued to improve, and continued to do his homework regularly. He is now out of therapy, appears to be keeping and enhancing his gains, and it looks as if he will not need further sessions (though a third round of RET sessions occasionally occurs with some difficult clients, since relapses may be multiple as well as singular). Assuming that this client retains his improved ways of thinking, emoting, and behaving, it would appear that RET can be successfully applied to relapsed clients, even when they have had a recurrence of what would seem to be psychotic symptoms.

CHAPTER 8

A Twenty-Three-Year-Old Girl, Guilty About Not Following Her Parents' Rules

ALBERT ELLIS, Ph.D.

This is a recording of the first session with Martha, an attractive twenty-three-year-old girl who comes for help because she is quite self-punishing, is both overly impulsive and compulsive, lies, is afraid of males, has no goals in life, and is very guilty about her relations with her father and mother—because they demand a great many things from her, including her adherence to a hard-shelled Baptist religion in which she no longer believes. Dr. Ellis, as is typical of rational-emotive psychotherapists, quickly zeroes in on her main problems and directly tries to show her that she need not be guilty about doing what she wants to do in life, even if her parents keep upsetting themselves about her beliefs and actions.

FIRST SESSION

C¹: Well, for about a year and a half since I graduated from college, I've had the feeling that something was the matter with me. Apparently—well, this was told me by somebody, and the more I think about it the more I think it's true: I seem to have a tendency toward punishing myself. I'm very accident-prone. I'm forever banging myself or falling down stairs, or something like that. And my relationship with my father is causing me a great deal of trouble. I've never been able to figure out where is the responsibility and what my relationship with my parents should be.

T²: Do you live with them?

C³: No, I don't. They live in Great Neck. I moved out in March.

T⁴: What does your father do?

C⁵: He is a newspaper editor.

T⁶: And your mother is a housewife?

C⁷: Yes.

T⁸: Any other children?

C⁹: Yes, I have two younger brothers. One is twenty; the other is sixteen. I'm twenty-three. The sixteen-year-old has polio, and the other one has an enlarged heart. My family was always very close. We never had much money, but we always had the feeling that love and security in life are what count. And the first thing that disturbed me was, when I was about sixteen years old, my father began to drink seriously. To me he had been the infallible person. Anything he said was right. And since I moved out and before I moved out, I've wondered where my responsibility to my family lies. Because if they would ask me to do something, if I didn't do it, I would feel guilty about it.

T¹⁰: What sort of things did they ask you to do?

C¹¹: Well, they didn't want me to move out; they felt that it just wasn't right for an unmarried girl to move out. Also, I'm very impulsive, I'm very compulsive; and I find it easier to lie than to tell the truth, if the truth is unpleasant. I think I'm basically afraid of men and afraid to find a good relationship with a man—I mean a relationship that would lead to marriage. My parents have never approved of anyone I have gone out with. In thinking about it, I wonder whether I, subconsciously maybe, went out of my way to find somebody they wouldn't approve of.

T¹²: Do you go with anyone now?

C¹³: Yes, two people.

T¹⁴: And are you serious about either one?

C¹⁵: Well, that I don't know. I really don't. One is sort of serious about me, but he thinks there's something the matter with me that I have to straighten out. I have also at various times been rather promiscuous, and I don't want to be that way.

T¹⁶: Have you enjoyed the sex?

C¹⁷: Not particularly. I think—in trying to analyze it myself and find out why I was promiscuous, I think I was afraid not to be.

T¹⁸: Afraid they wouldn't like you, you mean?

C[19]: Yes. This one fellow that I've been going with—in fact, both of them—said that I don't have a good opinion of myself.

T[20]: What do you work at?

C[21]: Well, I'm a copywriter for an advertising agency. I don't know if this means anything, but when I was in college, I never could make up my mind what to major in. I had four or five majors. I was very impulsive about the choice of college.

T[22]: What did you finally pick?

C[23]: I went to the University of Illinois.

T[24]: What did you finally major in?

C[25]: I majored in—it was a double major: advertising and English.

T[26]: Did you do all right in college?

C[27]: Yes, I was a Phi Beta Kappa. I graduated with honors.

T[28]: You had no difficulty—even though you had trouble in making up your mind—you had no difficulty with the work itself?

C[29]: No, I worked very hard. My family always emphasized that I couldn't do well in school, so I had to work hard. I always studied hard. Whenever I set my mind to do anything, I really worked at it. And I was always unsure of myself with people. Consequently, I've almost always gone out with more than one person at the same time. I think that it is, possibly, maybe a fear of rejection by one. Also, something that bothers me more than anything is that I think that I have the ability to write, and I wrote a lot when I was in college. Fiction, that is. And I've done a little bit since. But I don't seem to be able to discipline myself. Instead of spending my time wisely, as far as writing is concerned, I'll let it go, let it go, and then go out several nights a week—which I know doesn't help me. When I ask myself why I do it, I don't know.

T[30]: Are you afraid the writing wouldn't be good enough?

C[31]: I have that basic fear.

T[32]: That's right: it is a *basic* fear.

C[33]: Although I have pretty well convinced myself that I have talent, I'm just afraid to apply myself. My mother always encouraged me to write, and she always encouraged me to keep on looking for something better in everything I do. And from the time when I started to go out with boys, when I was about thirteen or fourteen, she never wanted me to get interested in one boy. There was always something better somewhere else. Go out and look for it. And if somebody didn't please me in all respects, go out and find somebody else. I think that this has influenced the feeling that I've had that I might be quite interested in one person, but I'm always looking for someone else.

T³⁴: Yes, I'm sure it probably has.

C³⁵: But I don't know what I'm looking for.

T³⁶: You seem to be looking for perfection, in a sense—which you're not going to find. You're looking for security, certainty.

I first obtain a moderate degree of background information from Martha—not for the ordinary kind of diagnosis (since I can quickly see that she is seriously disturbed), but to find a symptom that I can concretely use to show her what her basic philosophy or value system is and how she can change it. I thus ask her, in T³⁰, "Are you afraid the writing wouldn't be good enough?" because I assume, on the basis of rational-emotive theory, that there are only a few major reasons why she is not writing, and that this is probably one of them. Once she admits she has a fear of failure in writing, I emphasize that this is probably a general or basic fear—so that she will begin to see that her fear of failure is all-pervasive and explains some of the other dysfunctional behavior she has been indicating. As soon as I think I have a reasonably good chance to get in a therapeutic word, I stop Martha, in T³⁶, and flatly tell her that I think she's looking for perfection and certainty. I hope she will be somewhat startled by this statement and will want to go into it further: in which case I intend to show her that her writing fears (and other symptoms) largely stem from her perfectionism. As it happens, she does not appear ready yet to take up my hypothesis; so I bide my time for a while, knowing that I will sooner or later get back to forcing her to look at some of the philosophies behind her disturbed behavior.

C³⁷: Well, the basic problem I think that I have is that I seem to have lost sight of goals. I'm tied up in knots about—I'm worried about my family. I'm worried about money. And I never seem to be able to relax.

T³⁸: Why are you worried about your family. Let's go into that, first of all. What's to be concerned about? They have certain demands on you which you don't want to adhere to.

C³⁹: I was brought up to think that I mustn't be selfish.

T⁴⁰: Oh, we'll have to knock *that* out of your head!

C⁴¹: I think that that is one of the basic problems.

T⁴²: That's right. You were brought up to be Florence Nightingale—which is to be very disturbed!

C⁴³: I was brought up in a family of sort of would-be Florence Nightingales, now that I analyze the whole pattern of my family history. Maybe it was just a perversion of other desires. My parents got married because I was on the way. I really think that they loved each other. I don't know, but I think they did. They were pretty happy with each other up till a few years ago. When I was a little girl, I was my father's pet. Nobody ever spanked me, hardly anybody said a cross word to me. So I really don't think I was spoiled. My brother, Joe, who is twenty, had an enlarged heart, from which he has pretty well recovered as a result of an operation; and my parents are now sending him to college. My sixteen-year-old brother has had polio. When I was twelve, I developed an easily dislocatable shoulder; and there's always been one kind of ailment or another in my family. Always. And they have never been able to get out of debt. Never. They were hardly able to help me through college. I incurred all kinds of debts myself in college. And since then I've helped my family. My father became really alcoholic sometime when I was away in college. My mother developed a breast cancer last year, and she had one breast removed. Nobody is healthy.

T⁴⁴: How is your father doing now?

C⁴⁵: Well, he's doing much better. He's been going to AA meetings, and the doctor he has been seeing has been giving him tranquilizers and various other types of pills to keep him going. He spends quite a bit of money every week on pills. And if he misses a day of pills, he's absolutely unlivable. My mother feels that I shouldn't have left home—that my place is in Great Neck with them. I don't feel that, but there are nagging doubts, and there are nagging doubts about what I should—

T⁴⁶: Why are there doubts? Why *should* you?

C⁴⁷: I think it's a feeling I was brought up with that you always have to give of yourself. If you think of yourself, you're wrong.

T⁴⁸: That's a *belief.* It's a feeling because you *believe* it. Now, why
do you have to keep believing that—at *your* age? You believed
a lot of superstitions when you were younger. Why do you
have to retain them? We can see why your parents would
have to indoctrinate you with this kind of nonsense, because
that's *their* belief. But why do you still have to believe this
nonsense—that one should not be self-interested; that one
should be devoted to others, self-sacrificial? Who needs that
philosophy? All it's gotten you, so far, is guilt. And that's all
it ever *will* get you!

C⁴⁹: And now I try to break away. For instance, they'll call up
and say, "Why don't you come Sunday? Why don't you come
Friday?" And if I say, "No, I'm busy," rather than saying,
"No, I can't come, I will come when it's convenient," they
get terribly hurt, and my stomach gets all upset.

T⁵⁰: Because you tell yourself, "There I go again. I'm a louse for
not devoting myself to them!" As long as you tell yourself
that crap, then your stomach or some other part of you will
start jumping! But it's your *philosophy*, your *belief*, your *sentence to yourself*—"I'm no goddamned good! How could I do
that lousy, stinking thing?" *That's* what's causing your stomach to jump. Now that sentence is a false sentence. Why are
you no goddamned good because you prefer you to them? For
that's what it amounts to. *Who said* you're no damned good—
Jesus Christ? Moses? Who the hell said so? The answer is:
your parents said so. And you believe it because they said
so. But who the hell are they?

C⁵¹: That's right. You're brought up to believe that everything
your parents say is right. And I haven't been able to loose
myself from this.

T⁵²: You haven't *done* it. You're *able* to, but you haven't. And *you're*
now saying, every time you call them, the same crap to yourself. And you've got to see you're saying this drivel! Every
time a human being gets upset—except when she's in physical
pain—she has always told herself some bullshit the second
before she gets upset. Normally, the bullshit takes the form,
"This is terrible!"—in your case, "It's terrible that I don't want
to go out there to see them!" Or people tell themselves, "I
shouldn't be doing this!"—in your case, "I *shouldn't* be a selfish

individual!" Now, those terms—"This is terrible!" and "I *shouldn't* be doing this!"—are assumptions, premises. You cannot sustain them scientifically. But you *believe* they're true, without any evidence, mainly because your parents indoctrinated you to believe that they're true. It's exactly the same kind of assumption that people make that "Negroes are no goddamned good!" If you had been raised in the South, you would have believed that. But is it true because you would have been raised to believe it?

C[53]: No.

T[54]: Then why is it true that one should not be selfish, or should not stick up for oneself first, and should not consider one's parents or anybody else second, third, fourth, and fifth?

C[55]: That's absolutely right.

T[56]: Yes, but we've got to get you to believe it—that's the point. You don't *believe* that.

C[57]: I *want* to believe that.

T[58]: I know you want to; and once in a while you do believe it. But most of the time, very forcefully and strongly, you believe the crap with which you were indoctrinated. Not only believe it, but *keep* indoctrinating yourself with it. That's the real perniciousness of it. That's the reason it persists—not because they taught it to you. It would just naturally die after a while. But you keep saying it to yourself. It's these simple declarative sentences that you tell yourself every time you make a telephone call to your parents. And unless we can get you to see that you are saying them, and contradict and challenge them, you'll go on saying them forever. Then you will keep getting pernicious results: headaches, self-punishment, lying, and whatever else you get. These results are the logical consequences of an irrational cause, a false premise. And it's this premise that has to be questioned. If you do question it, you can't possibly sustain it.

As soon as Martha, in C[45], says that she has nagging doubts about staying at home with her parents, and that she's wrong if she thinks of herself first, I jump in with both feet and try to show her that this idea is only an opinion, that it cannot be empirically justified, and that it will lead to poor results. I am herewith being classically rational-emotive: not only explicating but attacking Martha's self-defeating premises and values, and trying to actively teach her how to attack them herself. I make a mistake, however, in T^{56}, by saying "We've got to get you to believe it." I could have better said: "It would be much preferable if we get you to believe it."

C^{59}: I get so mad at myself for being so illogical.

T^{60}: Now, you see, there you go again! Because you are not only saying that you *are* illogical, but that you *shouldn't* be. Why *shouldn't* you be? It's a pain in the ass to be illogical; it's a nuisance. But who says it's *wicked* for you to be wrong? That's what you're saying—that's *your parents'* philosophy.

C^{61}: Yes, and also there's the matter of religion. I was brought up to be a strict, hard-shelled Baptist. And I can't quite take it any more. This has been going on for— (*Pause*) Well, the first seeds of doubt were sown when I was in high school. Nobody answered my questions. And I kept asking the minister, and he didn't answer my questions. And when I went to college, I started reading. I tried very hard, the first two years in college. I went to church all the time. If I had a question. I'd ask the minister. But pretty soon I couldn't get any answers. And now I really don't believe in the Baptist Church.

T^{62}: All right, But are you *guilty* about not believing?

C^{63}: Not only am I guilty, but the worst part about it is that I can't quite tell my parents that I don't believe.

T^{64}: But why do you have to? What's the necessity? Because they're probably not going to accept it.

C^{65}: Well, they didn't accept it. I was going to get married to a Jewish fellow as soon as I graduated from college. And, of course, the problem of religion came up then. And I didn't stand up for what I believed. I don't know; rather than have scenes, I took the coward's way out. And when I spend Saturdays and Sundays with them now—which is rare—I go to church with them. And this is what I mean by lying, rather than telling the truth.

T^{66}: I see. You're probably going to extremes there—going to church. Why do you have to go to church?

C[67]: I always hate to create a scene.

T[68]: You mean you always sell your soul for a mess of porridge?

C[69]: Yes, I do.

T[70]: I don't see why you should. That leaves you with no integrity. Now it's all right to do whatever you want about being quiet, and not telling your parents about your loss of faith—because they're not going to approve and could well upset themselves. There's no use in throwing your irreligiosity in their faces. But to let yourself be forced to go to church and thereby to give up your integrity—that's bullshit. You can even tell them, if necessary, "I don't believe in that any more." And if there's a scene, there's a scene. If they commit suicide, they commit suicide! You can't really hurt them, except physically. You can't hurt anybody else except with a baseball bat! You can do things that they don't like, that they take too seriously, and that they hurt themselves with. But you can't really hurt them with words and ideas. That's nonsense. They taught you to believe that nonsense: "You're hurting us, dear, if you don't go along with what we think you ought to do!" That's drivel of the worst sort! They're hurting themselves by fascistically demanding that you do a certain thing, and then making themselves upset when you don't do it. You're not doing the hurting—they are. If they get hurt because you tell them you're no longer a Baptist, that's their doing. They're hurting themselves; you're not hurting them. They'll say, "How can you do this to us?" But is that *true*? *Are* you doing anything to them or are *they* doing it to themselves?

C[71]: No, I'm not.

T[72]: But you *believe* that you're hurting them. It's crap!

Classically, again, I try to show Martha, as is usually done in rational-emotive therapy that it is ethical to stick up for herself first, if she chooses to do so, and for her parents second. I also emphasize that people, including her and her parents, are not hurt by words, gestures, and attitudes (at point A) but by the nonsense they tell themselves about these verbalizations and meanings (at point B). I saw Martha a dozen years ago, when RET was a very young system of therapy. Today, I might very well take the same tack, but probably be less long-winded about it.

C[73]: And also, my mother thinks that I should be at home. I was contributing quite a bit of my paycheck every week. I got my first job when I graduated. My father started to work about the same time. He had been out of work. And I just gave them everything but what I absolutely needed. The debts that I had incurred when I was in college, I couldn't really start to pay back. Since then I've moved out, and I give them a little; but I just can't give them much any more—because I just simply can't. And besides that, I've gotten sick. I was sick twice this fall. And I have to get my teeth pulled now, and have to get a full upper plate put in. And I'm under financial strain. They make me feel—I guess I can't say *they* make me feel guilty.

T[74]: No; *you* do!

C[75]: The thing I make myself guilty about is the fact that my father doesn't earn enough money to support them.

T[76]: Why should *you* make yourself guilty because *he* doesn't earn enough money?

C[77]: All my life, ever since I can remember, I have. And I don't know where I got it from. This I would like to find out because maybe I can get rid of it. I've always felt that I had to make up for my father, because of his lack of financial success in the world. I don't know why I have the feeling.

T[78]: You have it, obviously, because somewhere along the line you *accepted* their indoctrination with this kind of philosophy—that you have to make up for your family's deficiencies. It doesn't matter exactly how they indoctrinated you; but you didn't get it from nowhere. Anyway, you let yourself be indoctrinated with this notion. They and society started it—for society helps indoctrinate you, too. Maybe it's a matter of shame: you think, "If everybody knows my father is so incompetent, they'll look down on us; and that would be terrible! So I have to make up for his lack in order to show people that we have a perfectly fine family."

C[79]: No, it isn't that. Someone was always sick. And if it wasn't one person sick, it was two. And this went on all the time. There was no time that I can remember when everybody was well. They've had doctors all the time. And when my brother Teddy was ill, my father spent a great deal of time going from doctor to doctor, and not concentrating on his—on his own career, I guess.

T^{80}: That may have been because of his own mental disturbance. He's probably always been mentally upset; alcoholics generally are.

C^{81}: He's always been supporting more people than he can. When his father died, my daddy was twelve, and he started working part time then. And then all through high school. He supported his mother and his sister all the way up till the time he married my mother. And then his mother made him feel guilty about getting married.

T^{82}: Yes, that's right; and he's been pre-alcoholic, in a sense, all his life, because he agreed with his mother that he should feel guilty. He now merely is more guilty than ever, and therefore has gone over the border into real alcoholism.

C^{83}: The constant pressures, the financial pressures, that were on him—

T^{84}: Which he really created—or at least went out of his way to accept!

C^{85}: Yes. Because he's a great writer and could make a lot of money that way. He could sell everything he writes. But why he doesn't, I don't know.

T^{86}: Because he's so disturbed.

C^{87}: He *is* disturbed.

T^{88}: He's always been. And probably, because you were the one member of the family who was relatively healthy physically, you felt, "I have to make up to the others for being this healthy!"

C^{89}: My mother always told me that. You see, I was always healthy until I developed my easily dislocatable shoulder. And my mother told me that my father almost came apart at the seams when I got afflicted, too. Because I was always the one he could look to for his security.

T^{90}: Yes, and that's exactly the point now. There's your answer: he looked to you for his security. That's where you may have got the concept that you had to be his security. There's their indoctrination. It's his expectation that you will take care of him and the family; and you've always tried to live up to that expectation.

C^{91}: I've always tried to live up to their expectations!

T^{92}: You're still trying to live *their* lives, instead of living *yours*.

C^{93}: I'm realizing that now. And I don't want to live their lives.

T^{94}: Well, I'm afraid that you have to be almost cruel and ruthless with people like your parents—because otherwise they'll exploit you forever: and you'll just be in the old morass. Because they're going to remain in a morass for the rest of their lives. I doubt whether they will ever change.

C^{95}: I feel that I went to college, and I was doing it practically on my own. My father always gave me five or ten dollars whenever he could; and he paid the phone bills. They tried, but they couldn't keep up with the expenses. I borrowed money, and I got some scholarships, and I worked in my freshman year. And I thought, "Now that I'm in college, I'm not a financial worry of theirs. Now everything will be all right. They'll be able to get on their feet. There are only four people to support." But it didn't happen.

T^{96}: You may never be in good financial circumstances, as far as I can see. Your father is too mentally disturbed.

C^{97}: They think everything will turn out well.

T^{98}: Yes, I'm sure. God is on their side!

C^{99}: I tried a little experiment with God—which was one of the things that made me break off from religion. I always used to pray for what I wanted, because anything you want you pray for. So I was always praying. Then one time I said, "I'll see what I can do without praying." So I studied instead; and I did better!

T^{100}: Right! But people like your parents will never take that risk of trying things without calling upon God to help them.

C^{101}: If there were a God, he never would have cursed anybody like he cursed my family—.

T^{102}: Yes, if there were a God, he'd be awfully cruel to do this to your family. Because you seem to have every ill in it: alcoholism, cancer, polio, an enlarged heart, a dislocatable shoulder—you name it! Every one of five people seems to be sorely afflicted. You could hardly have a worse setup.

C^{103}: I said once at the dinner table, "You know, somebody up there hates us!" (*Laughs*) I wanted to come to you because Ronald suggested it because you helped him get over his guilt about his mother. I had the feeling that I should go somewhere to find out what needed to be done. Because I don't want to waste any more of my life.

T¹⁰⁴: What needs to be done is relatively simple—but it's not easy to do. And that is—you've already done parts of what needs to be done. You have changed some of your fundamental philosophies—particularly regarding religion—which is a big change for a human being to make. But you haven't changed enough of your philosophy; you still believe some basic superstitions. Most people—whether Jew, Catholic, or Protestant—believe these superstitions, and your parents believe them even more than most people do, because they're more disturbed. The main superstitions are that we should devote ourselves to others before ourselves; that we must be loved, accepted, and adored by others, especially by members of our own family; and that we must do well, we must achieve greatly, succeed, do right. And you firmly believe these major superstitions. You'd better get rid of them!

C¹⁰⁵: How do I do that?

T¹⁰⁶: By seeing, first of all, that every single time you get upset— meaning guilty, depressed, anxious, or anything like that— every time you get some form of upset, some severe negative feelings, right before you got the feeling, you told yourself some superstitious creed—some bullshit. That, for example, you're no good because you aren't successful at something; or that you're a louse because you are unpopular, or are selfish, or are not as great as you should be. Then, when you see that you have told yourself this kind of nonsense, you have to ask yourself the question, "*Why* should I have to be successful? *Why* should I always have to be accepted and approved? *Why* should I be utterly loved and adored? Who said so? Jesus Christ? Who the hell was he?" There is no evidence that these things *should* be so; and you are just parroting, on faith, this nonsense, this crap that most people in your society believe. And it's not only your parents who taught it to you. It's also all those stories you read, the fairy tales you heard, the TV shows you saw. They all include this hogwash!

C[107]: I know. But every time you try to overcome this, you're faced with it somewhere else again. And I realize—I've come to realize—you know, the thing that made me try to straighten myself out was that I know I've got to learn to have confidence in my own judgment.

T[108]: While you've really got confidence in this other crap!

C[109]: Yes, I'm very unconfident.

T[110]: You have to be—because you believe this stuff.

I continue actively teaching and depropagandizing Martha. Not only do I deal with the irrational philosophies that she brings up, but I prophylactically mention and attack others as well. I keep trying to expose to her a few basic groundless ideas—such as the ideas that she must be loved and must perform well—and to show her that her symptoms, such as her self-sacrificing and her lack of self-confidence, are the natural results of these silly ideas.

C[111]: I have tremendous self-doubts about every part of my existence.

T[112]: Yes, you must, because you have so much of a belief that you must please others. If you have so much of this belief, you cannot have confidence in you. It's virtually impossible, for how can you do two opposite things at once—have confidence that you are a valuable person to yourself, no matter what others think, and believe that you are not valuable to you unless others approve of you? Confidence in yourself is really a high-class term for not giving that much of a damn what other people think of you. That's all it is. But you do care terribly about what other people think of you—about what your parents, especially, think. But also, probably, about what many other people think. Because if you were a poor daughter, what would the neighbors think? What would your friends think? You're really petrified!

C[113]: It's not the neighbors and friends. The thing that ties me up mostly is my parents.

T[114]: Yes, they're the primary ones. What would *they* think of you if you acted mainly in your own behalf? So what, if they think you're a louse? Let's even suppose that they disinherit you, excommunicate you from the family—

C[115]: Then I should think, "If they care that little about me, why should I care about them?"

T[116]: That's right. That would be tough! But it would just prove that they were benighted. It just would follow from their philosophy, which they're entitled to hold—however miserable it has made them. It would prove that they are fascistically trying to force you to believe this philosophy; and because they're failing, they excommunicate you. They're entitled to do so, of course; but you're entitled to say, "Who needs them?" Suppose, for example, you lived down south for awhile, that lots of people didn't like you because you weren't against Negroes, and that they called you a nigger-lover. What are you going to do—get terribly upset about them?

C[117]: No, that wouldn't bother me, because that never entered my life. I mean the fact that they hate Negroes. There are people who hate Negroes who never entered my life. Because I went to school with Negroes. Nobody ever told me that they were bad. If somebody ever said, "You're bad because you don't hate Negroes," that wouldn't bother me because that's not something—

T[118]: All right. But why should it bother you if somebody says you're bad because you don't put your parents' interests before your own?

C[119]: I guess because I've been indoctrinated with this idea.

T[120]: You believe *it*. It's exactly like hard-shelled Baptism. In fact, it has some of the aspects of orthodox religion; for this kind of religion says that the family comes first and the individual second; and that you're supposed to have twenty children and not use birth control, and so on. That's what many orthodox religions, like Catholicism and orthodox Judaism, teach. Everything for the church, the family—and somewhere, away underneath, the individual is buried.

C[121]: But the individual—whatever contributions he has to make, whatever his capabilities are—can be lost that way; and I don't want to be lost.

T[122]: Not only can he be, he must be lost that way.

C[123]: I don't want to be self-effacing!

T[124]: Right! Then why do you have to be? Who said you must be?

The answer is: your parents. Who the hell are they? Poor, sick, benighted individuals. They're not educated; they're not sophisticated. They're probably bright enough, but they're disturbed. Your father, as we said before, has probably been seriously upset all his life, in an undramatic manner. More recently, he became dramatically ill. But it doesn't come on like that. (*Snaps his fingers*) You can see the signs clearly over the years. And your mother has probably been fairly disturbed, too, though probably not as much as he. But that's the way it is: you were raised in a pretty crazy family. Does that mean you have to kowtow to their beliefs for the rest of your life?

C¹²⁵: No; I want to get away from it. I want to be myself. I don't want to be—

T¹²⁶: What's preventing you from being yourself? Nothing can prevent you right now, if you really want to be. You just would do better, every time the feelings of being weak arise, to trace them to the indoctrinations of your parents and of your society and your acceptance of these indoctrinations. And you'd better counter them—because you're suggesting to yourself, a hundred times a day now, those same creeds. You've taken them over, internalized them. And that's really fortunate. Because it's now become *your* belief—you can get rid of it. Not immediately—but you can. Just like you got rid of your religious views.

C¹²⁷: And I also want to find out—I suppose it's all basically the same thing—why I have been promiscuous, why I lie—

T¹²⁸: For love. You think you're such a worm that the only way to get worth, value, is to be loved, approved, accepted. And you're promiscuous to gain love, because it's an easy way: you can gain acceptance easily that way. You lie because you're ashamed. You feel that they wouldn't accept you if you told the truth. These are very common results; anybody who desperately needs to be loved—as you think you do with your crummy philosophy, will be promiscuous, will lie, will do other things which are silly, rather than do the things she really wants to do and rather than gain her own self-approval.

C¹²⁹: That's what I don't have; I don't have any.

T[130]: You never tried to get it! You're working your butt off to get other people's approval. Your parents' first, but other people's second. That's why the promiscuity; that's why the lying. And you're doing no work whatever at getting your own self-acceptance, because the only way you get self-respect is by not giving that much of a damn what other people think. There is no other way to get it; that's what self-acceptance really means: to thine *own* self be true!

In my response, T[130], I epitomize one of the main differences between RET and most other "dynamic" systems of psychological treatment. Whereas a psychoanalytically-oriented therapist would probably have tried to show Martha that her promiscuity and lying stemmed from her early childhood experiences, I, as a rational-emotive therapist, believe nothing of the sort. I assume, instead, that her childhood lying, for example, was mainly caused by her own innate tendencies toward crooked thinking—which in turn led her to react inefficiently to the noxious stimuli her parents may have imposed on her. What is important, therefore, is her own reactivity and not her parents' actions. I also believe, on theoretical grounds, that the reason for Martha's present promiscuity and lying is probably her current need to be inordinately loved; and she freely seems to admit (as she also previously did in C[19]) that my educated guess about this is true.

If I proved to be wrong in this guess, I would not be perturbed but would look for another hypothesis—for example, her promiscuity might be a form of self-punishment, because she thought she was unworthy on some other count. As a rational-emotive therapist, I am willing to take a chance on being wrong with my first hypothesis because, if I am right, I will usually save my client a good deal of time. Moreover, by taking a wrong tack, I may well help myself and the client get to the right tack. If, however, I try the psychoanalytic, history-taking path, in order to arrive at the "real" reasons for my client's behavior (1) I may never find what these "real" reasons are (for they may not exist, or years of probing may never turn them up); (2) I may still come up with the wrong reasons; and (3) I may sidetrack the client so seriously that she may never discover what her basic disturbance-creating philosophy is and therefore never do anything about changing it. For a variety of reasons, then, I take a very direct approach with Martha.

C¹³¹: You have to develop a sort of hard shell towards other people?

T¹³²: Well, it isn't really a callous shell. It's really that you have to develop your own goals and your own confidence so much that you do not allow the views and desires of others to impinge that much on you. Actually, you'll learn to be kinder and nicer to other people if you do this. We're not trying to get you to be against others, to be hostile or resentful. But you won't be Florence Nightingale, either! So you'd better get, not insensitive, but invulnerable. And the less vulnerable you get to what others think of you, actually the more sensitive, kindly, and loving you can often be. Because you haven't been so loving, really, but largely maintaining a façade with your parents. Underneath, you've been resentful, unloving.

C¹³³: I can be loving, though.

T¹³⁴: That's right. But you'd better be true to yourself first; and through being true to yourself—and not being anxious, depressed, and upset—then you'll be able to care more for other people. Not all people, and maybe not your parents. There's no law that says you have to love your parents. They may just not be your cup of tea. In fact, it looks like in some ways they aren't. Tough! It would be nice if they were; it would be lovely if they were people of your own kind, if you could love them and have good relationships. But that may never really be. You may well have to withdraw emotionally from them, to some extent—not from everybody, but probably from them somewhat—in order to be true to yourself. Because they tend to be leeches, fascists, emotional blackmailers.

C¹³⁵: Yes, that's the term: emotional blackmailers. This I know; this has been evidenced all through my life. Emotional blackmail!

At every point, I try to show Martha that she does not have to feel guilty for withdrawing emotionally from her parents and doing what she wants to do or thinking what she wants to think. I do not try to get her to condemn her parents or to be hostile to them. Quite the contrary! But I do consistently show her that they have their own problems and that she'd better resist their emotional blackmailing. As it turns out, she seems to have always known this; but my actively bringing it to her attention will presumably help her to act, now, on what she knows and feels. I am thereby helping her, through frank and therapist-directed discussion, to get in touch with her real feelings and to follow them in practice.

T^{136}: Right. And you've been accepting this blackmail. You had to accept it as a child—you couldn't help it, you were dependent. But there's no law that says you *still* have to accept it. You can see that they're blackmailing; calmly resist it, without being resentful of them—because they are, they are. It's too bad, but if they are, they are. Then their blackmail won't take effect. And they'll probably foam at the mouth, have fits, and everything. Tough!—so they'll foam. Well, there's no question that you can be taught to change. We haven't got any more time now. But the whole thing—as I said awhile ago—is your philosophy, which is an internalizing, really, of their philosophy. And if there ever was evidence of how an abject philosophy affects you, there it is: they're thoroughly miserable. And you'll be just as miserable if you continue this way. If you want to learn to *change* your philosophy, this is what I do in therapy: beat people's ideas over the head until they stop defeating themselves. That's all you're doing: defeating yourself!

I not only reemphasize, at the end of the session, that it is Martha's views, taken over from her parents, that are bolixing her up, but I keep utilizing material from her own life to consistently show her what is going on in her head, philosophically, and what she'd better do about changing her thinking. This twelve-year-old first interview with Martha indicates how RET, right from the start, encourages the therapist to talk much more about the client's value system than about her symptoms and how it uses the information she gives to highlight her own disturbance-creating ideas and to attack them. I think that this session also shows that although I do not hesitate to contradict Martha's assumptions at several points, I am essentially supportive in that I keep showing her (1) that I am on her side, (2) that I think I can help her, (3) that I am fairly sure what the real sources of her disturbances are, and (4) that if she works at seeing these sources and at doing something to undermine them, the chances are excellent that she will become much less upsettable. My "attack," therefore, is one that would ordinarily be called "ego-bolstering." Or, in RET terminology, it is one that is designed to help Martha fully accept rather than severely condemn herself.

To this end, I consistently have what Carl Rogers (1961) calls "unconditional positive regard" for Martha, for I accept her in spite of her difficulties and inanities, and believe that she is capable of overcoming her crooked thinking by living and working primarily for herself. I also show that I am on Martha's side, not because I personally find her attractive, bright, or competent, but because I feel that every human has the right to live primarily for herself and to consider others, including her parents, second.

SECOND SESSION

This is a recording of the second session with Martha, which takes place five days after the first session. It shows that she has already made some progress, has calmed down considerably, and is now in a better condition to work at some of her basic problems.

T[1]:   How are things?

C[2]:   Things are okay. I went to visit my parents on Monday night. And every time I was tempted to fall prey to their emotional blackmail, I remembered what you said, and I was able to fight it.

T[3]:   Fine!

C[4]:   My mother is having a rough time yet, because of having her breast removed. She hardly says anything. She's really in a world of fog. She gets confused, and she uses the confusion to give her a hold on the family. She was putting on a martyr act the other night; and usually I would have given in to her, but I said, "Quit being a martyr! Go to bed." She just looked at me as though I was a strange creature!

T[5]:   And you didn't get upset by it?

C[6]:   No, I didn't get upset by it. I had the feeling that I was doing the right thing. And that was, I think, the major accomplishment in the past few days.

T[7]:   Yes; well that was quite a good accomplishment.

C[8]:   Now if there are any bigger crises that will come, I don't know how I'll face them; but it looks like I can.

T⁹: Yes; and if you keep facing these smaller crises as they arise—and they tend to be continual—there's no reason why you shouldn't be able to face the bigger ones as well. Why not?

C¹⁰: I guess it's a case of getting into a good habit.

T¹¹: Yes, that's right: getting really to believe that no matter what your parents do, no matter how hurt they get, that's not your basic problem. You're not deliberately doing them in; you're just standing up for yourself.

As often occurs in RET, although this is only the second session, Martha is already beginning to implement some of the major ideas that were discussed during the first session and is beginning to change herself. I deliberately support her new notion that she can handle herself with her parents, and I keep reiterating that she does not have to react upsettedly to their views and behavior by getting upset. I thereby am approving her new patterns and rewarding or reinforcing her. But I am also repetitively teaching—taking every opportunity to reassert that she can think for herself and does not have to react negatively because her parents or others view her unfavorably.

C¹²: Well, something else has bothered me, I guess, during the last eighteen months. No, I guess after I finished school. I have the feeling that I can't express myself verbally as well as I used to do. I don't know why this is. Maybe I'm in an atmosphere where—well, you can't say that they aren't talking enough. But I really feel that I've lost something.

T¹³: Do you mean when you're talking to people in business or socially, you can't express yourself as well as you used to?

C¹⁴: Yes, I can't seem to find the right words.

T¹⁵: Well, part of it is probably true: because you've lost confidence in yourself during some of this while. And when you lose confidence in yourself, you will not be as good as you were in your performance. Then you look at your not being as good as you were—and you lose *more* confidence! That's the vicious circle that occurs. Now, if you'd stop worrying about how good you are at expressing yourself and just keep expressing yourself, most of your old ability would probably come back—

maybe all of it; you might even get better than you were. But you used to do it less self-consciously; and now you've become more self-conscious, more worried about how you're expressing yourself. We all make mistakes and blunders in expression. But you're taking yours too seriously. There's a famous experiment which is done with stutterers. You can take a stutterer, a very bad stutterer, and put earphones on him and play noise into the earphones so that he can't hear himself talk. Then you can give him something to read, and he often reads it without any stuttering!

C[16]:   Oh!

T[17]:   Because he can't worry; he can't know how badly or well he's reading. But if you take off the earphones again, he starts stuttering right away, because he's then able to listen to his voice; and he does a little stuttering for the first few words and then says to himself, "My Lord! This is terrible!" Then he starts stuttering, stuttering, stuttering. Now, you're paying too much attention to *how* you're expressing yourself; and *because* you're paying too much attention to it, you're not expressing yourself well.

My responses, T[15] and T[17], are really based on pure guesswork, stemming from RET theory. I know, from clinical experience and from theoretical constructs inducted from this experience, why most people fail to express themselves well and what they think about themselves when they fail, so I take the chance of assuming that Martha falls into the majority group and explain to her what is probably occurring in her case. If it transpires that I am wrong about her, I can always backtrack and look for a more realistic explanation. In the interest of economy, however, I hazard the guesses I make her, and wait to see how she will react to these hypotheses.

C[18]:   Something that I did wrong on Saturday—I found myself telling a lie, just a very, very minor thing. It wasn't a case where I had decided to tell a lie; it just came out without my realizing it.

T[19]:   Well, you're in the habit, probably. What were the circumstances?

C[20]:   Well, I had a date. I went up to Harlem. We met another couple—they were with us—and then my date got up to dance with the other girl. And the other fellow didn't ask me to dance. This happened a couple of times, and I got very annoyed. I felt that he didn't show any manners, and I was very upset about it.

T²¹: Was he dancing with his own date?

C²²: No, he didn't dance; well, he danced with her a couple of times, but I guess I felt neglected or something. And then on the way home the subject came up, and I said, "Oh, I told him how rude he was." I told my date that I told the other fellow how rude he was. And I hadn't said anything to him at all.

T²³: That's a very simple business to find out why you lied there. What you were saying to yourself was, "I should have told him this or something like this"—which, incidentally is wrong, as I'll show you in a minute. But let's, anyway, say it. You said to yourself, "I should have told him he was rude." And then you were ashamed that you didn't. So you told your boyfriend that you did. Because if he knew that you didn't, you would have been ashamed. Isn't that true?

C²⁴: Probably, because I would have said it. I wasn't sure what he would have thought.

T²⁵: Your boyfriend?

C²⁶: Yes.

T²⁷: But you were concerned with what *you* would have thought. You were sort of, in a sense, lying to yourself. Actually, I don't see why you had to be so concerned. Let's suppose this guy was rude. We don't know whether he actually was rude, incidentally, because he may have been afraid to dance with you—he may be a poor dancer, may be worried. But let's suppose it was just plain rudeness. Why haven't human beings got the right to be rude? Why *shouldn't* they be? It would be nice if they weren't; but if they are, why should you upset yourself?

C²⁸: You're right.

T²⁹: So you see: you were getting yourself upset about nothing. You were working yourself up into anger and saying, "I'll fix this guy's wagon!" And then you didn't fix his wagon, so you got angry at yourself for not fixing his wagon. So you lied to your date about it. That's what usually happens in these lies. You do something, or you don't do something, of which you're ashamed. And then you try to make it up with a lie—which won't do you any good whatsoever. Why *should* you be ashamed? Let's suppose another thing. Let's suppose the guy was deliberately, consciously rude to you, and let's suppose you had taken him to task for it. Actually, you would do better not to—because it's his problem. But let's suppose you did—which would mean that you made a mistake. So what's so horrible about you for making a mistake?

C[30]: Well, this is all a part of something that's bothered me for a long time. I'm always afraid of making a mistake.

T[31]: Why? What's the horror?

C[32]: I don't know.

T[33]: You're saying that you're a bitch, you're a louse when you make a mistake.

C[34]: But this is the way I've always been. Every time I make a mistake, I die a thousand deaths over it.

T[35]: You blame yourself. But why? What's the horror? Is it going to make you better next time? Is it going to make you make fewer mistakes?

C[36]: No.

T[37]: Then why blame yourself? Why are you a louse for making a mistake? Who said so?

C[38]: I guess it's one of those feelings I have.

T[39]: One of those *beliefs*. The belief is: "I am a louse!" And then you get the feeling: "Oh, how awful! How shameful!" But the feeling follows the belief. And again, you're saying, "I should be different; I *shouldn't* make mistakes!" Instead of: "Oh, look: I made a mistake. It's undesirable to make mistakes. Now, how am I going to stop making one next time?" If you'd use that line, you'd stop making the mistakes after a while.

As is usual in RET, I deliberately look for something that Martha says that will enable me to go far beyond the immediate events of her life and her dysfunctional emotional reactions about these events, and I soon find this thing. I show her that behind her lying about telling off a fellow who was rude to her was probably her feeling of shame about not telling him he was rude. I could have merely shown her that (1) she felt ashamed, and (2) there was no good reason for her to feel this way, since, at worst, she made a mistake in not speaking up, and she could have accepted herself with this mistake. But I deliberately go far beyond this and show her that she didn't have to take this person's rudeness seriously in the first place—as it probably had nothing intrinsically to do with her but mainly indicated that he had his own problems. Her upsetness, therefore, did not stem from point A, his rudeness, but from point B, her insisting to herself that he shouldn't be rude. I then go still further and show her that even if he were consciously and deliberately rude to her and even if she did take him to task, she would still be foolishly making herself angry about his having a problem.

By going beyond the immediate situation and letting Martha see some of the far-reaching consequences of her own thinking, I smoke her out and get her to admit the main thing I am trying to get at: that she's *always* afraid of making mistakes. I then have more concrete information to show her, again, that it's not the mistakes she makes at point A (the activating event) that upset her at point C (the consequence). Rather, it's the nonsense she tells herself at point B (her belief system): that she's a bitch, a louse for making such mistakes.

All through the session, therefore, I very consciously use Martha's material to reveal to her her basic irrational philosophies and how she can attack and change them. I try to interrupt her own viciously circular thinking: "I do poorly. Therefore, I'm a worm! therefore, I can only keep doing poorly. Therefore, I have to keep condemning myself for doing so badly." And I try to get her to replace it with something like: "I do poorly. I then wrongly berate myself because of my perfectionistic view about how well I *should* do. This self-berating helps me do much worse. Then I wrongly blame myself for doing worse. Now I can look at what I'm mistakenly believing, can accept myself with my fallibilities, and can gradually work at correcting my errors and probably do better."

C⁴⁰: Well, this is the way it was in school, if I didn't do well in one particular thing, or even on a particular test—and little crises that came up—if I didn't do as well as I had wanted to do.

T⁴¹: Right. You beat yourself over the head.

C⁴²: Yes.

T⁴³: But why? What's the point? Are you supposed to be perfect? Why the hell shouldn't human beings make mistakes, be imperfect?

C⁴⁴: Maybe you always expect yourself to be perfect.

T⁴⁵: Yes. But is that *sane*?

C⁴⁶: No.

T⁴⁷: Why do it? Why not give up that unrealistic expectation?

C⁴⁸: But then I can't accept myself.

T⁴⁹: But you're saying. "It's shameful to make mistakes." *Why* is it shameful? Why can't you go to somebody else when you make a mistake and say, "Yes, I made a mistake"? Why is that so awful?

C⁵⁰: I don't know.

T⁵¹: There *is* no good reason. You're just *saying* it's so. Recently I wrote an article for a professional publication, and they accepted it, and they got another psychologist to write a critique of it. He wrote his critique—a fairly savage one—and he pointed out some things with which I disagree, so I said so in my reply. But he pointed out some things which he was right about; where I had overstated my case and made a mistake. So, I merely said about this in my rejoinder, "He's right; I made a mistake here." Now, what's the horror? Why shouldn't I make a mistake? Who the hell am I—Jesus Christ? Who the hell are you—the Virgin Mary? Then, why shouldn't you be a human being like the rest of us and make mistakes?

C⁵²: It might all go back to, as you said, the need for approval. If I don't make mistakes, then people will look up to me. If I do it all perfectly—

T⁵³: Yes, that's part of it. That, is the erroneous belief; that if you never make mistakes everybody will love you and that it is necessary that they do. That's right. That's a big part of it. But is it true, incidentally? Suppose you never did make mistakes—*would* people love you? They'd sometimes hate your guts, wouldn't they?

C⁵⁴: And yet, not all the time. There are times—this is rare, I grant you—but sometimes I'll stand up, take a stand on something that other people don't like. But this is so rare!

T⁵⁵: Yes, but what about the times when you know you're wrong?

Let's take those times—that's what we're talking about. You know you're wrong, you made a mistake, there's no question about it. Why are you a louse at *those* times? Why is it shameful to admit your mistake? Why can't you accept yourself as a fallible human being—which we all are?

C⁵⁶: (*Pause*) Maybe I have done this on the idea that if I keep telling myself how perfect I am, I won't realize how imperfect I am.

T⁵⁷: Yes, but why shouldn't one accept the fact that one is imperfect? That's the real question. What's shameful about being imperfect? Why must one be a goddamned angel—which you're trying to be?

C⁵⁸: Probably there's no good reason.

T⁵⁹: No. Then why don't you look at *that*? There's no good reason. It's a definitional thing, saying "To be good, to be perfect. To be a worthwhile human being, I must be perfect. If I have flaws, I'm no damned good." And you can't substantiate that proposition. It's a senseless proposition; but you believe it. The reason you believe it is your society believes it. This is the basic creed of your silly society. Certainly, your parents believe it. If they knew one-sixtieth of your errors and mistakes—especially your sex errors!—they'd be horrified, wouldn't they?

C⁶⁰: Yes.

T⁶¹: You have the same silly horror! Because *they* think you ought to be a sexless angel, *you* think you ought to be.

C⁶²: (*Silence*)

T⁶³: The devil knows that they're not very good judges. But you're taking their idiotic judgments—the same judgments that have driven your father to drink and made your mother utterly miserable. They both have been miserable all your life. That's what perfectionism leads to. A beautiful object lesson there! Anybody who is perfectionistic tends to become disturbed, unhappy—ultimately often crazy. The gospel of perfection!

C⁶⁴: That's what I have to work on. Because I don't want to get like they are.

T⁶⁵: No, but you are partly like they are already—we've got to change that. It isn't a matter of getting—you've already got!

> Let's face it. You don't do the same kind of behavior as they do, but you hate yourself when you don't. You make the mistakes; they don't make them. But then you say, "I'm no good! How could I have done this? This is terrible! I'm not Florence Nightingale. I go to bed with guys. I do bad things. I make blunders. How awful!" That's the same philosophy that they have, isn't it? And it's an impossible philosophy, because we'd really literally have to be angels to live up to it. There *are* no angels! Not even your parents!

I keep showing Martha that she is quite unrealistic and perfectionistic—and that as long as she continues to be, she will inevitably get the poor results she is getting. I try to demonstrate that her negative view of herself is merely the result of a definition; she is "no good" because she *defines* herself, when she is imperfect, as being no good.

I make something of a mistake, probably, when I tell Martha that she believes she is worthless largely because her parents and her society teach her to believe this. I fail to note—as I noted in detail in the final chapter of *Reason and Emotion of Psychotherapy* (Ellis, 1962), which was published a few years after this session with Martha occurred—that practically all humans seem to be born with a tendency to believe this sort of drivel; that they must be pretty perfect and are no good if they are not; and that therefore their parents and their society are easily able to convince them that this is "true."

Clinically, however, I felt when I talked to Martha that she was already prejudiced against her parents' views and that she might therefore see the perniciousness of her own ideas if I emphasized how close to those of her parents they were. As a rational-emotive therapist, I am a frank propagandist, since I deliberately use appeals that I think will work with a given client. But I only propagandize in accordance with what appears to be the empirical reality; that people do define themselves as worthless slobs and that they then do obtain behavioral results. I do not propagandize only to win Martha's approval, but to dramatically (emotively) bring to her attention the realities of life.

Rational-emotive therapists are sometimes accused of foisting on their clients their own prejudiced views of the world. Actually, they try to base their views on reasonably objective considerations—on the facts of human existence and the usual nature of people. And they teach individuals with disturbances to look at these facts and to realistically accept and work with them. But they may teach through dramatic or emotive methods, in order to put a point over more effectively, taking into consideration that clients generally hold their wrong-headed views in a highly emotionalized, not easily uprootable manner.

C[66]: (*Pause*) I guess that's this great fear of failure. That might have been what was keeping me from concentrating on writing, which I really want to do. I'm afraid that I might make a mistake, you know.

T[67]: Yes, that's the other grim tragedy. Two things happen if you have a terrible, grim fear of failure. One is, as you just said, you get anxious, unhappy, ashamed. Two, you don't live; you don't do the things you want to do. Because if you did them, you might make a mistake, an error, be a poor writer—and wouldn't that be awful, according to your definition? So you just don't do things. That's your parents again. How could they be happy, when they haven't done anything? And you have been following the same general pattern. You haven't taken it to their extremes as yet, but it's the same bullshit, no matter how you slice it. And in your case you're afraid to write; because if you wrote, you'd commit yourself. And if you committed yourself, how horrible *that* would be!

C[68]: I've done a lot of thinking about it, since the last time I saw you. And I've gone at the typewriter with sort of a fresh burst of enthusiasm. I'm really anxious to get to it—I want to get home from work so I can. Nothing big has happened, but I feel as though if I concentrate on it and keep feeling this way, all I have to do is to keep working at it.

T[69]: And one of two things will happen. Either you'll become a good writer, with enough work and practice; or you'll prove that you're not—which would be a good thing, too. It would be far better to prove you're not a good writer by working at it than not to write. Because if you don't write, you may go on for the rest of your life hating yourself; while if you really work solidly day after day, and you just haven't got it in this area, that's tough. So you won't be a writer—you'll be something else. It would be better to learn by that experience.

C[70]: That's right. Because—I don't know—I felt so different, sitting at the typewriter and working at it, that it got to be enjoyable.

T[71]: It will!

C[72]: But it was painful before.

T[73]: It was painful because you were *making* it painful by saying, "My God! Look what would happen if I failed! How awful!" Well, anything would become painful if you kept saying that.

C[74]: Another thing that bothers me, I guess—it's the whole pattern of behavior; the way everything has been in my life. It's a sort of—"Go ahead and do it now, and then something will come along and take care of it." Like my parents always said, "We'll go ahead and do this, even though we don't have the money for it, and it'll come from somewhere."

T[75]: Right: "In God we trust!"

C[76]: This is the way I went to college. But I made it.

T[77]: That's right: *you* made it. It wasn't God; it was you.

C[78]: And God had nothing to do with it! (*Laughs*)

T[79]: That's right.

C[80]: And I find myself acting still in this way, and not being able to plan things. And even if I plan them, little things, they don't seem to come out anyway. But I still keep doing things haphazardly, thinking, "Well, go ahead and do it; and it will come from somewhere."

T[81]: Yes; but *will* it?

C[82]: No, it won't. God helps those who help themselves.

T[83]: And if you plan and scheme and plot, then a lot of things will ultimately work out. Because you planned and schemed and plotted and worked. But you're believing in magic here, aren't you?

C[84]: And when I tell myself, "Don't be silly; you can't do it, so don't," I'm tempted to go ahead and do it anyway.

T[85]: Yes, because you're telling yourself stronger and louder: "It'll take care of itself. Fate will intervene in my behalf. The Lord will provide!"

C[86]: And I get mad at myself for doing it—

T[87]: That's illegitimate! Why not say, "Let's stop the crap!" instead of getting mad at yourself? How will getting mad at yourself help?

C[88]: It doesn't. It just causes more tension.

T[89]: That's exactly right. It doesn't do any good whatsoever. Let's cut out all the self-blame. That doesn't mean cut out all criticism. Say, "Yes, I am doing this wrongly, so how do I not do it wrongly?"—instead of: "I am doing it wrongly; what a louse I am! I'm no good; I deserve to be punished!"

I persist at showing Martha that she can take chances, do things badly, and still not condemn herself. At every possible turn, I get back to her underlying philosophies concerning (1) failing and defining herself as a worthless individual and (2) unrealistically relying on the world or fate to take care of difficult situations. She consistently describes her feelings, but I bring her back to the ideas behind them. Then she seems to accept my interpretations and to seriously consider working against her disturbance-creating ideas. My persistence and determination may importantly induce her to tentatively accept my explanations and to use them herself.

It may be noted, in this connection, that I am probably setting a good *un*neurotic example for Martha and serving as a good model for her. Modeling, as Bandura (1970) has shown, is an important part of social learning and, hence, of psychotherapy. Whereas individuals with disturbances usually fail to persist and seem determined to avoid anxiety-provoking situations, I keep displaying persistence and nonavoidance with her—thereby implying that she can behave similarly.

Also, I keep reinforcing Martha's sane viewpoints (as when she remarks, "God has nothing to do with it!") and contradicting her insane views (as when she implies that she has to get mad at herself when she acts foolishly). So, to some extent, I am helping "condition" her to a different mode of thinking and reacting. Mostly, however, I am not trying to induce her to adopt a more scientific approach to life through simple "conditioning" or "suggestion."

C[90]: When I am particularly worried about anything, I have very strange dreams. I have dreams that I can't relate what the problem is, but I have them several times a week.

T[91]: There's nothing unusual about that. They're probably anxiety dreams. All the dreams say—if you told me what they are, I could show you right away—the same kind of things you're saying to yourself during the day. They're doing it in a vague and more abstract way. But that's all they are, just repetitious of the crap you're telling yourself during the day. In dreams, our brain is not as efficient as it is when we're awake; and therefore it uses symbols, vague representations, indirectness, and so on. But the dreams tell us the same crap we think during the day.

C[92]: I had a dream last week that disturbed me. I dreamed that I ran off somewhere with my boss, and his wife found us in bed; and I was so upset over that—I really was. Because I never consciously thought of my boss in a sexual way.

T[93]: That doesn't mean that that's what the dream represented, that you thought of your boss in a sexual way. There's a more obvious explanation of the dream. All the dream is really saying is: you did the wrong thing and got found out.

C[94]: I never thought of that.

C[95]: That's all it was saying, probably. And what's one of the wrongest things you can do in our society? Have intercourse with your boss and have his wife find out! That's all. It probably has little to do with sex at all; and you're probably not going around unconsciously lusting after your boss.

C[96]: No, I don't think I am.

T[97]: No. But it would be the wrong move, if you did have sex with him; it might, of course, jeopardize your job. So that's all you're saying in your dream: if I do the wrong thing, I'm no goddamned good; I may lose my job; I may get terribly penalized; and so on. That's what you say all day, isn't it? Why should you not translate it into dreams at night? It's the same crap!

In RET, dreams are not overemphasized and are often used only to a small extent; for, as I say to Martha, they are hardly the royal road to the unconscious (as Freud [1963] believed), but seem to be rather distorted and muddled representations of the same kind of thinking and feeling that the individual tends to do during his waking life. Since they are experienced in symbolic, vague, and ambiguous ways, and since they can easily be misinterpreted (according to whatever biases the individual therapist happens to hold), the rational-emotive practitioner would rather stick with the client's conscious thoughts, feelings, and behaviors and with the unconscious (or unaware) thoughts and feelings that can be deduced from them. Dreams are rather redundant material, and can consume a great deal of therapeutic time if they are taken too seriously. Moreover, long-winded dream analysis can easily (and dramatically!) distract the client from what he'd better do most of all: look at his philosophies of life and work hard at changing them. So when dreams are used in RET, they are put in the framework of its general theory. It is assumed that they encapsulate some idea—either a rational and hopeful idea (for example, that the individual can do better and get better) or·an irrational, catastrophizing, or depressing idea (for example, in Martha's case, that she might do the wrong thing with her boss, get penalized, and prove that she is "no damned good"). This idea is sought out, explained by the therapist, and then counterattacked.

C⁹⁸: That dream did worry me.

T⁹⁹: That's interesting. You got worried about the dream—

C¹⁰⁰: I got worried about the dream because I thought this must mean—

T¹⁰¹: —that's right: that "I'm lusting after my boss, and isn't that terrible!" Well, suppose you were lusting after your boss. Let's just suppose, for example—

C¹⁰²: No, I didn't think, "Wouldn't that be terrible!" I thought, "Well, I don't—consciously."

T¹⁰³: Yeah? So?

C¹⁰⁴: And then I thought. "Maybe I am—unconsciously."

T¹⁰⁵: So suppose you were? Let's suppose you were unconsciously lusting after your boss; not consciously, but unconsciously. What's the hassle?

C¹⁰⁶: (Pause) I don't know.

T¹⁰⁷: Why would that be bad? You'd just be unconscious of some of your lustful thoughts. Well, who isn't? What you should be saying—let's suppose the dream were indicating that you were lusting after your boss, and you understood the dream and found that out—is "Well, isn't that interesting! I'm lusting after my boss unconsciously. So do me something!" You see—you're always ready to beat yourself over the head. "Isn't it terrible! What a louse I am!" Millions of girls are unconsciously lusting after their bosses. Well, what's wrong with that? As long as they're sane enough not to do much about it, not to get into trouble. But you were saying: "Oh, no! I'm unaware of it. Isn't this awful! I'm doing something over which I have no control!"

C[108]: It sounds so silly when you say it, but I guess that's it.

T[109]: It *is* silly, when you bring it out and look at it in the light.

C[110]: So many of those things that bother people are—

T[111]: Yes, absolutely!

I at first misinterpret Martha's problem because I think that she thinks she is a terrible person for lusting after her boss, when she really seems to think that she is doing something she can't control and that her lack of control is terrible. I then try to show her how and why it is not horrible for her to have desires of which she is unaware and cannot control.

The beauty of the rational-emotive approach is that no matter what the client seems to be upset about, the therapist can quickly demonstrate that there is no good reason for her upset. Thus, if Martha's dream represents (1) her lusting after her boss, (2) her being out of control, or (3) any other kind of mistake, RET theory holds that she cannot be a rotter and that she therefore need not be terribly anxious, guilty, angry, or depressed. She creates her disturbed feelings, not from the dream events, nor from her foolish motives that may be revealed in these events, nor from the happenings in her real life, nor from anything *except* her own attitudes about these events, motives, or happenings. And I, as her therapist, am concerned much more with her attitudes than with the things that are transpiring in her waking or sleeping life. So if RET is consistently followed, *any* emotional problem may be tracked down to its philosophic sources (or the ways in which the individual blames herself, others, or the world); and these philosophies may then be challenged, attacked, changed, and uprooted.

C[112]: Another thing that bothers me: I mentioned before that I was afraid of men, I think. But most of the real friends I have made have been members of the opposite sex. I always found it difficult to make friends with women. I've never particularly liked very many of them. And in one way I've felt very comfortable with the men I made friends with. Yet, when I go out with somebody or date somebody for a while,

I really become unsure of myself with that person—and afraid.

T^{113}: Afraid you'll do the wrong thing and that he won't like you?

C^{114}: Yes, I guess so.

T^{115}: It's the same crap, isn't it? "If I do the wrong thing, if I make a mistake, he won't like me; and wouldn't that be terrible! I'll be utterly bereft because he'll reject me!"

C^{116}: (*Silence*)

T^{117}: Why would you be bereft? Let's suppose you did the wrong thing, and he didn't like you. You make a few mistakes and he says, "To hell with this, dear! I'm breaking this up now." Why would that be terrible?

C^{118}: Well, I suppose if I really cared for the person, then I would really think it's terrible. But I think I let myself get too emotionally tied up with the person I go out with—so that I do tend to emotionally rely on the person.

T^{119}: Emotionally dependent?

C^{120}: Yes.

T^{121}: Yes, that's right. But isn't dependency the same thing? You're saying, "I can't stand on my own two feet, and I need to rely on this person." Isn't that what it means?

C^{122}: Yes.

T^{123}: *Why* do you need to rely? Why can't you stand on your own two feet? Even if you loved the person, why do you have to be at his mercy—the mercy of whether he would return your love and would help you?

C^{124}: One shouldn't be. One should be able to—this is something my mother always encouraged me to be: be able to stand on your own two feet. Because if you rely on a man too much, sooner or later he's going to run out on you.

T^{125}: Well, that's not entirely true—

C^{126}: No, it's not entirely true, but I can see how that thought has some—

T^{127}: Yes, she really said a little more than that. She said "He's going to run out on you—and that would be dreadful!"

C^{128}: Well, then the ring would be on and—

T^{129}: And that would be awful!

C^{130}: Not that it would be, but that *you* would be—

T^{131}: You'd be worthless.

C^{132}: No, not that you'd be worthless; but that you'd be stranded.

T¹³³: Desolate, deserted, incapable of taking care of yourself! All right, is that *true*?

C¹³⁴: I suppose if I were married and had children, it would be more true than—

T¹³⁵: Yes, but even that—let's suppose the worst. Suppose you were married and had two or three children, and your husband ran out on you. It would certainly be a pain in the neck, but why would you be desolate, destroyed?

C¹³⁶: The worst problem would be the financial problem—how to take care of them.

T¹³⁷: All right, but children don't starve to death these days. So you'd temporarily have to get the city to help you.

C¹³⁸: When you look at these things like that, they make so much sense!

T¹³⁹: That's right. You're catastrophizing all over the place, because your mother has completely catastrophized. She's not going to stop that. As I said, always try to look on the worst side of it. Suppose you were deserted, left penniless, and so on. Hell!—it certainly would be an awful nuisance, but look at the number of women who have been deserted in the past ten years—have they all dropped dead or starved?

C¹⁴⁰: No.

T¹⁴¹: Then what's the great hassle?

C¹⁴²: I guess there isn't any.

T¹⁴³: But your mother thinks there is, and you unthinkingly accept her thought—because you don't question her catastrophizing.

C¹⁴⁴: I sure have to do a lot of revamping of my thinking.

I try to show Martha that it would not be dreadful, as her mother said it would be, if she were deserted by a man—it would merely be highly inconvenient. And I deliberately try to get her to see that even if the worst possible marital problem occurred, and she and her three children were deserted by her husband, it would not be (except by definition) catastrophic. This is one of the most frequently used techniques in RET: the therapist helps the client to get down to the rock-bottom core of her catastrophizing and shows her that no matter what happens, she would still not be utterly lost.

The rational-emotive therapist, like many other kinds of therapists, will sometimes help clients like Martha see that there is very little probability that certain unfortunate events (such as loss of love, accidents, or economic deprivations) will occur. But, more effectively than virtually any other practitioner, he also is able to show the client that even if such events *do* transpire—and, of course, they always *could*—it still would not be "horrible" or "terrible."

Thus, I try to convince clients such as Martha that nothing is "awful." Because "awfulness," "horror," or "terribleness," when accurately defined, include not only the idea of great inconvenience or disadvantage—which certainly may exist—but also the idea of the illegitimacy or unnaturalness of the client's being disadvantaged and her theologically-based belief that she ought not, must not be inconvenienced. If I were seeing Martha today, I would more strongly emphasize this point to her. I would also try to show her that as long as she believes that it is "awful" and "horrendous" to be deserted by a man, she will tend (1) to obsessively think about this "terrible" hazard, (2) wrongly convince herself that there is a high probability (instead of a mere possibility) of its occurrence, and (3) perhaps act in such a panicked manner with her most attractive boyfriends that she will actually encourage them to find her anxiety obnoxious and to desert her.

RET, then, usually gives the individual a deeply philosophic answer to the problems that she is beset with throughout her life. Whereas certain forms of behavior modification, such as Wolpe's (1958; Wolpe and Lazarus, 1966) desensitization method, teach the client that she need not be overconcerned about this or that, the rational-emotive approach teaches her that she need not catastrophize about anything. Even if real, overt hazards exist in her life (such as the possibility of her dying of some disease), she can learn to convince herself that (1) she probably won't suffer in the worst ways she can imagine, (2) if she, by some outside chance, does suffer in this manner there is no earthly (or godly) reason why she shouldn't, and (3) while she is still alive, the chances are high that she can still enjoy herself in spite of her real handicaps, even though she may well not be as happy as she would be without them. RET promulgates a radically different way of looking at troubles, problems, and dangers—one which was partly originated by Epictetus, Marcus Aurelius (Hadas, 1964), and other Stoic philosophers, but which does not posit any fate or god to which the human being should blindly subject himself. It encourages the individual to see potential and actual life difficulties for what they are—problems to cope with, instead of "horrible" threats to total existence and entire happiness.

T[145]: That's right. You have to do a lot of revamping of your thinking. And you're a very bright girl—you *can* do it. You've done quite well in this one week, so far. All you have to do is continue that. If you can get through school and achieve Phi Beta Kappa, you can certainly do some thinking for yourself—even though you weren't raised to. You were raised *not* to think for yourself; but you've done some independent questioning in regard to religion, and you've done it pretty much on your own. Why can't you do it in regard to the rest of these crappy philosophies?

C[146]: Well, I'll have to, Because—talk about catastrophes—I could really screw up other things for myself if I just keep on going this way.

T[147]: That's right; that's what you were heading for—screwing up everything for yourself.

C[148]: I could have gone on saying, "I always knew it would be like this." When I get very, very upset about something—well, not every time, but if something seems like a tragedy, and I just can't face it, and I don't know what I'm going to do, especially when I get all disturbed about money—there are times when I think, "Everything is disorganized. I need something to organize my life. Maybe I should go join a church." Then I think, "What a fool I am!"

T[149]: Right.

C[150]: The only organization can come from within myself, not—

T[151]: Exactly.

C[152]: —from outside sources.

T[153]: Right. The church isn't going to help you; you have to think for yourself. The only way you got *dis*organized was giving up thinking for yourself, and taking over a great deal of your parents' thinking. Not all of it, fortunately.

C[154]: Now I see what a lot of these mistaken beliefs are!

T[155]: Right.

C[156]: I have to do something more about that.

T[157]: Exactly.

I again attempt to reinforce Martha by pointing out better ways of thinking and behaving to her, having her act on some of these ways, then approving of her actions. However, I am trying not merely to reinforce her behavior, as would be the case in pure behavior therapy. Instead, I am attempting to reinforce her independent thinking. This may seem paradoxical. For reinforcement, as I have previously noted in this book, usually helps the individual to be more suggestible—to go along with what others want her to do, in order to win these others' approval. It therefore tends to result in *less* independent thinking. I use some principles of reinforcement with Martha, but at the same time I use them to help her become *less* suggestible: first, to her parents and people like them, and finally even to me. Unless she makes this final move and even comes to think independently of me, she has merely exchanged one kind of dependency for another, and is not too different from the way she was before. So although I recognize the dangers (as well as the advantages) of reinforcement, as a rational-emotive therapist I use it to uproot basic suggestibility and thus eventually to help Martha become less reinforceable, less conditionable, and more self-directing.

C[158]: Well, today I guess you could say that I reverted—well, I haven't come very far, so I couldn't have reverted back very far, but today—I've been dating two fellows at the moment. One of them called me today, and he said that he was going to do something tonight. And I had thought that he was going to see me, though he hadn't said anything about it. And I had this unreasonable fit of annoyance. Then I said, "Why should I get annoyed? It's no problem of mine. I have no right to feel that way." As though I expect everybody to bend to my will, and I don't give in return.

T[159]: That's right, exactly. But at least you caught that—didn't you?

C[160]: Yes.

T[161]: Fine.

C[162]: I felt like a stupid jerk when I realized what I was doing.

T[163]: You're not a stupid jerk. You're a human being who makes errors. We all do. Why shouldn't you? Nobody is intelligent all the time. We're all fallible.

C[164]: I didn't know what to say to you when I came in tonight. I didn't know where to start.

T[165]: You normally start the way you did, telling me the progress you've made and—what we're particularly interested in—your lack of progress, the times where the new thinking didn't work, so we can go over it, and get it so it does work. Just like a music lesson. A piano teacher comes and you play your lessons, show what progress you've made; but you also show where you fouled up, where you didn't do so well. And the teacher corrects you; and you try again next week; and the process is repeated until corrections aren't needed any more. You've learned a way of playing the piano. Here, you learn a new philosophy of life, a new way of thinking.

C^{166}: Last night a fellow called me up. I'm not interested in this person, and he asked me out. I've done this several times. I know I should probably say to him, "Don't call me," or "I'm not interested," or—

T^{167}: "I'm going steady with somebody."

C^{168}: I don't do this.

T^{169}: Why don't you? What are you telling yourself to stop yourself from doing this?

C^{170}: I don't know. That I'd better hang on to this one, because another one is going to leave sooner or later; and maybe this one might be worthwhile.

T^{171}: But is that true?

C^{172}: No, it is not true.

T^{173}: If that were true, it would not be so crazy.

C^{174}: But it's not true. And this is something I've always done.

T^{175}: But you're sort of saying, "Since I'm such a rotter, even though I've got two guys at the moment, they're bound to find me out and desert me. Then I'll have this guy. I couldn't possibly get a better guy than this—who is a pain in the ass. But he's around and will have me." Isn't that what you're saying?

C^{176}: Yes.

T^{177}: Bullshit, isn't it?

C^{178}: Yes.

T^{179}: All right, that's what you've got to see. That's what we have to teach you more and more to see—that every time you foul up, act idiotically, you're telling yourself some nonsensical thing. It usually begins with the premise, "Since I am a slob—"

C^{180}: I think I did something else today that's based on that philosophy. I'm not sure. I got on the bus this morning, and I thought I didn't lock the door. I could remember putting the key in the lock, but I couldn't remember turning it. And I worked myself up into such a tizzy over that that I went home at lunchtime to see if I locked the door.

T[181]: All right, but what's the hassle? There again, let's suppose you hadn't locked it—it's possible—

C[182]: But the reason I was so fussed about the door was that I had left the window ajar previously, and the apartment was robbed. But before that, and with some other thing, I'm always running back to see whether I turned the lights out, turned the gas off—

T[183]: Yes, but when you left the door unlocked, how many times did you leave it unlocked?

C[184]: I probably neglected to lock it several times.

T[185]: All right; so one of those times you were robbed—for leaving the window, not the door, open. It's sort of by accident, but it did happen. So if you do leave the door unlocked, what are the chances that somebody will come around, try it, and rob your apartment again? It's possible, but not highly probable. And even let's suppose there's a good chance of this happening. Let's suppose you left the door unlocked, and somebody did come around and rob you. There's no use worrying about it. The thing to do is calmly to go back at lunchtime and see. But why give yourself such a rough time? Will that make the chances of robbery any better or worse?

C[186]: I was in a tizzy all morning over it.

T[187]: You *put* yourself into a tizzy over it. Now, what's the hassle?

C[188]: There was no reason to do it.

T[189]: No, there *was* no reason to give yourself such a hard time. You're saying to yourself, "I might have made a mistake, and that would be awful!" That's what you're really saying. "I deserve to suffer for that stupid mistake I made of not locking the door." The same crap! Always blaming yourself—always trying to be perfect. Never allowed to act crazily or stupidly. Because that's what you define as good: "I am a good girl. I am worthwhile when I am perfect. When I make the slightest blunder, I'm a louse; I'm no damned good!"

C[190]: (*Long pause*) Yes. Maybe this comes from the things my parents told me when I was a child: "Be a good girl; do exactly what we say; make us proud of you."

T^{191}:   Right; that's where it started. But it *now* comes from the
           fact that you're not challenging that old philosophy. You're
           not around them that much any more; but now *you're* repeat-
           ing this drivel to yourself. That's why it continues!

I keep showing Martha—with material from her own life—that
she seems to keep worrying about how things will turn out but is
really consistently preoccupied with the irrational idea that she
would be a worthless person if she didn't make them turn out favora-
bly. No matter what kind of incident she relates, I usually return
to the same basic theme: she may make some kind of error, and
she thinks she has to damn herself if she does. She seems to agree
with me almost every time, and even to bring out new material
soon after my interpretations, which indicates the same irrational
belief—that she must be perfect and is a terrible girl if she is not.
Either I am accurately targeting Martha's real problem or else
I am brainwashing her. It is unlikely, from the material she brings
up, that the latter is true. But even if I were convincing her, somewhat falsely, that she is perfectionistic and that she'd better learn
to forgive herself for her errors, I am likely to help her considerably
with this idea. I might not be revealing and attacking her main
problem, if this occurred. But then her chief symptoms would tend
to remain, and I would be eventually forced to surrender my major
hypothesis about their causation and to look for other ideas that
were truly causing her upset.

C^{192}:   (*Long pause*) I guess the main thing is to keep in mind the
           fact that a lot of the thoughts I have—that is, whenever I
           get a thought like that, it's one of these invalid thoughts,
           and I'd better challenge it.
T^{193}:   That's right, to see that it is invalid. First you start with
           the feeling—the upset. Then you know, on theoretical grounds,
           that you have an invalid thought, because you don't get nega-
           tive feelings without first having some silly thought. Then
           you look for the thought—which is pretty obvious most of
           the time. You're invariably blaming yourself or saying that
           something is horrible when it isn't. Then you say, "Why am
           I a louse? Why is this horrible? Why would it be dreadful
           if such-and-such a thing happened?" Challenge it; question
           it; counter it. That's the process. And if you go through that

process, your thoughts can't persist. Because they're *your* irrational thoughts now. They're no longer your parents' ideas. *You* have internalized them.

C¹⁹⁴: (*Long pause*) I guess it has to be done.

T¹⁹⁵: Yes, it has to be done—for your sake. And you will get immense benefit from doing it—as you've already been deriving this week. It felt good when you acted that way, didn't it?

C¹⁹⁶: Since I have been back at the typewriter again, I've been thinking differently. I can see myself falling back, as I used to be able to do, into a clear pattern of thought. I mean, I'm not just thinking in symbols and metaphors, but am able to describe things incisively, or at least have descriptive impressions of things.

T¹⁹⁷: Yes. That's because you're letting yourself go—you're not pouncing on yourself so much. You're giving yourself leeway to think up these descriptions, which you could have done a few weeks ago but you weren't doing because you were worried about other things—about "Am I doing the writing well?" and so on.

C¹⁹⁸: Yes, you're right. Not that I've done very much in this last week, but I do feel like I'm loosening up more.

T¹⁹⁹: That's very good progress in one week's time! All you have to do is keep that up—and go a little further.

C²⁰⁰: And another thing I've done: I haven't called up my father because I felt I had to. And he hasn't called me—so that means something.

T²⁰¹: Fine! When would you like to make the next appointment?

Toward the close of this second session, Martha indicates that she is already making good progress. Her improvements, of course, may be concomitant with but not necessarily the result of the therapeutic points that I made during the first session and of her thinking about and working on these points in between the two sessions. But it does seem likely that, especially in relation to her handling of her relations with her parents and her decreased guilt about these relations, she is now considerably less upset than she was the previous week; and it also looks as though I had specifically helped her in this respect.

Martha's apparent progress represents a common occurrence in

RET. After one or two active-directive sessions, clients frequently report that something they thought they were never able to do before is now in their repertoire. This does not mean that they are truly "cured" of their emotional disturbances. But it often does seem to mean that they are well on the way to resolving at least one or two major aspects of these disturbances.

Even if clients such as Martha are quickly helped, this hardly means that all or most individuals who try rational-emotive encounters are similarly relieved; many of them, of course, are not. I assume, however, that a certain large minority of people can almost immediately profit by the RET approach; and I assume that a given individual with whom I am talking may be one of this minority. If my assumption proves to be correct, fine! If it does not, I am prepared, if necessary, to doggedly continue with the approach for as many sessions as are desirable—until the client finally begins to see that she is causing her own upsets, that she can observe the specific meanings and beliefs by which she causes them, that she can vigorously and consistently dispute and challenge these beliefs, and that she can thereby become considerably less disturbed.

THIRD SESSION

The third session with Martha was uneventful. Because she was afflicted with some expensive physical ailments and had financial difficulties, she decided to discontinue therapy for a time.

FOURTH SESSION

This is a transcript of the recording of the fourth session with Martha, which takes place nine months after the third session. She had expected to come back to therapy sooner than she actually did, but she was able to get along nicely and didn't feel impelled to return until she had a specific problem to discuss. She now comes with this problem—her relations with men.

T^1:   How are things with you?
C^2:   Pretty well, I would say. I've been hearing good things about you from some of the people I sent to see you. From Matt, in particular. He thinks that you've helped him immensely.
T^3:   I'm glad that he thinks so.
C^4:   And I see that you're making yourself comfortable, as usual.

That's the way I found you last time: shoes off, feet up.

T⁵: Yes; that's the way I usually am.

C⁶: I came to you back in January because I needed some help in writing; and also I didn't know how to handle my parents.

T⁷: Yes.

C⁸: Well, I think I solved those two problems fairly well. I get along very well with my parents now. Not because I'm giving in to them at all. I've sort of established myself as a human being, apart from them completely. And I also found some other work. I was working, as I told you, for an advertising agency. But it didn't have any interest for me at the time. I was terribly bored, and I felt I could write on my own. But I was afraid. Then I got an idea for a novel, and a publisher has taken an option on it, and I've been working on it ever since. It will be published in the spring by the same publisher who has been having such success recently with several young novelists.

T⁹: I see. That's fine!

C¹⁰: So that's all working out very well. But there's something that is bothering me, that I thought you could help me with. I've been thinking of getting married. I've been thinking of marriage in general, first of all. But before that—maybe I'm not quite sure that I really know how to love anybody. Not that I consider that there's a formula. But I've always, in a way, been somewhat afraid of men. The other thing is that there is someone·in particular who would like to marry me. And—maybe I'd better tell you how this all happened.

T¹¹: Sure.

C¹²: In trying to analyze it—in trying to figure it out—I guess it all started to go back to my father. My father was a nice guy, but he has been alcoholic since I was twelve; and he has been getting worse since I last saw you. But I was absolutely adoring to my father when I was a little girl. And then I realized he was a human being, and he fell off the pedestal. Now I don't know how much can be attributed to that, but I don't think I ever trusted a man. I guess I was afraid that if I really went for somebody and sort of devoted myself to that person completely, and if that person thought he owned me, sooner or later he would walk out on me. And this has always terrified me, no matter what kind of associations I've had. I always have to keep one step ahead of them.

T¹³: All right; it *would* terrify you if you keep saying to yourself, "They'll find out how worthless I am and leave me!"

C¹⁴: I guess you're right.

T¹⁵: And if you get rid of that fear—and as you said yourself, a couple of minutes ago, it is a fear—then you can be pretty sure that you'll love someone. I don't know *whom* you'll love— this person you're talking about, who wants to marry you, or anybody else—but I'm sure you have the *capacity* to love if you're not absorbed in, "Oh, my God! What a louse I am! When is he going to find it out?" See?

C¹⁶: Well, the fellow I've been going with is certainly a very nice person. But when I met him, I was terrified of him because it came over me, "Uh-oh! I'd better watch out for him!" I put him immediately in this category—"Beware of him!" Once he was in this category—"Beware of him!"—it didn't matter how I acted. This sort of released me from acting the way I ordinarily would think of acting. I have not really been playing fairly and squarely with him. I've broken with him a couple of times. But a couple of weeks ago I saw him again; and he told me that he loved me, and he'd like to marry me, but I'd better get some help and figure out why I think that men are so untrustworthy. He had just undergone therapy for a year and a half. First he went to Dr. ——, then he went to Dr. ——. I think he discussed me with both of them. And they both told him that I needed some help for myself before I could consider any serious steps with any man. I don't know whether he is the right person. It sounds like the great beautiful dream that I always had. But I would like to be married—I really would. I don't think it's just because of loneliness. I think I find something missing—there isn't someone to share things with.

T¹⁷: There's no reason you shouldn't get married, when you overcome this fear—and when you really get sent by somebody. As I said a few minutes ago, I'm sure you will. I still don't know whether this particular guy will be it, but maybe he is. How long have you known him?

C¹⁸: Oh, I met him a year ago in May.

T¹⁹: And what does he do?

C²⁰: He's head of the writing department in an agency.

T²¹: How old is he?

C²²: He's thirty-three. I'm twenty-three.

T²³: Has he been married before?

C²⁴: No, he's never been married. Up until a very short time ago, he never wanted the responsibility of marriage. I think he was so involved with himself that he never wanted to give himself to anyone. He concentrated on building a reputation for himself as a department head. And any woman that he became involved with was only in his way. Consequently, he dated all sorts of people that he would never consider marrying. This I got from what he has told me about the people he has dated, and also from what he told me about his therapy.

T²⁵: I take it that he is getting along all right with his job?

C²⁶: Oh, yes; he's very successful.

T²⁷: And he has friends?

C²⁸: Yes, quite a few.

T²⁹: And how do you get along with him when you're with him?

C³⁰: Up until recently, when I started to see him again, I was still afraid that if I were not on my guard with him, he would just walk out on me—and even if I married him, he would walk out on me. And now I can see him again. I think I can realize that these fears that I have are unfounded—that there is something within me that is keeping me from him, except maybe as a dependency on him and also as a crutch. I also see that he's really interested in me now. He cares for me, and it's not just sex.

T³¹: How are your sex relations with him?

C³²: Oh, pretty good.

T³³: Do you enjoy them?

C³⁴: Yes, though I don't get an orgasm all the time.

T³⁵: Few girls are completely satisfied every time. Is he a good lover?

C³⁶: Yes.

T³⁷: All right. Also, you have not felt too comfortable, and that may have had something to do with your not being satisfied all the time. If you were more free and less fearful, you might more often be satisfied.

C[38]: I guess so.

T[39]: I think it's quite possible, if you really let yourself go. But you're inhibited, you're holding yourself back—not in all ways, but in many ways—because of your fears. From what you've said so far, it doesn't look like a bad situation.

C[40]: Another thing that I seem to do: every time I get interested in someone, I find myself looking at other men. And I think that this might not be a real interest in other men. This might be that I'm trying not to face the relationship and the fact that I'm afraid of men.

T[41]: Yes, that's possible. But it's also possible that if you think of one man in terms of marrying him and you still get interested in other men, you may not be so sure as yet, in terms of your experience, that it should be the first one. And therefore you'd like to try others. Because you haven't had that many involvements during your life, and therefore you might want to have more of a fling—more trials before you get married. So some of what you feel may be normal, and some of it may be your fear of getting involved. The basic problem still is getting you to be unfearful—to realize yourself that you don't *have* to be afraid of anything. And then I don't see why you can't make it with this guy—or some other guy. I'm not sure which one. So far this fellow looks all right. The only odd thing is that he's thirty-three years old and hasn't had too much of a relationship with anyone yet. But now he's had some help, and it looks like he's getting a lot healthier than he was; so that's fine.

C[42]: Well, I would like to overcome this, because I don't like the position where I know I am afraid to put my faith in it—with him or anybody else. I don't want to be afraid of them—that they might leave me.

T[43]: That's right. For what can they do? The basic thing they can do, as you said before, is reject you. Now, let's suppose that they do. Let's suppose that you went with this guy, and you really let yourself go with him, and he finally did reject you, for whatever his reasons might be. How does that prove that you're no good, that you're worthless—which is your conclusion—how does that prove it?

C[44]: I could always suppose that he was the one who had short-comings, rather than me.

T[45]: But let's suppose he doesn't have serious shortcomings, and he rejects you. How does that still prove you're worthless? Let's suppose he's a perfect doll, and then he finds out certain things about you and spurns you. Now what does that prove?

C[46]: I don't know.

T[47]: All it proves is that he doesn't like you for having these deficiencies. It proves, in other words—assuming that he's objective about your deficiencies and is not inventing them—that you have certain defects. But how does having these defects prove that you're worthless? Or that you're thoroughly inadequate, that you're no good?

C[48]: It doesn't.

T[49]: That's exactly right! And yet that's what you automatically think every single time: that it does mean something bad about *you*. That's what your parents believe: that if you are deficient and somebody finds it out, that proves that you're worthless, as a total human. Isn't that their philosophy?

C[50]: I guess so.

T[51]: They've told you that in so many words, so many times—as you told me they did awhile ago. When they found out something about you that they didn't like—such as your not running to their beck and call—you were not just a daughter who didn't like them that much (which is all that was evident); no, you were a louse—no good! They called you every name under the sun. They tried to make you guilty, you told me. Over the phone, they'd call you several times—and so on. Isn't that right? They assume that when someone is deficient in their eyes, that person is a slob. That's their philosophy: that unless you're an angel, you are no good.

C[52]: I guess I just carried it with me. I let myself carry it with me.

T[53]: That's right. You've let yourself carry it with you—which is normal enough. Most people do. But look at the results! If it had good results, if it really made you happy, we might say, "Go carry it!" But the result is the normal result—or the abnormal result, in your case. You can't give to a man because you're always worrying, "How worthless I am! And how soon will he see it? And before he sees it, maybe I'd better do something to get rid of him." Which is your logical conclusion from an irrational premise, the premise being that if people do find your deficiencies and therefore reject you, you're totally no good. Actually, there are *two* premises here. One, that they'll find your deficiencies and therefore will reject you—which is quite an assumption!—two, that if they do reject you, you're no damned good. These are two completely irrational premises. They're not supported by any evidence. But you believe them—and millions of people believe them, as you do—on blind faith. They are essentially the same premises as that of original sin: that you were born in sin, and you're going to be found out as a sinner, and all your sinning is going to be revealed on Judgment Day; therefore, the only thing you can do is keep atoning and repenting all your life, or else keep hiding your sinfulness from other people even if you can't hide it from God. Again, this is your parents' philosophy.

C⁵⁴: Yeah; mine is just as foolish as theirs.

T⁵⁵: Yeah—the same thing!

I try to show Martha that it is not her boyfriend but her own attitudes about herself that are upsetting her, and that no matter how defective she is in this or any other respect, and no matter how badly her boyfriend (or anyone else) rejects her, she can still fully accept herself and try to better her relationships. Although I am therefore ruthless about insisting that she acknowledge her deficiencies, I am (in a typical RET manner) highly supportive about the possibility of her unconditionally accepting herself. Because of its essential supportiveness, because the rational-emotive practitioner *always* accepts the client with her failings and tries to induce her similarly to accept herself, RET can be exceptionally direct, evocative, and defense-stripping. Ordinary experiential therapists and encounter groups can afford to be ruthlessly revealing and confronting because they usually intersperse self-exposure with the therapist's or the group's giving the individual pronounced love, warmth, or approval (Burton, 1969). In RET, the therapist generally does not give this kind of affection (since there is the always existing danger that the client will, in getting it, wrongly think he is "good" *because* the therapist or group cares for him). Instead, the rational-emotive therapist (and group) tries to give unconditional acceptance, that is, complete tolerance and lack of condemnation of the client no matter what his faults are. I think an incisive reading of these sessions with Martha will show that I am rarely loving or warm to her but that I frequently show full acceptance of her.

C⁵⁶: How do I go about convincing myself that this is wrong?

T⁵⁷: The first thing you'd better do before you convince yourself that this is wrong is to convince yourself—that is, fully admit to yourself—that you very strongly have this belief. You can't very well tackle a belief and change it unless you fully admit that you have it. After seeing this, the second thing is to see the degree—which is enormous and intense—to which you have it. You can at first do this by inference—by observing your behavior and asking yourself what ideas lie behind it. For your behavior itself is not necessarily fearful. It may take the form of your *feeling* in a state of panic; or it may be defensive.

C⁵⁸: Well, my behavior is mostly defensive.

T⁵⁹: All right. Then we have to start with your defensive behavior. Look at it, question it, challenge it, and see—by inference, at first—that it could only be this way if you *were* fearful. For why would you be defensive if you were not, underneath, also afraid of something? If we can get you to see how many times a day you're unduly restricted, defensive—and therefore fearing—until you see the real frequency and intensity of your fears, then at least we get you to see what the cancer really is. You can't really understand the cancer without seeing the depths of it. Okay, we have the first step, then, which is to make you see fully what the depths of your cancerous ideation are. Then, as you begin to see this, the second step is to get you to calmly assess it. The first cancer is your defense and your fear behind it. The second cancer is—and this is the reason why so many people *are* defensive—if you admit to yourself, "My God! What a terribly fearful person I am!" you will then tend to blame yourself for *that*. In other words, you say on level number one, "My heavens, I'm a wrongdoing person, am therefore terribly worthless, and I'd better not let anyone know this." So you become defensive because your real philosophy is: "What a worthless slob I am because I'm imperfect; I have deficiencies; I have faults." So the first level is to make yourself fearful because of your feelings of worthlessness—the philosophy that human beings who are deficient are no damned good. Then, as a derivative of that first level, you come to the second level: "Because I'm deficient, because I'm fearful, because I'm neurotic, I'm a louse and am worthless for *that* reason. So I'd better deny that I'm really that fearful (*a*) because people will find out about it and hate me and (*b*) because I'll use my fear to prove to myself what a louse I am."

So first we have to get you to admit the fact that you're fearful, defensive, and so on—that you are a perfectionist who tends to bring on feelings of worthlessness. Then we have to get you to see that by admitting your fear and defensiveness you're not a louse for having these traits; and to get you to see that simply because you have a *feeling* you're worthless doesn't mean that you really *are*. So we have to get you to (*a*) admit that you feel like a skunk; (*b*) objectively perceive—and not blamefully perceive—that you believe you're one; and (*c*) (which is really just an extension of (*b*) start tackling your concept of being a skunk.

In other words, once you start admitting that you're fearful, you have to concretely look for the simple exclamatory sentences by which you create your fears. Because people have emotions and feelings, but these are the results of sentences, phrases, meanings that they tell themselves. Human beings communicate in some kind of language, and you have to find the concrete language you're using to create, and to indoctrinate yourself over and over with, your fears. You experience these fears originally because you took over, largely from your parents and from society, the belief that if you're deficient, you're no good. And you keep saying this in some kind of internalized language. Now you have to look at the concrete language—the actual words, phrases, and meanings that you say to yourself—and analyze your internalized communication, parse it for its logic.

Because your sentences, your concepts are illogical. One of your main beliefs, for example, is, "Because I am deficient,

I am worthless." Now the first part of this sentence is very often true—you *are* deficient in various ways. But does this deficiency prove your *worthlessness*? No! And if you feel worthless—which you do when you're so afraid and guilty in connection with your parents or relating to a male—then you can dig out your own sentence, "Because I am deficient, I am worthless," and challenge it, question it, look it in the eye—and then beat it down logically.

Which really means, instead of saying, "My God! Every time I'm deficient I'm no good; and if my boyfriend found that out, it would be terrible!" you can say to yourself, "All right. So I'm deficient. What's the horror? How does that prove I'm worthless? What difference does it *really* make? Why should a human being blame herself for having deficiencies? Why can't I either change the deficiency—which is sometimes possible—or live with it? If I have the wrong color eyes and my boyfriend doesn't like it, I'm certainly not going to change that!" And so on.

In other words, instead of unthinkingly accepting these irrational premises which your parents indoctrinated you with, and society too, you have to look at them and think about them—question and challenge them. Now if we can get you to go through these processes of admitting your feelings first—facing your fears behind the defenses and acknowledging your feelings of worthlessness behind the fears—and get you to parse your self-condemning ideas, to see of what they consist, to find your exact sentences and challenge their meanings, you'll win out. For *you* are telling you these beliefs right now; nobody else is telling you very much. Your parents do—but in a minor way. That's not major any more—*you* are. So if you challenge your beliefs, they must change—those irrational meanings, those self-sentences, they've got to go away. Because *you're* the only one who is sustaining them. Now that's the problem; and you've already done part of this. As a result of the few sessions we've had—three times, isn't it?

C[60]: Three times.

T[61]: Yes, three times. You've done this in one aspect of your life, in regard to your parents. Because they were saying, "What a worthless slob you are for not coming to see us," and you were saying to yourself, "Oh, yes, I am a worthless slob because I'm not bowing low to my parents." You were then feeling terrible, depressed; you were practically suicidal when I first saw you some ten months ago—in January of this year. Okay, you've done it there, in that important area of your life. You've challenged your own sentences. You said, "Yes, I am not the greatest daughter in the world to them; but that does not prove I am a worthless slut. It just proves that I am not the greatest daughter in the world, and I don't have to be. If they don't like it, that's too damned bad."

And as a result of those few sessions and your own thinking, you're not bothered much by your parents any more, and they're acting much better—which I told you they would. Because you were rewarding them before for their nonsense. Okay, now we'd better get you to broaden that. What you'd better do now is no different—it's more important, because your parents eventually would die anyway. You'd get over the problem with them then. But you're not going to die for a long time; and you're going to live with this fear, these defenses, these feelings of worthlessness, these constrictions—unless we can get you to do about them what we got you to do about your parents.

It's a little more difficult in this area, because we don't have them savagely beating you over the head—which is easy for you to see and fight against. We have *you* cruelly berating yourself—which is not easy to see. But we can see the unhappy results: your disturbed feelings. And if we can start with them, get you to admit them, there's no reason you can't work this problem through in a similar manner. It'll probably take a little more time, but it's the most valuable thing you have to do.

C⁶²: I know, because I feel that this is a very important thing right now. And not just right now, but for the rest of my life.

T⁶³: Right. Eventually you're going to marry, as you said; and even if you never marry this fellow—or you do—you're going to have to face this problem with yourself.

C⁶⁴: Well, then, should I do this: every time during the day that

I think that I'm being defensive about something, sort of be watchful for it? Then analyze whatever it is that I say to myself?

T⁶⁵: Just ask yourself calmly, at first, when you get a queasy feeling, whether it's a direct fear. Because you're still going to get those overt fears at times. But especially when it's a defense—when you're saying to yourself something like, "Oh, what does it matter if so-and-so doesn't care for me? I can get somebody else." Then ask yourself right away: "Now, look. Did I really mean that? Or was I using that as a defense against my fear of his leaving me?" Or when you find yourself looking at other men—like the illustration you gave before—ask yourself, "Am I really that interested in the other man?" Because you may be—they may be attractive. "Or, really, am I hiding my fear of losing so-and-so by this maneuver?"

Just calmly question your own thoughts and actions, when it seems likely that they may be defensive. Now, sometimes you'll find that you're not being defensive. Don't think that everything you do is a defense! Because then you'll get mixed up. There are some things we do for true, non-defensive motives. You might even say to yourself, "That guy over there is unusually attractive, and if I only knew him and he turned out to be as bright and sane as he looks on the surface, maybe he would be better for me than my boyfriend." Because your boyfriend, I'm sure, has his flaws; and you might be able to find a better one.

You can usually tell whether you're defensive by looking at the evidence. For example, if you occasionally look at another fellow and say, "He seems to be pretty good; I wonder what he's like," there's no reason to suspect that you are setting up defenses. But suppose every time you're out with your boyfriend, you keep looking interestedly at practically every other fellow you meet. Then it looks suspicious; then it looks like it isn't just a matter of your naturally comparing your boyfriend to somebody who might be better. It's probably more of your running away stuff.

But also, as I said before, all of your feelings won't be defenses. Sometimes you're really going to feel the emotion itself, without the defenses—such as, emotions of depression, anger, anxiety, guilt, and overexcitement. Any negative feeling, whatever it is, we're interested in. Every time, I contend, when you get a negative feeling, you get it because the split second before you feel it you have told yourself something. And this something, in general, is that something is or may be terrible. *That's* why you're getting the negative response.

If you say that something is or may be good, you're going to get the feeling of joy, elation, love, or something like that. But every time you get depression, anxiety, or guilt, you think, "Something is terrible!" And very often that something is *you.* "If *I* do this, it should be perfect!" At other times, when you get angry, you tell yourself, "*That* son-of-a-bitch is doing this, and *that* is terrible!"

So we want you to look at these feelings—and that doesn't necessarily mean the second you experience them. Because it might be ten minutes later that you get a chance to track them back. You might be angry for ten minutes, without even realizing it and without doing anything about it. But you can then, after the fact, say: "Now, look. I was just angry (or anxious, or guilty). What did I say to me to create this feeling?" And you start looking for these things that you said to yourself. Then you can find them, parse them, and show yourself just how irrational they are. If you can't find them, that's what I'm here for. Any time you get a feeling that you can't track down—a negative feeling—make a note of it and bring it in to me. I'll ask you about the circumstances in which it occurred, and the chances are that I'll be able to track it down very quickly to the ideas you've been telling yourself—because I've had so much experience in doing this. And, incidentally, it can't be one of ten thousand things you've told yourself; for all these ten thousand are really derived from a few basic things which are fairly easy to find.

It may be particularly noted that, from C[56] to T[65], I do by far the most talking and act very much like a teacher who is lecturing to one individual student. After Martha asks how she is to convince herself that her own philosophy of life produces inefficient results, I outline, in detail, the process she'd better take in this respect.

When she notes that a great deal of her behavior is defensive, instead of doing what many therapists (especially those of psychoanalytic or experiential persuasion) would do and showing her that these defenses will have to be emotively unblocked in the course of many sessions, I quickly explain to her what defenses are, how they arise, and how she can work against them. I thereby give her a kind of homework assignment: to question her thoughts and actions, in her real life, and to teach herself to distinguish between defensive and non-defensive behaviors.

I explain defense-expunging to Martha because I feel that even if she comes for many therapeutic sessions and continually is shown how defensive she is, she will hardly surrender her defensiveness until she regularly and vigorously attacks it herself. Frequently, this material which I teach Martha would be done in question-and-answer form, as in a Socratic dialogue (Diaz-Guerrera, 1959). Thus I might ask, "Let's suppose that you are out with your boyfriend and that you compare his traits to others, find them usually to be superior, but conclude that you'd better give him up for one of these others. What would that probably indicate?" If Martha did not see that this kind of behavior might well indicate defensiveness, I would keep questioning her and challenging her answers, until she did begin to see this clearly.

Because, however, Martha is quite bright, because she easily seems to understand the points I make and quickly starts acting on some of them, I choose to do more lecturing and less questioning. I assume that I shall thereby save her time and give her more material to work with in between sessions. Today, as was not true a dozen years ago, I also often employ tape recordings with clients and give them a recorded tape or cassette of each session to take home with them to replay several times. In this type of session, I frequently do a considerable amount of lecturing, knowing that the client will get the repetitive advantages of my explanations as he keeps rehearing the tape.

I prophylactically warn Martha that she'd better not assume that everything she does is pathological and look for hidden meanings all the time. For she may become attracted to some other fellow because he *is* attractive and not because she is afraid to become too involved with her present boyfriend. In this regard, the rational-emotive therapist tries to avoid the common psychotherapeutic error of encouraging the client to suspect virtually all her motives and actions, and thereby to become obsessed with analyzing herself about all kinds of unimportant events and feelings.

C⁶⁶: Well, this is part of the major problem that I brought up
        before: that in the other aspects I was doing poorly in, I
        seemed to have no goal—that I'd lost sight of my goal. And
        also that in my relationship with my parents I was telling
        myself how incompetent I was and how terrible I was; and
        you say that it was a low opinion that I had of myself.

T⁶⁷: That's right.

C⁶⁸: And this is an extension of that.

T⁶⁹: That's right; that is the major thing. Your problems with your
        parents were a big aspect, but the less crippling aspect of
        your general problems. Because you live with yourself all your
        life—you don't live with your parents.

C⁷⁰: Well, this has bothered me for many years.

T⁷¹: Yes, practically all your life. In fact, I have a theory that the
        basic problem is biological as well as social: that we tend, as
        children, normally to blame ourselves and others, but particu-
        larly ourselves; and that unless something happens to jolt us
        out of this self-condemning, we keep doing it forever. And
        we have to work, forcefully and vigorously, to jolt ourselves
        out of doing this. Because, according to the principles of iner-
        tia, human beings will keep doing a thing largely because
        they've previously done it. And this is the natural tendency
        of practically all people, as far as I know: to convince them-
        selves that "because I am imperfect, I'm worthless!"

C⁷²: But actually, your parents bring you up that way. Because
        you are naughty, you stand in a corner; you don't get your
        supper; you get spanked; or someone says to you, "That wasn't
        very nice; that wasn't very good!"

T⁷³: That's right. They don't only spank you—that wouldn't be
        so bad, because then they would just penalize you—but they
        also say, "You're no good!" And the attitude they take in doing
        the spanking is an angry attitude; and the whole implication
        of the anger is that you're worthless. People do this in order
        to train you, when you're a child; and it's a very effective
        method of training. But look at the enormous harm it does!
        Incidentally, one of the main reasons we would want you to
        undo your self-blaming tendencies is that if you do get mar-
        ried and have children, you will tend to do the same kind
        of thing to them that was done to you—unless you see very

clearly what was done to you and what you're doing now to continue it.

C⁷⁴: And also, I'm absolutely terrified of being somebody's mother.

T⁷⁵: Yes, that's right. Just look how incompetent you might be, and how you might screw it up! And wouldn't *that* be awful!

C⁷⁶: You know, I've been asking myself that a hundred thousand times.

T⁷⁷: All right; but those are the times we have to clip. Let's just take that sentence, "Suppose I was somebody's mother and brought my child up badly." That's what you're saying. How are you *ending* the sentence?

C⁷⁸: Wouldn't that be awful! Wouldn't I be terrible!

T⁷⁹: That's right. Now is that a logical conclusion to make from the observed facts? Even let's suppose the facts were true—that you did bring up a child badly. Let's suppose that. Would it still follow that you'd be a worthless slob?

C⁸⁰: No, it wouldn't. Because I'd be defining—that's what it is—I'd be defining *worthless* in terms of whatever it is I lack, whatever it is that I do badly in.

T⁸¹: That's right. The equation you'd be making is: my deficiency equals my worthlessness. That's exactly the equation—and it's a definition. Now is it a *true* definition?

C⁸²: No.

T⁸³: It's a true or an accurate definition if you *make* it true—if you *insist* that it's true.

C⁸⁴: But it's not necessarily a correct one.

T⁸⁵: That's right. And what happens when you make that definition?

C⁸⁶: Then you feel worthless, because you define yourself as worthless.

T⁸⁷: Yes, pragmatically, you defeat yourself. If it were a definition that led to good results, that might be fine. But *does* it lead to that?

C⁸⁸: No. Because you tend to look at everything negatively, rather than—I hate to say positively, because it sounds like "positive thinking," and that's not it.

T⁸⁹: Yes, let's say it makes you look at things negatively rather than objectively.

C⁹⁰: Yes, objectively.

From responses T[77] to T[89], I resort to a questioning dialogue, instead of my previous type of straight lecturing and explaining. I keep asking Martha various questions about what she's telling herself, what results she is thereby getting, and whether the things she is saying to herself and the definitions she is setting up about her behavior are really accurate. She shows, by her answers, that she is following what I have previously explained and that she can probably use this material in her future living.

Unless the rational-emotive therapist gets around, at some point in the therapeutic process, to questioning the client and receiving some feedback from her, there is no evidence that she really understands his main points. She may nod her head, agree verbally with him, and seem to be going along with everything he says. But until she begins to stop and think about what he is teaching and begins to give back to him the main RET messages in her own words, little may be accomplished. It is highly important, therefore, that the therapist check the client from time to time to see whether she has a real understanding of what he is talking about or whether she is merely yessing him and giving empty lip service to some of the concepts he is discussing with her.

T[91]:   That's exactly right. Instead of saying, objectively, "I have this deficiency; now let me see what I can do about it, because it's undesirable to retain it," or instead of saying, as I said before, "Let me see how I can accept myself even if I can't change my deficiency," you're telling yourself, "I'm a slob for having this defect!" That's your definition. Now, the odd thing is that almost everybody in the United States unthinkingly accepts this same definition; and practically no one sees that it is a definition. They think it's a fact. Isn't that amazing? As I always say, if the Martians or the Venusians ever make it to this earth, they're going to be shocked!

C[92]:   (laughs) Yes, they are.

T[93]:   Amazing, no one seems to question it!

C[94]:   No, each child does as his mommy says.

T[95]:   Also, a child will lots of times define himself as a blackguard on his own. Because if he fails and does so lots of times—as he inevitably will—even if Mommy didn't call him a slob, he would probably tend to think he is worthless. It's sort of a normal, natural conclusion for a young child, who can't think straight because of his youth, to say, "Because I failed at A, B, C, and D, I'm bound to fail at X, Y, and Z; and therefore I'm thoroughly incompetent at everything." That's what we call overgeneralization; and human beings, especially young children, tend to overgeneralize. Now, unfortunately, we also help them to do this, in our society—in fact, in most societies. But they might well do it without social help, though probably to a lesser degree. Anyway, it behooves us to help them to think in a less overgeneralized manner. We'd better take the child who tends to overgeneralize and calmly show him, a thousand times if necessary, "Look, dear, because you did A, B, C, and D mistakenly, that doesn't mean—"

C⁹⁶: "—that you're going to do X, Y, and Z wrongly."

T⁹⁷: That's right! "And even if you do A, B, C, and D badly, and also do X, Y, and Z wrongly, that doesn't mean that you're a louse. It means, objectively, that you have deficiencies. So you're not Leonardo da Vinci. Tough!" But we don't teach them anything of the kind.

C⁹⁸: No. "You have to excel in everything. If you don't, that's bad!"

T⁹⁹: "That's terrible!" We don't even say it's bad. Because it is, of course, objectively bad; it's inconvenient; it's a nuisance when you fail; and you will get certain poor results if you keep failing. But it doesn't say anything about you personally, as a *human being*, except that you're the kind of a creature who often fails. It doesn't say that you're a worm—unless you define it so.

C¹⁰⁰: Well, I think I'll know what to look for.

T¹⁰¹: Yes. It will take a little practice. It won't take very long, I'm sure, in your case, because you see the outlines, and I think you're very able to do this kind of thinking, which is highly important. Many people deliberately shy away from doing it, so they never see it. They're hopeless because, in a sense, they don't *want* to see it; they want the world to change, or others to change, rather than wanting to change themselves. But you want to see it, and you have seen a large hunk of it already, in dealing recently with your parents. Considering the short length of time that I saw you and that you've been working on it, you've done remarkably well. Now there's no reason why you can't see the bigger hunk of it—which applies to you much more than to your relations with your father and mother.

So you go off and look for these things we've been talking about. As I said, make a list, if you're not going to remember the things that come up during the week that you bother yourself about. Make a list of the major times when you feel upset, or when you believe you acted defensively instead of feeling overtly upset. Look for these things; come in, and we'll talk about them. I'll check what you find, just as I'd check your lessons if I were teaching you how to play the piano. You'll then be able to see your own blockings more clearly. There's no reason why not.

I continue to be encouraging to show Martha that she has been able to make good progress so far and that she should be able to continue to do so. But I stress that she well may not be able to do this entirely on her own at the present time and that therefore it would be best if she kept coming in to see me, to check her own impressions of what is bothering her and to make sure that she works concertedly against her internalized philosophies that lead her astray.

C[102]: Because I know I need this right now. I mean I can feel the need for it. Logically, I know that my hang-up with relating to males is a big stumbling block; and this is something I have to overcome.

T[103]: Yes. What I would advise you to do is to see me every week or so for therapy, or every other week or so; and also, if possible, join one of my therapy groups for awhile, where you'll see and relate to others who have similar problems to yours. You may get some insight into some of the things you're doing by watching them and showing them how to solve some of their difficulties. That's another helpful way, because we're often just too close to ourselves. But if we see the same kind of behavior in someone else, we say, "Ah, I do that, too!"

C[104]: When do the groups meet?

T[105]: I have eight different therapy groups. They meet at different times. When are you available?

C[106]: I work until 6:30 in the evening.

T[107]: All right. Most of my groups are evening groups. The only groups with openings right now are the Monday group at 8:45 P.M. and a new Wednesday group at 7:00.

C[108]: I think probably Wednesday would be the best. But I can't start just yet.

T[109]: All right, let me know when you can start. Once you do start, you have to come regularly once a week to group; and then you can attend individual sessions on a more irregular basis, any time that you want to have them. Being in the group usually means that you can cut down on the individual sessions.

C[110]: All right; I'll let you know about the group when I am ready to join it.

T[111]: When would you like an individual session?

C[112]: Would Thursday night be all right?

T[113]: I can see you at 10:00 P.M.

C[114]: All right.

T[115]: And you just think about these things we have been discussing. And when you do come to the group, you may not say anything for a couple of sessions, but may merely listen. But the more you speak up, about your own problems and about theirs, the more you will get out of it. Your group is just starting, so things may be a little confused at first; but it will get straightened out after a few weeks. As I said, with this combination of individual and group therapy, I'm sure you'll get onto your basic problems and work against them quite quickly—especially since you know already that you are able to benefit so much from just those first sessions.

C[116]: I wanted to come back after the third one, but I was waiting to have my tonsils out and I was having a very bad time with them, and also financially. Then I got terribly anemic and went to the doctor once a week for liver shots; and everything sort of fell in on me physically at that time. But I realize that those three sessions did me so much good. It took me about two months to have the problem with my parents all straightened out. And I also got the idea for the novel, and I've been working very hard on it ever since.

T^{117}: You've been using the material that I gave you. As long as
        you do this kind of homework, things will work. Okay, I'll
        see you next week, then.

The client came for one more individual session and several group
sessions of therapy, and then felt that she was doing very well and
that she could manage things on her own. She returned, over the
years, for another session from time to time, mainly to discuss the
problems of her parents, her husband, her children, or other close
associates. More than twelve years have now passed since the last
session of her original series of interviews, and she continues to
get along in life remarkably well. She is still in touch with me at
intervals, largely to refer her friends and relatives for therapy sessions. She has reality (rather than emotional) problems with her
parents; she is happily married and has two lively and seemingly
little-disturbed children; she gets along well with her husband, in
spite of his personal hang-ups; and she keeps writing successful books
and taking great satisfaction in her work. She is hardly free from
all disturbances, since she still has a tendency to become overwrought
about people treating her unfairly. But she seems almost fully to
accept herself, and most of her original problems are solved or kept
on a level of minimum upset. She still marvels at, and keeps telling
her new acquaintances about, the relatively few sessions of RET
that helped her to look at, understand, and change her basic anxiety-creating and hostility-inciting philosophy of life.

References

Adler, A. *Understanding Human Nature.* New York: Garden City Publishing Company, 1927.

Adler, A. *The Science of Living.* New York: Greenberg Publishers, 1929.

Adler, A. *What Life Should Mean to You.* New York: Blue Ribbon Books, 1931.

Ansbacher, H. L., & Ansbacher, R. *The Individual Psychology of Alfred Adler.* New York: Basic Books, 1956.

Appleton, W. S. The Struggle to Concentrate. *American Journal of Psychiatry,* 1969, *126,* 256-259.

Arbuckle, D. S. *Counseling and Psychotherapy: An Overview.* New York: McGraw-Hill, 1967.

Ard, B. N., Jr. *Counseling and Psychotherapy. Classics on Theories and Issues.* Palo Alto, Calif.: Science and Behavior Books, 1966.

Ard, B. N., Jr. The A-B-C of Marriage Counseling. *Rational Living,* 1967, *2*(2), 10-12. (a)

Ard, B. N., Jr. Assumptions Underlying Marriage Counseling. *Marriage Counseling Quarterly,* 1967, *2,* 20-24. (b)

Ard, B. N., Jr. Rational Therapy in Rehabilitation Counseling. *Rehabilitation Counseling Bulletin,* 1968, *12,* 84-88.

Ard, B. N., Jr. A Rational Approach to Marriage Counseling. In Ard, B. N., Jr., & Ard, C. C. (Eds.), *Handbook of Marriage Counseling.* Palo Alto, Calif.: Science and Behavior Books, 1969, Pp. 115-119.

Argabrite, A. H., & Nidorf, L. J. Fifteen Questions for Rating Reason. *Rational Living,* 1968, *3*(1), 9-11.

Austin, J. J. *Educational Evaluation.* (Rev. ed.) Livonia, Mich.: Research Concepts, 1964.

Bandura, A. *Principles of Behavior Modification.* New York: McGraw-Hill, 1969.

Barber, T. X. The Effects of "Hypnosis" and Motivational Suggestions on Strength and Endurance: A Critical Review of Research Studies. *British Journal of Social and Clinical Psychology,* 1966, *5,* 42-50.

Barber, T. X., & Calverley, D. S. Empirical Evidence for a Theory of "Hypnotic" Behavior: The Suggestibility-enhancing Effects of Motivational Suggestions, Relaxation-Sleep Suggestions, and Suggestions That the Subject will Be Effectively "Hypnotized." *Journal of Personality,* 1965, *33* (2), 256-270.

Barber, T. X., & Calverley, D. S. Toward a Theory of "Hypnotic" Behavior: Experimental Analyses of Suggested Amnesia. *Journal of Abnormal Psychology,* 1966, *71*(2), 95-107.

Bard, J. A. Some Data of Possible Interest to Psychotherapists. Unpublished, 1965.

Beck, A. T. *Depression: Clinical, Experimental and Theoretical Aspects.* New York: Hoeber-Harper, 1967.

Beck, A. T., & Hurvich, M. S. Psychological Correlates of Depression. 1. Frequency of "Masochistic" Dream Content in a Private Practice Sample. *Psychosomatic Medicine,* 1959, *21,* 50-55.

Beck, A. T., & Stein, D. The Self Concept in Depression. Unpublished study. Cited by A. T. Beck, *Depression: Clinical, Experimental and Theoretical Aspects.* New York: Hoeber-Harper, 1967.

Becker, J. Achievement-related Characteristics of Manic-Depressives. *Journal of Abnormal and Social Psychology,* 1960, *60,* 334-339.

Becker, J., Spielberger, C. D., & Parker, J. B. Value Achievement and Authoritarian Attitudes in Psychiatric Patients. *Journal of Clinical Psychology,* 1963, *19,* 57-61.

Bedford, S. The "New Morality" and Marriage Counseling. In Ard, B. N., Jr., & Ard, C. C. (Eds.), *Handbook of Marriage Counseling.* Palo Alto, Calif.: Science and Behavior Books, 1969. Pp. 83-87.

Bone, H. Two Proposed Alternatives to Psychoanalytic Interpreting. In Hammer, E. (Ed.), *The Use of Interpretation in Treatment.* New York: Grune and Stratton, 1968. Pp. 169-196.

Bourland, D. D. The Un-Isness of Is. *Time*, May 23, 1969, 69.

Brainerd, C. J. Personal Worth and Perception of One's Parents. *Rational Living*, 1970, 4(1), 17-19.

Branden, N. *The Psychology of Self-Esteem*. Los Angeles: Nash, 1969.

Breen, G. J. Active-Directive Counseling in an Adult Education Setting. *Journal of College Student Personnel*, July 1970, 279-283.

Breznitz, S. Incubation of Threat: Duration of Anticipation and False Alarm as Determinants of the Fear Reaction to an Unavoidable Frightening Event. *Journal of Experimental Research in Personality*, 1967, 2, 173-179.

Burkhead, D. E. *The Reduction of Negative Affect in Human Subjects: A Laboratory Test of Rational-Emotive Psychotherapy*. Ph.D. Thesis, Western Michigan University, 1970.

Burton, A. (Ed.). *Encounter*. San Francisco: Jossey-Bass, 1969.

Callahan, R. J. Overcoming Religious Faith: A Case History. *Rational Living*, 1967, 2(1), 16, 21.

Carlson, W. A., Travers, R. M. W., & Schwabe, E. A., Jr. A Laboratory Approach to the Cognitive Control of Anxiety. Paper presented to the American Personnel and Guidance Association Convention, Las Vegas, March 31, 1969.

Cassidy, W. L., Flanagan, N. B., & Spellman, M. Clinical Observations in Manic-Depressive Disease. *Journal American Medical Association*, 1957, 164, 1535-1546.

Conklin, R. C. *A Psychometric Instrument for the Early Identification of Underachievers*. M.A. Thesis, University of Alberta, 1965.

Conner, A. M. *An Evaluation of the Effectiveness of Rational-Emotive Therapy with a Group of Probationers*. M.A. Thesis, Pacific Lutheran University, May 1970.

Cooke, G. The Efficacy of Two Desensitization Procedures: An Analogue Study. *Behavior Research and Therapy*, 1966, 4, 17-24.

Coué, E. *My Method*. New York: Doubleday, Page, 1923.

Davison, G. C. Relative Contributions of Differential Relaxation and Graded Exposure to in vivo Desensitization of a Neurotic Fear. *Proceedings of the 72nd Annual Convention of the American Psychological Association*, 1965, 209-210.

Davison, G. C. Anxiety under Total Curarization: Implications for the Role of Muscular Relaxation in the Desensitization of Neurotic Fears. *Journal of Nervous and Mental Disease*, 1967, 143, 443-448.

Davison, G. C., Goldfriend, M. R., & Krassner, L. A Postdoctoral Program in Behavior Modification: Theory and Practice. *American Psychologist*, 1970, 25, 767-782.

Davison, G. C., & Valins, S. Maintenance of Self-attributed and Drug-attributed Behavior Change. *Journal of Personality and Social Psychology*, 1969, 11, 25-33.

Davitz, J. *The Language of Emotion*. New York: Academic Press, 1969.

Deane, G. E. Human Heart Rate Responses During Experimentally Induced Anxiety: Effects of Instruction on Acquisition. *Journal of Experimental Psychology*, 1966, 67, 193-195.

Diamond, L. Defeating Self-Defeat: Two Case Histories. *Rational Living*, 1967, 2(1), 13-14. (a)

Diamond, L. Restoring Amputated Ego. *Rational Living*, 1967, 2(2), 15. (b)

Diaz-Guerrera, R. Socratic Therapy. In Standal, S. W., & Corsini, R. J. (Eds.), *Critical Incidents in Psychotherapy*. Englewood Cliffs, N.J.: Prentice-Hall, 1959.

DiLoreto, A. *A Comparison of the Relative Effectiveness of Systematic Desensitization, Rational-Emotive and Client-Centered Group Psychotherapy in the Reduction of Interpersonal Anxiety*. Ph.D. Thesis, Michigan State University, 1968.

Dua, P. S. Comparison of the Effects of Behaviorally Oriented Action and Psychotherapy Reeducation on Introversion-Extraversion, Emotionality, and Internal-External Control. *Journal of Counseling Psychology*, 1970, 17, 567-572.

Ellis, A. Outcome of Employing Three Techniques of Psychotherapy. *Journal of Clinical Psychology*, 1957, 13, 344-350.

Ellis, A. *Reason and Emotion in Psychotherapy.* New York: Lyle Stuart, 1962.

Ellis, A. *Homosexuality: Its Causes and Cure.* New York: Lyle Stuart, 1965.

Ellis, A. The Nature of Disturbed Marital Interaction. *Rational Living,* 1966, *1*(1), 22-26.

Ellis, A. *Is Objectivism a Religion?* New York: Lyle Stuart, 1968.

Ellis, A. *How to Live with a Neurotic.* New York: Crown Publishers and Award Books, 1969. (a)

Ellis, A. *The Art and Science of Love.* New York: Lyle Stuart and Bantam Books, 1969. (b)

Ellis, A. A Weekend of Rational Encounter. In Burton, A. (Ed.), *Encounter.* San Francisco: Jossey-Bass, 1969. Pp. 112-127. (c)

Ellis, A. Teaching Emotional Education in the Classroom. *School Health Review,* November 1969, 10-13. (d)

Ellis, A. *Sex Without Guilt.* New York: Lyle Stuart and Lancer Books, 1970.

Ellis, A. Psychotherapy and the Value of a Human Being. In Davis, J. W. (Ed.), *Value and Valuation: Essays in Honor of Robert S. Hartman.* Knoxville: University of Tennessee Press, 1971. (a)

Ellis, A. Rational-Emotive Therapy. In Jurjevich, R. M. (Ed.), *Directive Psychotherapy.* Miami: University of Miami Press, 1971. (b)

Ellis, A. The Value of a Human Being: A Psychotherapeutic Appraisal. *Existential Psychiatry,* in press. (a)

Ellis, A. The Humanistic Approach to Psychotherapy. *The Humanist,* in press. (b)

Ellis, A. *Emotional Education.* New York: Julian Press, in press. (c)

Ellis, A. Emotional Education with Groups of Normal School Children. In Ohlsen, M. M. (Ed.), *Counseling Children in Groups.* New York: Holt, Rinehart and Winston, in press. (d)

Ellis, A., & Gullo, J. M. *Murder and Assassination.* New York: Lyle Stuart, 1971.

Ellis, A., & Harper, R. A. *A Guide to Successful Marriage.* New York: Lyle Stuart and Hollywood: Wilshire Books, 1968.

Ellis, A., & Harper, R. A. *A Guide to Rational Living.* Englewood Cliffs, N.J.: Prentice-Hall and Hollywood: Wilshire Books, 1970.

Ellis, A., Wolfe, J. L., & Moseley, S. *How to Prevent Your Child from Becoming a Neurotic Adult.* New York: Crown Publishers, 1966.

Eysenck, H. J. (Ed.). *Experiments in Behavior Therapy.* New York: Macmillan, 1964.

Falck, H. S. Thinking Styles and Individualism. *Bulletin of the Menninger Clinic,* 1969, *33,* 133-145.

Folkins, C. H. Temporal Factors and the Cognitive Mediators of Stress Reaction. *Journal of Personality and Social Psychology,* 1970, *14,* 173-184.

Frank, J. The Influence of Patients' and Therapists' Expectations on the Outcome of Psychotherapy. *British Journal of Medical Psychology,* 1968, *41,* 349-356.

Freud, S. *Collected Papers.* New York: Collier Books, 1963.

Friedman, A. S., Cowitz, B., Cohen, H. W., & Granick, S. Syndromes and Themes of Psychotic Depression: A Factor Analysis. *Archives of General Psychiatry,* 1963, *9,* 504-509.

Fritz, C. E., & Marks, E. S. The NORC Studies of Human Behavior in Disaster. *Journal of Social Issues,* 1954, *10,* 26-41.

Garfield, S. L., Gershon, S., Sletten, I., Sundland, D. M., and Ballou, S. Chemically Induced Anxiety. *International Journal of Neuropsychiatry,* 1967, *3,* 426-433.

Garfield, Z. H., Darwin, P. L., Singer, B. A., & McBreaty, J. F. Effect of "in vivo" Training on Experimental Desensitization of a Phobia. *Psychological Reports,* 1967, *20,* 515-519.

Geer, J. H., Davison, G. C., and Gatchel, R. J. Reduction of Stress in Humans Through Non-veridical Perceived Control of Aversion Stimulation. *Journal of Personality and Social Psychology,* 1970, *16,* 731-736.

Geis, H. J. Guilt Feelings and Inferiority Feelings: An Experimental Comparison. *Dissertation Abstracts,* 1966, *13,* 8515.

Geis, H. J. The Psychology of Dieting. *Rational Living,* Fall, 1970, *5*(1), 23-33.

Glass, D. D., Singer, J. E., & Friedman, L. N. Psychic Cost of Adaptation to an

Environment Stress. *Journal of Personality and Social Psychology*, 1969, *12*, 200-210.

Glasser, W. *Reality Therapy*. New York: Harper, 1965.

Glicken, M. D. Counseling Children. *Rational Living*, 1966, *1*(2), 19-25.

Glicken, M. D. Mental-Health Clinics: Trick or Treatment? *Rational Living*, 1967, *2*(2), 16-17.

Glicken, M. D. Rational Counseling: A New Approach to Children. *Journal of Elementary Guidance and Counseling*, 1968, *2*(4), 261-267.

Gliedman, L. H., Nash, E. H., Imber, S. D., Stone, A. R., & Frank, J. D. Reduction of Symptoms by Pharmacologically Inert Substances and by Short-Term Psychotherapy. *Archives of Neurology and Psychiatry*, 1958, *79*, 345-351.

Gordon, J. E. (Ed.). *Handbook of Clinical and Experimental Hypnosis*. New York: Macmillan, 1967.

Greenwald, H. (Ed.). *Active Psychotherapy*. New York: Atherton Publishers, 1967.

Grossack, M. M. Why Rational-Emotive Therapy Works. *Psychological Reports*, 1965, *16*, 465.

Grossack, M. M., Armstrong, T., & Lussiev, G. Correlates of Self-Actualization. *Journal of Humanistic Psychology*, 1966, *6*, 87.

Gullo, J. M. Useful Variations on RET. *Rational Living*, 1966, *1*(1), 44-45. (a)

Gullo, J. M. Counseling Hospitalized Patients. *Rational Living*, 1966, *1*(2), 11-15. (b)

Gustav, A. "Success Is——." Locating Composite Sanity. *Rational Living*, 1968, *3*(1), 1-6.

Hadas, M. (Ed.) *Essential Works of Stoicism*. New York: Bantam Books, 1964.

Hampson, J. L., Rosenthal, D., & Frank, J. D. A Comparative Study of the Effects of Mephenesin and Placebo on the Symptomatology of a Mixed Group of Psychiatric Outpatients. *Bulletin of Johns Hopkins Hospital*, 1954, *95*, 170-177.

Harper, R. A. Marriage Counseling as Rational Process-oriented Psychotherapy. *Journal of Individual Psychology*, 1960, *16*, 197-207. (a)

Harper, R. A. A Rational Process-oriented Approach to Marriage Counseling. *Journal of Family Welfare*, 1960, *6*(4), 1-10. (b)

Harper, R. A. Moral Issues in Marital Counseling. In Silverman, H. L. (Ed.), *Marital Counseling*, Springfield, Ill.: Charles C Thomas, 1967. Pp. 325-335.

Hartman, B. J. An Entrancing Suggestion. *Rational Living*, 1967, *2*(2), 25.

Hartman, B. J. Sixty Revealing Questions for Twenty Minutes. *Rational Living*, 1968, *3*(1), 7-8.

Hartman, R. S. *The Measurement of Value*. New York: General Electric Company, 1959.

Hartman, R. S. *The Measurement of Value*. Carbondale: Southern Illinois University Press, 1967.

Hauck, P. A. The Neurotic Agreement in Psychotherapy. *Rational Living*, 1966, *1*(1), 31-34.

Hauck, P. A. *The Rational Management of Children*. New York: Libra, 1967. (a)

Hauck, P. A. Challenge Authority—For Thy Health's Sake. *Rational Living*, 1967, *2*(1), 1-4. (b)

Hauck, P. A. An Open Letter to Us. *Rational Living*, 1968, *3*(1), 29-30.

Hauck, P. A. Can Rational-Emotive Therapy Serve the Christian? *Journal of Pastoral Counseling*, 1969, *4*(1), 31-38.

Herzberg, A. *Active Psychotherapy*. New York: Grune and Stratton, 1945.

Hudson, J. W. Value Issues in Marital Counseling. In Silverman, H. L. (Ed.), *Marital Counseling*. Springfield, Ill.: Charles C Thomas, 1967. Pp. 164-176.

Janov, A. *The Primal Scream*. New York: Delta Books, 1971.

Jellinek, E. M. Clinical Tests on Comparative Effectiveness of Analgesic Drugs. *Biometrics Bulletin*, 1946, *2*, 87.

Jones, M. C. The Elimination of Children's Fear. *Journal of Experimental Psychology*, 1924, *7*, 382-390.

Jones, R. G. *A Factored Measure of Ellis' Irrational Belief System, with Personality and Maladjustment Correlates*. Ph.D. Thesis, Texas Technological College, August 1968.

Jordan, B. T., & Kempler, B. Hysterical Personality: An Experimental Investigation of Sex-Role Conflict. *Journal of Abnormal Psychology*, 1970, *75*, 172-176.

Jourard, S. M. *Disclosing Man to Himself.*

Cincinnati: Van Nostrand Reinhold, 1968.

Jurjevich, R. M. (Ed.). *Directive Psychotherapy.* Miami: University of Miami Press, 1971.

Kamiya, J. Conscious Control of Brain Waves. *Psychology Today,* 1968, *1*(11), 57-61.

Karst, T. O., & Trexler, L. D. Initial Study Using Fixed-Role and Rational-Emotive Therapy in Treating Public-Speaking Anxiety. *Journal of Consulting Psychology,* 970, *34,* 360-366.

Kemp, C. G. Influence of Dogmatism in Counseling. *Personnel and Guidance Journal,* 1961, *39,* 662-665.

Kilty, K. M. *Attitudinal Affect and Behavioral Intentions.* Urbana: University of Illinois Group Effectiveness Research Laboratory, Technical Report No. 65, 1968.

Kilty, K. M. On the Relationship Between Affect and Cognition. *Psychological Reports,* 1969, *25,* 215-219.

Kilty, K. M. Some Determinants of the Strength of Relationship Between Attitudinal Affect and Cognition. *Journal of Social Psychology,* 1970, 1-24.

Konietzko, K. Self-Help Wanted: Internal Reprogrammer. *Rational Living,* 1968, *3*(2), 27-30.

Krippner, S. Relationship Between Reading Improvement and Ten Selected Variables. *Perceptual and Motor Skills,* August 1964, 15-20.

Lafferty, J. C. Values That Defeat Learning. *Proceedings Eighth Inter-Institutional Seminar in Child Development.* Dearborn, Michigan: Edison Institute, 1962.

Lafferty, J. C., Dennerll, D., & Rettich, P. A Creative School Mental Health Program. *The National Elementary Principal,* April 1964, *43*(5), 28-35.

Lang, P. J., Sproufe, L.A., & Hastings, V. E. Effects of Feedback and Instructional Set on the Control of Cardiac Variability. *Journal of Experimental Psychology,* 1967, *75,* 425-431.

Lazarus, A. A. Behavior Therapy and Beyond. New York: McGraw-Hill, 1971.

Lazarus, R. S. *Psychological Stress and the Coping Process.* New York: McGraw-Hill, 1966.

Levitt, E. E., Den Breeijen, A., & Persky, H. The Induction of Clinical Anxiety by Means of a Standardized Hypnotic Technique. *American Journal of Clinical Hypnosis,* 1960, *2,* 206-214.

Levitt, E. E., Persky, H., & Brady, J. P. *Hypnotic Induction of Anxiety: A Psychoendocrine Investigation.* Springfield, Ill.: Charles C Thomas, 1964.

Lidz, T., Corneilson, M.S., Terry, C., & Pleca, S. Intrafamilial Environment of the Schizophrenic Patient. II The Transmission of Irrationality. *Archives Neurology and Psychiatry,* 1958, *79,* 305-316.

Litvak, S. B. Attitude Change by Stimulus Exposure. *Psychological Reports,* 1969, *25,* 391-396. (a)

Litvak, S. B. A Comparison of Two Brief Group Behavior Therapy Techniques on the Reduction of Avoidance Behavior. *Psychological Record,* 1969, *19,* 329-334. (b)

Loeb, A., Beck, A. T., Diggory, J. C., & Tuthill, R. Expectancy Level of Aspiration, Performance and Self-Evaluation in Depression. *Proceedings of the Annual Convention of the American Psychological Association,* 1967, *2,* 193-194.

McConaghy, N. Penile Volume Change to Moving Pictures of Male and Female Nudes in Heterosexual and Homosexual Males. *Behavior Research and Therapy,* 1967, *5,* 43-48.

McGrory, J. E. Teaching Introspection in the Classroom. *Rational Living,* 1967, *2*(2), 23-24.

Maes, W. R., & Heimann, R. A. *The Comparison of Three Approaches to the Reduction of Test Anxiety in High School Students.* Final Report project 9-1-040. Washington: Office of Education, Bureau of Research, United States Department of Health, Education and Welfare, October 1970.

Marcia, J. E., Rubin, B. M., & Efran, J. S. Systematic Desensitization: Expectancy Change or Counter Conditioning? *Journal of Abnormal Psychology,* 1969, *74,* 382-387.

Masters, W. H., & Johnson, V. E. *Human Sexual Inadequacy.* Boston: Little, Brown, 1970.

Maultsby, M. C., Jr. The Pamphlet as a Therapeutic Aid. *Rational Living,* 1968, *3*(2), 31-35.

Maultsby, M. C., Jr. The Implications of Successful Rational-Emotive Psychotherapy for Comprehensive Psychosomatic Disease Management. Unpublished, 1969. (a)

Maultsby, M. C., Jr. Systematic Written Homework in Psychotherapy. A Clinical Study of Eighty-seven Unselected OPD Patients. Unpublished, 1969. (b)

Maultsby, M. C., Jr. Psychological and Biochemical Test Change in Patients Who Were Paid to Engage in Psychotherapy. Unpublished, 1969. (c)

Maultsby, M. C., Jr. Routine Tape Recorder Use in RET. *Rational Living*, 1969, *5*(1), 8-23. (d)

Meath, J. A., Feldberg, T. M., Rosenthal, D., & Frank, J. D. A Comparative Study of Reserpine and Placebo in the Treatment of Psychiatric Outpatients. Unpublished, 1954. Cited in Frank, J. D., *Persuasion and Healing*. Baltimore: Johns Hopkins University Press, 1961.

Meehl, P. E. *Psychologists' Opinions as to the Effects of Holding Five of Ellis' "Irrational Ideas."* Minneapolis: Research Laboratories of the Department of Psychiatry, University of Minnesota. Report No. PR 66-7, 1966.

Miller, N. E. Learning of Visceral and Glandular Responses. *Science*, January 31, 1969, *163*, 34-45.

Mowrer, O. H. Preparatory Set (Expectancy)—A Determinant in Motivation and Learning. *Psychological Review*, 1938, *45*, 62-91.

Mowrer, O. H. *The New Group Therapy.* Princeton, N.J.: Van Nostrand, 1964.

Nisbett, R. E., & Schacter, S. Cognitive Manipulation of Pain. *Journal of Experimental and Social Psychology*, 1966, *2*, 227-236.

Nomikos, M. S., Opton, E. M., Jr., Averill, J. R., & Lazarus, R. S. Surprise Versus Suspense in the Production of Stress Reaction. *Journal of Personality and Social Psychology*, 1968, *2*, 204-208.

O'Connell, W. E., & Hanson, P. G. Patients' Cognitive Changes in Human Relations Training. *Journal of Individual Psychology*, 1970, *26*, 57-63.

Overall, J. E., & Gorham, D. Basic Dimensions of Change in the Symptomatology of Chronic Schizophrenics. *Journal of Abnormal and Social Psychology*, 1961,

63, 597-602.

Pastore, N. A Neglected Factor in the Frustration-Aggression Hypothesis: A Comment. *Journal of Psychology*, 1950, *29*, 271-279.

Pastore, N. The Role of Arbitrariness in the Frustration-Aggression Hypothesis. *Journal of Abnormal and Social Psychology*, 1952, *47*, 728-731.

Patterson, C. H. *Theories of Counseling and Psychotherapy.* New York: Harper and Row, 1966.

Patterson, C. H. A Current View of Client-centered or Relationship Therapy. *Counseling Psychologist*, 1969, *1*(2), 2-25.

Paul, G. L. *Insight Versus Desensitization in Psychotherapy: An Experiment in Anxiety-Reduction.* Stanford, Calif.: Stanford University Press, 1966.

Payne, R. W., & Hirst, H. L. Overinclusive Thinking in a Depressive and a Control Group. *Journal of Consulting Psychology*, 1957, *21*, 186-188.

Peale, N. V. *The Power of Positive Thinking.* Greenwich, Conn.: Fawcett Publications, 1962.

Perls, F. *Gestalt Therapy Verbatim.* Lafayette, Calif.: Real People Press, 1969.

Pollaczek, P. Administrative Council—In-Service Program. Lecture No. 2 and No. 3. Mimeographed. Garden City, New York: Garden City Schools, 1967.

Pottash, R. R., & Taylor, J. E. Discussion of Albert Ellis, "Phobia Treated with Rational-Emotive Psychotherapy." *Voices*, 1967, *3*(3), 39-40.

Rand, M. E. Rational-Emotive Approaches to Academic Underachievement. *Rational Living*, 1970, *4*(2), 16-18.

Raskin, N. J. The Psychotherapy Research Project of the American Academy of Psychotherapists. *Proceedings of the 73rd Annual Convention of the American Psychological Association*, 1965, 253-254.

Raskin, N. J. Diversity, Congruence and Confidence. Paper presented at the American Psychological Association Convention, New York City, September 3, 1966.

Reich, W. *Character Analysis.* New York: Orgone Institute Press, 1949.

Rimm, D. C., & Litvak, S. B. Self-Verbalization and Emotional Arousal. *Journal of Abnormal Psychology*, 1969, *74*, 181-187.

Rimm, D. C., & Medeiros, D. C. The Role of Muscle Relaxation in Participant Modeling. *Behavior Research and Therapy*, 1970, *8*, 127-132.

Ritter, B. The Group Desensitization of Children's Snake Phobias Using Vicarious and Contact Desensitization Procedures. *Behavior Research and Therapy*, 1968, *6*, 1-6.

Rogers, C. R. *On Becoming a Person*. Boston: Houghton-Mifflin, 1961.

Rogers, C. R. *Carl Rogers on Encounter Groups*. New York: Harper and Row, 1971.

Rokeach, M. *Three Christs of Ypsilanti*. New York: Alfred A. Knopf, 1964.

Roper, P. The Effects of Hypnotherapy on Homosexuality. *Canadian Medical Association Journal*, February 11, 1967, *96*, 319-327.

Rosenthal, D., & Frank, J. D. Psychotherapy and the Placebo Effect. *Psychological Bulletin*, 1956, *53*, 294-302.

Russell, B. *The Conquest of Happiness*. New York: Bantam Books, 1968.

Sahakian, W. S. Stoic Philosophical Psychotherapy. *Journal of Individual Psychology*, 1969, *25*, 32-35.

Salzinger, K., & Pisoni, S. Reinforcement of Verbal Affect of Normal Subjects During the Interview. *Journal of Abnormal and Social Psychology*, 1960, *60*, 127-130.

Schacter, S., & Singer, J. E. Cognitive, Social and Physiological Determinants of Emotional State. *Psychological Review*, 1962, *69*, 379-399.

Schutz, W. *Joy*. New York: Grove Press, 1967.

Shapiro, M. B., Neufield, I., & Post, F. Experimental Study of Depressive Illness. *Psychological Reports*, 1962, *10*, 590.

Shapiro, M. B., & Ravenette, E. T. A. A Preliminary Experiment on Paranoid Delusions. *Journal of Mental Science*, 1959, *103*, 295-312.

Sharma, K. L. *A Rational Group Therapy Approach to Counseling Anxious Underachievers*. Ph.D. Thesis, University of Alberta, 1970.

Sparks, L. *Self-Hypnosis: A Condi-tioned-Response Technique*. New York: Grune and Stratton, 1962.

Spielberger, C. D., & Gorscuh, R. L. *Mediation Process in Verbal Conditioning*. Washington: Report of the United States Public Health Service Grants, MH 7229, September 1966.

Spielberger, C. D., Parker, J. B., & Becker, J. Conformity and Achievement in Remitted Manic-Depressive Patients. *Journal of Nervous and Mental Disease*, 1963, *137*, 162-172.

Steffy, R. A., Meichenbaum, D., & Best, J. A. Aversive and Cognitive Factors in the Modification of Smoking Behavior. *Behavior Therapy and Research*, 1970, *8*, 115-125.

Sullivan, R. Experimentally Induced Somatagnosia. *Archives of General Psychiatry*, 1969, *20*, 71-78.

Taft, G. L. A Study of the Relationship of Anxiety and Irrational Ideas. Ph.D. Thesis, University of Alberta, 1965.

Tillich, P. *The Courage to Be*. New York: Oxford University Press, 1953.

Tosi, D. J., & Carlson, W. A. Client Dogmatism and Perceived Counselor Attitudes. *Personnel and Guidance Journal*, 1970, *48*, 657-660.

Valins, S. Cognitive Effects of False Heart-Rate Feedback. *Journal of Personality and Social Psychology*, 1966, *4*, 400-408.

Valins, S. Emotionality and Information Concerning Internal Reactions. *Journal of Personality and Social Psychology*, 1967, *6*, 458-463.

Valins, S. *The Perception and Labeling of Bodily Changes as Determinants of Emotional Behavior*. In Black, P. (Ed.), *Physiological Correlates of Emotion*. New York: Academic Press, 1970.

Valins, S., & Ray, A. A. Effects of Cognitive Desensitization on Avoidance Behavior. *Journal of Personality and Social Psychology*, 1967, *7*, 345-350.

Velten, E. A Laboratory Task for Induction of Mood States. *Behavior Research and Therapy*, 1968, *6*, 473-482.

Wagner, E. E. Techniques of Rational Counseling. *High Spots*, 1963, *3*(6), 2.

Wagner, E. E. Counseling Children: Two Accounts. *Rational Living*, 1966, *1*(2), 26-30.

Wenger, M. A., Averill, J. R., & Smith,

D. D. B. Autonomic Activity During Sexual Arousal. *Psychophysiology*, 1968, *4*, 468-478.

White, A. M., Fichtenbaum, L., and Dollard, J. Measurement of What the Patient Learns from Psychotherapy. *Journal of Nervous and Mental Disease*, 1969, *149*, 281-293.

Wolf, S. Effects of Suggestion and Conditioning on the Action of Chemical Agents in Human Subjects—The Pharmacology of Placebo. *Journal of Clinical Investigation*, 1950, *29*, 100-109.

Wolf, S., & Pinsky, R. H. Effects of Placebo Administration and Occurrence of Toxic Reactions. *Journal of the American Medical Association*, 1954, *155*, 339-341.

Wolfe, J. L. Emotional Education in the Classroom. *Rational Living*, 1970, *4*(2), 23-25.

Wolpe, J. *Psychotherapy by Reciprocal Inhibition*. Stanford, Calif.: Stanford University Press, 1958.

Wolpe, J., & Lazarus, A. A. *Behavior Therapy Techniques*. London: Pergamon Press, 1966.

Yablonsky, L. *The Tunnel Back: Synanon*. New York: Macmillan, 1965, and Baltimore: Penguin Books, 1967.

Zajonc, R. B. Attitudinal Effects of Mere Exposure. *Journal of Personality and Social Psychology*, 1968, *9*, (Monogr. Suppl. Part 2).

Zingle, H. W. *Therapy Approach to Counseling Underachievers*. Ph.D. Thesis, University of Alberta, 1965.

Melvin Powers
SELF-IMPROVEMENT
LIBRARY

ASTROLOGY

_____ASTROLOGY: A FASCINATING HISTORY P. Naylor	2.00
_____ASTROLOGY: HOW TO CHART YOUR HOROSCOPE Max Heindel	2.00
_____ASTROLOGY: YOUR PERSONAL SUN-SIGN GUIDE Beatrice Ryder	2.00
_____ASTROLOGY FOR EVERYDAY LIVING Janet Harris	2.00
_____ASTROLOGY GUIDE TO GOOD HEALTH Alexandra Kayhle	2.00
_____ASTROLOGY MADE EASY Astarte	2.00
_____ASTROLOGY MADE PRACTICAL Alexandra Kayhle	2.00
_____ASTROLOGY, ROMANCE, YOU AND THE STARS Anthony Norvell	2.00
_____MY WORLD OF ASTROLOGY Sydney Omarr	3.00
_____THOUGHT DIAL Sydney Omarr	2.00
_____ZODIAC REVEALED Rupert Gleadow	2.00

BRIDGE & POKER

_____BRIDGE BIDDING MADE EASY Edwin Kantar	5.00
_____BRIDGE CONVENTIONS Edwin Kantar	4.00
_____HOW TO IMPROVE YOUR BRIDGE Alfred Sheinwold	2.00
_____HOW TO WIN AT POKER Terence Reese & Anthony T. Watkins	2.00

BUSINESS, STUDY & REFERENCE

_____CONVERSATION MADE EASY Elliot Russell	2.00
_____EXAM SECRET Dennis B. Jackson	2.00
_____HOW TO BE A COMEDIAN FOR FUN & PROFIT King & Laufer	2.00
_____HOW TO DEVELOP A BETTER SPEAKING VOICE M. Hellier	2.00
_____HOW TO MAKE A FORTUNE IN REAL ESTATE Albert Winnikoff	3.00
_____HOW TO MAKE MONEY IN REAL ESTATE Stanley L. McMichael	2.00
_____INCREASE YOUR LEARNING POWER Geoffrey A. Dudley	2.00
_____MAGIC OF NUMBERS Robert Tocquet	2.00
_____PRACTICAL GUIDE TO BETTER CONCENTRATION Melvin Powers	2.00
_____PRACTICAL GUIDE TO PUBLIC SPEAKING Maurice Forley	2.00
_____7 DAYS TO FASTER READING William S. Schaill	2.00
_____STUDENT'S GUIDE TO BETTER GRADES J. A. Rickard	2.00
_____STUDENT'S GUIDE TO EFFICIENT STUDY D. E. James	1.00
_____TEST YOURSELF — Find Your Hidden Talent Jack Shafer	2.00
_____YOUR WILL & WHAT TO DO ABOUT IT Attorney Samuel G. Kling	2.00

CHESS & CHECKERS

_____BEGINNER'S GUIDE TO WINNING CHESS Fred Reinfeld	2.00
_____BETTER CHESS — How to Play Fred Reinfeld	2.00
_____CHECKERS MADE EASY Tom Wiswell	2.00
_____CHESS IN TEN EASY LESSONS Larry Evans	2.00
_____CHESS MADE EASY Milton L. Hanauer	2.00
_____CHESS MASTERY — A New Approach Fred Reinfeld	2.00
_____CHESS PROBLEMS FOR BEGINNERS edited by Fred Reinfeld	2.00
_____CHESS SECRETS REVEALED Fred Reinfeld	2.00
_____CHESS STRATEGY — An Expert's Guide Fred Reinfeld	2.00
_____CHESS TACTICS FOR BEGINNERS edited by Fred Reinfeld	2.00
_____CHESS THEORY & PRACTICE Morry & Mitchell	2.00
_____HOW TO WIN AT CHECKERS Fred Reinfeld	2.00
_____1001 BRILLIANT WAYS TO CHECKMATE Fred Reinfeld	2.00

Melvin Powers
SELF-IMPROVEMENT
LIBRARY

Melvin Powers
SELF-IMPROVEMENT
LIBRARY

MAKING MONEY AT THE RACES David Barr	2.00
PAYDAY AT THE RACES Les Conklin	2.00
SMART HANDICAPPING MADE EASY William Bauman	2.00

HYPNOTISM

ADVANCED TECHNIQUES OF HYPNOSIS Melvin Powers	1.00
ANIMAL HYPNOSIS Dr. F. A. Völgyesi	2.00
CHILDBIRTH WITH HYPNOSIS William S. Kroger, M.D.	2.00
HOW TO SOLVE YOUR SEX PROBLEMS WITH SELF-HYPNOSIS Frank S. Caprio, M.D.	2.00
HOW TO STOP SMOKING THRU SELF-HYPNOSIS Leslie M. LeCron	2.00
HOW TO USE AUTO-SUGGESTION EFFECTIVELY John Duckworth	2.00
HOW YOU CAN BOWL BETTER USING SELF-HYPNOSIS Jack Heise	2.00
HOW YOU CAN PLAY BETTER GOLF USING SELF-HYPNOSIS Heise	2.00
HYPNOSIS AND SELF-HYPNOSIS Bernard Hollander, M.D.	2.00
HYPNOSIS IN ATHLETICS Wilfred M. Mitchell, Ph.D.	2.00
HYPNOTISM (Originally published in 1893) Carl Sextus	3.00
HYPNOTISM & PSYCHIC PHENOMENA Simeon Edmunds	2.00
HYPNOTISM MADE EASY Dr. Ralph Winn	2.00
HYPNOTISM MADE PRACTICAL Louis Orton	2.00
HYPNOTISM REVEALED Melvin Powers	1.00
HYPNOTISM TODAY Leslie LeCron & Jean Bordeaux, Ph.D.	2.00
HYPNOTIST'S CASE BOOK Alex Erskine	1.00
MEDICAL HYPNOSIS HANDBOOK Drs. Van Pelt, Ambrose, Newbold	2.00
MODERN HYPNOSIS Lesley Kuhn & Salvatore Russo, Ph.D.	3.00
NEW CONCEPTS OF HYPNOSIS Bernard C. Gindes, M.D.	3.00
POST-HYPNOTIC INSTRUCTIONS Arnold Furst	2.00
How to give post-hypnotic suggestions for therapeutic purposes.	
PRACTICAL GUIDE TO SELF-HYPNOSIS Melvin Powers	2.00
PRACTICAL HYPNOTISM Philip Magonet, M.D.	1.00
SECRETS OF HYPNOTISM S. J. Van Pelt, M.D.	2.00
SELF-HYPNOSIS Paul Adams	2.00
SELF-HYPNOSIS Its Theory, Technique & Application Melvin Powers	2.00
SELF-HYPNOSIS A Conditioned-Response Technique Laurance Sparks	2.00
THERAPY THROUGH HYPNOSIS edited by Raphael H. Rhodes	3.00

JUDAICA

HOW TO LIVE A RICHER & FULLER LIFE Rabbi Edgar F. Magnin	2.00
MODERN ISRAEL Lily Edelman	2.00
OUR JEWISH HERITAGE Rabbi Alfred Wolf & Joseph Gaer	2.00
ROMANCE OF HASSIDISM Jacob S. Minkin	2.50
SERVICE OF THE HEART Evelyn Garfield, Ph.D.	2.50
STORY OF ISRAEL IN COINS Jean & Maurice Gould	2.00
STORY OF ISRAEL IN STAMPS Maxim & Gabriel Shamir	1.00
TONGUE OF THE PROPHETS Robert St. John	3.00
TREASURY OF COMFORT edited by Rabbi Sidney Greenberg	2.00

MARRIAGE, SEX & PARENTHOOD

ABILITY TO LOVE Dr. Allan Fromme	2.00
ENCYCLOPEDIA OF MODERN SEX &	

Melvin Powers
SELF-IMPROVEMENT
LIBRARY